D1245843

# CAMPAIGN CRAFT

# CAMPAIGN CRAFT

## The Strategies, Tactics, and Art of Political Campaign Management

*Fifth Edition*

## MICHAEL JOHN BURTON, WILLIAM J. MILLER, AND DANIEL M. SHEA

PRAEGER™

An Imprint of ABC-CLIO, LLC
Santa Barbara, California • Denver, Colorado

**Library of Congress Cataloging-in-Publication Data**

Burton, Michael John.
  Campaign craft : the strategies, tactics, and art of political campaign management / Michael John Burton, William J. Miller, and Daniel M. Shea. — Fifth edition.
     pages cm
  Includes bibliographical references and index.
  ISBN 978-1-4408-3732-6 (alk. paper) — ISBN 978-1-4408-3733-3 (ebook)  1. Campaign management—United States.  I. Miller, William J., 1984–  II. Shea, Daniel M.  III. Title.
  JK2281.B87  2015
  324.70973—dc23       2015006879

ISBN: 978-1-4408-3732-6
EISBN: 978-1-4408-3733-3

19  18  17  16  15     1  2  3  4  5

This book is also available on the World Wide Web as an eBook.
Visit www.abc-clio.com for details.

Praeger
An Imprint of ABC-CLIO, LLC

ABC-CLIO, LLC
130 Cremona Drive, P.O. Box 1911
Santa Barbara, California 93116-1911

This book is printed on acid-free paper ∞

Manufactured in the United States of America

# Contents

# Part IV: THE FUTURE OF ELECTIONEERING

# List of Figures and Tables

## Figures

## Tables

# Preface

A fifth edition of *Campaign Craft* prompts me to think about how and why this unique book has enjoyed such a rich history. Over nearly two decades, the book has been in the hands of thousands of readers (though its strong presence on college syllabi hints that many readers were involuntary). I enjoy talking to scholars and professionals who use this book. I once heard from a docent of the political arts who had assigned *Campaign Craft* to his novices in a newly democratic nation. Now *that's* a cool measure of success!

Dan Shea wrote the first edition of *Campaign Craft* on his own. He had experience in New York politics and a degree in campaign management before entering a doctoral program at the State University of New York at Albany. When Dan began teaching campaign management at the University of Akron's Ray C. Bliss Institute of Applied Politics, he could not find a suitable text. There were books on voter behavior and electoral systems, and how-to guides intended for practitioners, but no campaign management text that quite understood the political science literature. The goal then, as now, was to merge the two worlds: *Campaign Craft* offers a deep exploration of campaign management grounded in serious political science. In my opinion, the book took off in the 1990s because academic campaign management programs took off simultaneously. *Campaign Craft* was the right product at the right time.

I have known Dan since we were graduate students at SUNY–Albany, sharing a cheap, grad-school apartment with him. (Dan is an avid hunter so our refrigerator was a good place to find wildlife.) After coursework at Albany, I left upstate New York for a series of jobs in Washington, DC. I worked on a congressman's staff and in the office of Vice President Al Gore—and when I left to take a teaching job at Ohio University, Dan graciously asked me to get on board with *Campaign Craft*.

I like to think my contribution to the project is an injection of diffidence. Working in DC at the locus of competing interests, convictions, and predictions rendered the problem of "decisions under uncertainty" instinctual. Close readers of successive editions may find creeping ambivalence: On one hand, strategy $X$ might work; on the other hand, strategy $Y$ might be better.

Each edition of *Campaign Craft* benefited from helpful research assistants. One of those research assistants is Will Miller, who was an undergraduate at Ohio University, then a graduate student (when he served as my research assistant), then a colleague (when he briefly served as an instructor), and then a coauthor on a number of publications, now to include *Campaign Craft*. I saw Will's enthusiasm on a research project that ended with a trip to Wright-Patterson Air Force base so we could inspect historic presidential planes up close. I saw Will's analytic prowess when, as part of his wedding weekend in small-town Georgia, we took a "ghost tour" of local neighborhoods. (Bayesian theory suggests that false-positives likely dominated posterior probabilities, so, maybe not much real evidence of phantoms.)

With each update, I begin with a hope we can slide out the old anecdotes and findings and slip new material into the empty places. The job is never so easy. First, scholarship on campaign management and strategy is dynamic. *Campaign Craft* was first published before the rise of field experimentation that has become a major presence in electoral research. Second, because political campaigns follow the logic of an arms race—each side is trying to gain advantage over the other and "final answers" are superseded by novel questions— the strategies, tactics, and art of political campaign management are in a perpetual state of self-reinvention.

The five years since our fourth edition of *Campaign Craft* have seen—

- The emergence of super PACs and an overall rise in campaign money
- New questions about the strength and durability of campaign finance regulations
- Intensified partisanship and polarization
- Increased politicization of judicial elections

- Debates over ballot access and voter integrity
- Professionalization of down-ballot contests
- The rise of quantitative analysis in political campaigns.

A version of *Campaign Craft* that leans forward to the second half of the present decade must account for these changes, and more.

Past editions of *Campaign Craft* have benefited mightily from the help of research assistants and personal friends: Molly Park, Steven "The Book" Petrovic, David Boisture, James Moore, Diana Warth, Craig Berger, Dominic Ionta, Kevin Wahlmark, William J. Miller, Mark Ondrejech, Nicholas Garlinghouse, Enrique Buron, Jaime Emmons, Caitlyn Zachry, Saskia van Wees, and Louise Koons.

For the current edition, we owe deep thanks to Alex Banks, who did a standout job tracking down cites and keeping us on track, and Michael Wood, a friend and political operative who read the text in its entirety and added helpful comments. Also, thanks to Nellie Lavalle for helping with final checks of the manuscript.

Thank you to Gordon Hammy Machado and Ezhil R. Kuppan for their assistance with editing and creating the book you see before you. And thanks to Steve Catalano and Bridget Austiguy-Preschel with Praeger for continuing to see the value in this work.

Most importantly, we thank everyone who taught us the craft of campaigning while tolerating our mistakes.

*Michael John Burton*
*Department of Political Science*
*Ohio University*

# INTRODUCTION

# Consultant-Centered Campaigns

The presidential election of 1896 was an epic battle. It set Democrat William Jennings Bryan, a fiery politician from Nebraska, against Republican William McKinley, the even-tempered governor of Ohio. Bryan's oratory was in the classical tradition. Economic hardship was dividing the nation, Bryan argued, and a monetary policy like the one McKinley offered, which proposed to link the national currency to gold bullion, was a vital threat to the working class. In an impassioned speech to the Democratic Convention, Bryan declared, "You shall not press upon the brow of labor this crown of thorns, you shall not crucify mankind upon a cross of gold" (Bryan 1913, 249). Taking his "Silver Democrat" message to 26 states, speaking to an estimated 5 million people, distancing his policies from the failures of the incumbent administration, Bryan cast himself as a champion of the "common man" (Dinkin 1989, 114).

Sensing trouble, McKinley harnessed the ingenuity of his long-time friend and political godfather Marcus A. Hanna, arguably the first modern campaign consultant, who fashioned the McKinley campaign along "business principles" (Troy 1996, 105). Hanna approached captains of industry for campaign cash, gathering about $3.5 million, more than anyone had raised in a presidential race to that date (Glad 1964, 169; Jones 1964, 283). He organized separate bureaus for Germans, African Americans, wheelmen, merchants, and even women, a group that did not yet enjoy universal suffrage. Hundreds of speakers were deployed and countless pamphlets were distributed, some written in the home languages of newly arrived immigrants.

Nineteenth-century political custom held that presidential incumbents should not plead their own case on the campaign trail. Wandering the countryside in search of votes suggested weakness and would give Bryan a chance to outperform McKinley. Hanna therefore orchestrated a series of finely tuned "pilgrimages" that had the air of a contemporary campaign. The candidate would not go to the people; the people would come to the candidate.

The whole affair became a national phenomenon. It was said that "the desire to come to Canton has reached the point of mania" (Troy 1996, 105). Railroad moguls transported those wishing a journey to McKinley's front porch in Canton, Ohio (Jamieson 1996, 18). From midsummer through November, McKinley gave more than 300 speeches and saw perhaps a million callers at his door. People snatched twigs, grass, stones, and shards of the now-famous front porch to keep as souvenirs.

Election Day brought victory. McKinley won the presidency with 51 percent of the vote to Bryan's 47 percent. It was a respectable win, thanks, in large measure, to the innovative tactics of Mark Hanna.

McKinley's triumph came in the early days of electronic communication—telephones were a novelty and radio was still in the offing—and the stage was set for astonishing change. Television would be introduced following World War II and within a decade two-thirds of the nation's households would own at least one TV set. In the 1960s, satellite communication became standard fare on television newscasts. In the 1980s, CNN made television news a 24-hour commodity. And in the 1990s, the Internet gave instant access to in-depth information from around the globe. The culture became wired, and then wireless. College students carry smartphones, take and share photos, play music, locate restaurants and reviews, send and receive tweets, and message friends around the globe. "Cord cutters" are watching movies, documentaries, campaign commercials, and candidate gaffes on Netflix, YouTube, Chromecast, and Roku.

New technologies are changing education, transportation, personal communication, and electoral politics. Voters are tracked by ever-growing databases and increasingly precise microtargeting programs. In 2008, Barack Obama's campaign amassed nearly 3 million cell phone numbers by announcing that voters could receive breaking news of the vice presidential pick via SMS text (Pérez-Peña 2009). In 2012, Obama used online data and sophisticated algorithms to personalize his messaging (Issenberg 2012a). In 2014, conservative groups were building voter databases outside the confines of the traditional American party system (Allen and Vogel 2014). Although the strategic goals of professional campaigning do not change, the tools of the trade are in a permanent state of revolution.

This chapter discusses the "new style" of electioneering, the role of political parties in contemporary elections, consultant-centered campaigns, scholarship on campaign management and strategy, and the organization of this book.

## New-Style Electioneering

Campaigns were once run by family members, friends, and party activists who canvassed neighborhoods and street corners handing out pamphlets. Ward heelers cajoled friends and posted yard signs. In the 1950s, this sort of "retail" politics was the way of the world. Massachusetts pol Tip O'Neill, who would later make his mark as Speaker of the House of Representatives, could view politics as a sociable affair: Hands were shaken, deals were made, and no one gave up a vote until asked (O'Neill and Novak 1987). In retirement O'Neill lamented, "If I were running today, I probably would have to use all the modern techniques of political campaigning: hiring a political consultant, polling extensively and making ads targeted to TV audiences" (O'Neill and Hymel 1994, xi–xii).

O'Neill's career spanned the twilight of retail electioneering. The shift toward professionalism that began with Mark Hanna's work in 1896 was hastened by Dwight D. Eisenhower's 1952 bid for the White House. With advertising gimmicks like name repetition, Eisenhower's team produced a catchy jingle that went, "Ike for president, Ike for president; you like Ike, I like Ike, everybody likes Ike for president." By the mid-1960s, mass-market strategies like random-sample surveys were colonizing American politics. Carefully constructed random-sample surveys appeared more effective than conferring with party leaders, and television could reach a huge audience with comparative ease.

A contemporary political professional might dismiss handshake-and-pamphlet electioneering as "old style." Old-style campaigning was characterized by a personalized retail politics practiced by political operatives and party bosses. "New-style" campaigning, a notion outlined by Robert Agranoff (1972), broke with that past. The new style was marked by a new individualism, with new players, new incentives, new tactics, and new resources—none of which was dominated by the major political party organizations. As a novel campaign industry began taking hold in the early 1970s, there were, by Agranoff's count, 30 branches of the campaign profession (1972, 17). A directory of political consultants now lists 70 categories of consultancy, from "Ad Testing" to "Voter Registration" (Political Pages Directory 2014). One estimate has 5,000 to 10,000 professionals working in campaigns (Johnson, forthcoming).

Television is the archetype of Agranoff's new-style campaigning. The congressional class of 1974 had a whole novel political look—young, energetic political outsiders with blow-dried hair. To win, candidates had to go on TV, a costly medium requiring specialized expertise. Television demanded professionals who could "edit on the action." Few operatives knew how to backlight a candidate without creating a halo effect. The language of ad production—with its "Nagras," "Chroma Keys," and "crystal syncs"—was utterly foreign to old-style campaign managers. Political campaigns had to outsource the production of television ads to those who already knew the business.

The new style hinged on money, in part because independent professionals expect direct payment for their labors, preferably up front or in real time. Consultants make their living by piecework, by the hour, or by a share of expenditures. Some are incentivized by a "victory bonus." Party affiliation is important to the consulting industry as a matter of trust, if nothing else, but campaign consulting is unmistakably profit-driven. The top 150 consulting firms received $466 million out of $1.2 billion spent on the federal elections up through June of the 2011–2012 cycle (see Fineman and Blumenthal 2012). By the end of the cycle total expenditures across the board, including advertising, amounted to $6.3 billion (Choma 2013).

A second reason for the importance of money goes to a crucial difference between money and volunteers. If a campaign organization is short on volunteers to staff an Election Eve phone bank, it can buy the services of a telemarketing firm. If, however, the campaign is short on money for television airtime, it cannot pay for the ad slots with surplus volunteers.

Consultants looking to spend money have a wide range of options. Television, radio, and the Internet can touch more people in a few seconds than party foot soldiers could reach in a month. Twenty-first-century computers crunch through voter lists and let campaign consultants produce mail, raise money, target voters, and generate news releases. Candidates "meet" with large numbers of people via Internet video conferences. Campaign clips are produced for Web-exclusive distribution, and someone needs to know how to do this job cost-effectively. Digitally generated "robo calls" are moving onto a turf once occupied by dedicated volunteers. Social media help citizens become campaign operatives as the amateur politicos share messages, stories, and factoids with their personal friends (and online "friends") so long as professionals offer the appropriate tools.

The mainstay of political rhetoric in the time of Bryan and McKinley was the full-blown campaign speech; today's voters see 15-second television spots, 6-second sound bites, 5-word SMS texts, 140-character tweets, 6-second Vines, 3-second GIFs repeating themselves over and over, and a steady stream of Facebook updates. And many voters are watching and interacting with several screens at a time. Nielsen reports that 84 percent of smartphone and tablet owners are using these devices as second-screens while watching television simultaneously (Nielsen 2014).

Much of this media is filled with content generated by political professionals. (Anyone can add a hashtag to the vocabulary; can everyone make it go viral?) More information is available to contemporary voters than ever before—with candidate Web sites, bloggers, and instant access to news archives, the potential of an intensely informed electorate has never been greater)—then again, some will argue, with McGinniss, that in a new era, "style becomes substance" (1969, 30).

## The Parties

Agranoff's focus on new-style campaigning was linked to political changes in the years following Eisenhower's presidential term: The two major political parties appeared to be in decline.

During the "Golden Age of Parties," candidates did not run campaigns so much as stand for election. Office seekers were expected to contribute to their own electoral efforts, perhaps with a donation to the machine, but day-to-day operations were left to party operatives. Political machines drew power from the allocation of government jobs and other tangible benefits, often relying on immigrants who found opportunity in the party. Reformers pushed back by advocating civil service rules (which reduced patronage), the secret ballot (which rendered vote promises unenforceable), and direct primary elections (which removed the selection of nominees from the hands of party leaders). Many good-government groups called for nonpartisan municipal elections. Decreased immigration, increased mobility, and broad-based public education loosened the grip of old-style party machines. After decades of erosion, respected journalist David Broder declared, "The party's over" (1972).

In the new-style, "The candidate, rather than the party," wrote Agranoff, "tends to be the chief focus of today's campaign communication" (1972, 4). Candidates were running for office with help from political consultants who made their services available on the open market. Voter partisanship was at a lull, candidates were frequently blasting the party apparatus and committing apostasy when expedient. In later years, a common sense would emerge that campaigns had become "candidate centered."

And yet, the national parties and thousands of state and local party organizations persisted. A study of the parties from 1960 through 1980 found, contrary to popular belief, that most party organizations remained vibrant (Gibson et al. 1983; Cotter et al. 1984). Although a good deal of money was pouring in to candidate campaigns from interest groups, political parties remained the largest single source of assistance to candidates. Office seekers relied on party organizations to carry petitions, assemble volunteers, find money, make telephone calls, and canvass door-to-door. Some claimed, "the party goes on" after all (Kayden and Mahe 1985; see also Crowder-Meyer 2009; Roscoe and Jenkins 2014).

The parties were morphing into "service-oriented" organizations that allocated money and expertise (Kolodny and Dulio 2003; Shea 1999; Roscoe and Jenkins 2014; White and Shea 2004, 101–126). Political scientist Paul Herrnson notes that House and Senate campaign committees offer "assistance in specialized campaign activities such as management, gauging public opinion, issue and opposition research, and communications" (2012, 111). State-level party operatives might join candidates in the field, helping the candidate's campaign organization (and perhaps looking over its shoulder). Herrnson writes, party committees can serve as "brokers," linking "candidates and interest groups, the individual contributors, the political consultants, and the powerful incumbents who possess some of the money, political contacts, and campaign experience that candidates need" (2012, 111).

## Consultant-Centered Campaigns

While contemporary campaigns are not quite party-centered, neither are they strictly candidate-centered. In many ways they are consultant-centered. Founding scholar of campaign communications research Dan Nimmo argued that electoral contests were becoming titanic battles between warring campaign professionals (1970). Candidates put their names on the ballot and make key decisions, but the organizational structures supporting candidates are largely populated by political consultants (see Johnson 2015). The old-style party boss pledging government jobs is long gone. Campaigns are now run by people who know the strategies, tactics, and art of political campaign management—that is, by campaign professionals. Everything from fundraising to direct mail to television advertising to grassroots work can be coordinated by members of the new campaign intelligencia.

The rise of political intellectuals would have flabbergasted practitioners of old-style politics. Experience, not schoolwork, was the driving force of New York's legendary Tammany Hall. Tammany leader George Washington Plunkitt made the point clear:

> We ain't all bookworms and college professors. If we were, Tammany might win an election once in four thousand years. Most of the leaders are plain American citizens, of the people and near the people, and they have all the education they need to whip the dudes who part their name in the middle and to run City Government. We got bookworms, too, in the organization. But we don't make them district leaders. We keep them for ornaments on parade days. (Riordon 1995, 45)

Yet recent years have seen the ranks of political professionals augmented with graduate school alumni holding diplomas in data analysis, field experimentation, psychology, and statistical modeling, and specialized degrees in campaign management.

Consultants have their own professional organization. The American Association of Political Consultants (AAPC) charges yearly dues, holds well-attended conferences, maintains a code of ethics, and bestows industry honors—the "Pollie" awards (American Association of Political Consultants 2012). While Jon Stewart's *Daily Show* might poke good fun at a Pollie for "Best Use of a Yard Sign," professionals assembled at an annual conference of the AAPC can learn about the latest campaign techniques while they bulk up on business contacts. Vendors showcase their latest wares and consultants chat with one another. Between meetings, attendees might be seen skimming *Campaigns & Elections*, which covers the industry for professionals, or going online to check out vendors' websites.

The business of consulting is driven by a logic of proliferation. Direct mail illustrates the point. Figuring out how to size, sort, and seal a mailing is just the beginning, as direct mail depends on clean data, fast stuffing, and well-built lists. To get a mailing right, a campaign operative must learn how to "merge and purge," "de-dupe," and practice "good data hygiene." Once the operative has mastered the legal, technical, creative, and organizational demands of the mail business, there is no point in restricting expertise to a single candidate. Expanding to a larger group of clients reduces per-unit costs and increases profits. New technologies will allow a smart mail strategist to customize the mailing per the values and interests of specified voter segments.

Ironically, the waning of old-style one-to-one relationships and the rise of mass outreach strategies cleared the way for a *new*, new-style of customized voter contact. It is a business dynamic anticipated by mass-customization in manufacturing (see Pine 1993; Tseng and Jiao 2001). The key is "modularity."

Strategists build standardized components that will fit diverse situations. Campaign scholars Judith Trent, Robert Friedenberg, and Robert Denton write, "[C]andidates adapt" to varied political audiences with "speech modules." Each module is "a single unit of speech," Trent, Friedenberg, and Denton explain, and "typically, candidates will have a speech unit, or module, on each of the ten to twenty issues on which they most frequently speak" (2011, 186). A campaign's talking points are recycled from one event to the next with minor variations in phrasing. They are used in letters, brochures, op-eds, debates, social media, or any other textual communication. Old-style retail campaigning involved a direct relationship with voters; early new-style campaigns used a mass-marketing approach; and the *new*, new style, in which consultants narrowly target their message to members of a broad audience, adapting processes on demand, exemplifies mass customization (see Figure I.1).

Modularization can be seen throughout the campaign process. Electoral data come in standardized formats, campaign commercials have consistent regularity, and news releases have a customary format. When a staffer learns how to coordinate sound and video at small events, this expertise can be adapted to larger settings. A smart advance person soon figures out by repetition which pieces of the technology—electronics, wiring, and so forth—are unique to local vendors and which are standardized nationwide. Once the transferable elements of sound and video production are understood, the

**Figure I.1**
**Party-, Candidate-, and Consultant-Centered Campaigns**

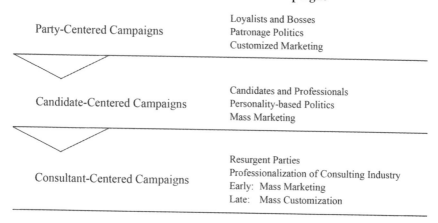

| Party-Centered Campaigns | Loyalists and Bosses<br>Patronage Politics<br>Customized Marketing |
| Candidate-Centered Campaigns | Candidates and Professionals<br>Personality-based Politics<br>Mass Marketing |
| Consultant-Centered Campaigns | Resurgent Parties<br>Professionalization of Consulting Industry<br>Early:  Mass Marketing<br>Late:   Mass Customization |

technique has been, in effect, modularized, and the swift production of large events is enabled. A presidential campaign staffer can rapidly assemble an immense campaign rally with satellite trucks, lights, and a handsome backdrop because each piece of the puzzle has already been used several times before.

The professionalization of political campaigns depends on efficient modularization. Profits accrue from the act of recycling techniques from one campaign to the next. Political professionals develop generalized statistical models intended to guide electoral targeting and get-out-the-vote operations for a variety of campaigns. They specialize in particularized types of campaign messages or field tactics. A consultant who had written "around 150 speeches" notes that he "regard[s] all of those speeches as variations on one single speech." Each speech had six component parts: "Four parts were set in advance, and the remaining two were prepared especially for each event." The candidate would say something about the locale of the speech—"I am happy to be here today in your hometown"—and proceed to "say something like, 'I remember how once upon a time the situation was such and such. . . . (filler N. 2)'" (Maor 2001, 35; ellipses in the original).

James Carville has opined, "In campaign politics an idea is like a fruitcake at Christmas—there's not but one, and everybody keeps passing it around" (Matalin and Carville 1995, 35).

There is danger in predictability. The general who fights the next war like the previous one risks ignominious defeat, but if modularized components are continually remixed and rematched, with new techniques replacing those that have become outmoded, a consultant's methods can remain strategically viable. To win—and profitability is maximized by repeated victory—campaign operatives must keep their techniques current. They should probably broaden their knowledge by working on a variety of campaigns, meeting with other consultants, and keeping up with innovations in their chosen subfield. In other words, consultants should become "professionals" insofar as their careers revolve not around individual candidates but campaigns and elections per se.

## Scholarship

This book is not a how-to manual for managing campaigns; it is a rational reconstruction of the logic of electioneering. While a campaign guidebook is principally concerned with exactly what works in what context and when, a rational reconstruction looks at why political professionals do the things they do and why the business and practice of campaigning have changed the way they have.

At the center of the study of campaigns is the question: *Do campaigns matter?* Early work on voter behavior suggested campaign activities might not play a large role in electoral results. A voter's ballot choice is highly predictable early in the campaign season based on socio-economic status and party attachment. A typical contest's outcome is highly predictable. Electoral forecasts that take account of incumbency status, economic conditions, and other influences outside the control of campaign organizations can usually figure out the winner well before Election Day (even as media attention dwells on the most uncertain of these contests). Maybe campaigns don't matter, or don't matter much.

Political scientists speak of the "minimal effects" of electioneering, but minimal does not mean absent. Thomas Holbrook argued, "[E]lection outcomes and voting behavior can be explained with just a few variables, none of which are related to the campaign," and yet, according to Holbrook, "campaigns do matter" (1996, 156). "Prevailing attitudes about the economy and the incumbent administration" create an "equilibrium" (157), something like a natural level of partisanship. Support for a candidate is sometimes out of equilibrium at the outset of a campaign. A front-runner who has fallen behind expectations has an obvious mission, namely, to "move public opinion toward the expected outcome" (157). Holbrook's perspective: Campaign effects are minimal, but real, and they can make a difference.

Scholars who see a strong role for noncampaign influences understand the limitations of forecasting models. James Campbell (2008) argued that precampaign "fundamentals" such as incumbency and the economy constrain the outcome of presidential contests but they do not always determine outcomes. Campbell has estimated "unsystematic campaign developments" at "less than two percentage points of the vote" although they have sometimes run as high as five percentage points (78). John Sides and Lynn Vavreck have found strong evidence for the influence of fundamentals, but the power of conditions beyond a candidate's control is contingent on a decision to take advantage of those conditions (2013, 186–187). Abundant experimental research shows that voters can be nudged into voting (see Green and Gerber 2008; Green et al. 2013). Leading scholar Gary Jacobson argues that the question now is not *whether* campaigns matter, but *how* (2015). Well-resourced, forward-thinking candidates need to apply their skills competently if they are to maximize their chances for victory on Election Day. While the marginal value of any particular strategy may be difficult to estimate—the number of potential factors is all but countless—the assumption that good strategy can make a difference appears to drive the behavior of campaign organizations.

A strong literature covers the practice of electioneering. Several books emerged in the 1970s, most notably those of Agranoff (1972), Joseph Napolitan (1972), and James Brown and Philip M. Seib (1976). In the 1980s, Larry Sabato (1981), Marjorie R. Hershey (1984), Ann Beaudry and Bob Schaeffer (1986), and Barbara L. and Stephen A. Salmore (1989) described the inner workings of political campaigns. Later, Edwin Diamond and Stephen Bates (1992) and Karen S. Johnson-Cartee and Gary A. Copeland (1991) examined campaign advertising; Gary W. Selnow (1994) took account of computer technology in modern elections. Stephen C. Craig and David B. Hill highlight perspectives by scholars and practitioners in an edited volume that lets students of politics talk about theory and practice (2010).

More recently, John S. Klemanski, David A. Dulio, and Michael Switalski have examined state legislative campaigns (2015). Dulio has also looked at political consulting as a business (2004), as has Stephen Medvic, one of the early observers of political consulting (2001). Dennis Johnson's *No Place for Amateurs* (2007),

*Campaigning in the Twenty-First Century* (2011), and *A History of Political Consulting* (2016) analyze the consulting industry as it rose from an ad hoc business model to a mature profession.

Specialized work covers many topics. Costas Panagopoulos wrote an early analysis of *Politicking Online* (2009). The *Routledge Handbook of Political Marketing* (2011) was edited by Jennifer Lees-Marshment, who coedited *Political Marketing in the United States* (2014) with Brian Conley and Ken Cosgrove. James A. Thurber and Candice Nelson have kept students of campaign politics updated on the business of campaigning (1995, 2000, 2004, 2010, 2013). Robert V. Friedenberg (1997) outlined communications consulting, and Nelson, Dulio, and Medvic have edited a provocative volume on campaign ethics (2002), while Ronald Keith Gaddie (2004) asks why anyone would want to run for office in the first place. Jeffrey M. Stonecash (2008) demystifies the campaign polling process, and Michael J. Malbin (2006) continues to produce some of the most important analyses of campaign finance at the Campaign Finance Institute. Seminal research into congressional elections by Paul S. Herrnson (2012) and Gary Jacobson (2013) is critical to the study of campaigns. Primary elections are examined by Robert Boatright (2014). Kelly Dittmar (2015) reviews the distinctive conditions women face when they run for office, with particular consideration to the challenges facing consultants and candidates.

Beyond scholarship, a variety of campaign manuals give practical advice. Judge Lawrence Grey's *How to Win a Local Election* tells campaign operatives, "A coat of clear varnish can extend the life of a sign, and one good tip is to take the stack of signs as they come from the printer and use a roller with varnish to seal all the edge" (2007, 203). Catherine Shaw's *The Campaign Manager* (2014), S.J. Guzzetta's *The Campaign Manual* (2010), and Christine Pelosi's *Campaign Boot Camp, 2.0* (2012) are informative primers for nuts-and-bolts understanding. Hal Malchow's *Political Targeting* (2008) is more advanced than most instructional materials and is perhaps most useful to experienced professionals.

While campaign guidebooks explore tactical matters in detail, it is not their mission to place new-style politics in a broad, historical, analytical context. Work that examines scholarship, not practice, can miss the constraints and opportunities facing practitioners; the trees get lost in the forest. *Campaign Craft* hopes to bridge the gap. This volume combines theoretical knowledge with practical information about the nature and function of real-world elections. Each chapter reviews a slice of new-style electioneering to find a logic of campaign behavior. The goal of the present book is to clear away some of the mystery surrounding a sometimes enigmatic, frequently exasperating, and always intriguing aspect of American politics.

## Organization of the Book

Each of the following chapters is designed to help students of American politics understand the history and logic of political campaigns in this new age of high-tech, consultant-centered electioneering. Every electoral contest presents a unique set of challenges. Financial limitations prevent any campaign from undertaking a first-rate targeting operation *and* the deepest possible opposition research *and* the best voter targeting, survey techniques, media strategy, *and* grassroots operation. Strategic thinking involves tough choices on resource allocation; the optimal mix of expenditures might become obvious to the campaign team in distressing hindsight. Far from outlining the perfect strategy or a set of "best practices," *Campaign Craft* is intended to explain what a political campaign organization might be doing and why the organization might be doing it that way—the logical calculus driving competitive campaigns.

The focus of the book will be on elections below the presidential level: statewide, congressional, and local contests. Few consultants are lucky enough or skilled enough to plan media buys, organize direct mail, or raise funds in the higher echelons of a presidential campaign. Although this book will feature "presidentials" throughout the text—these elections epitomize campaign strategy and readers know the plots and players—for the most part the book will contemplate strategies, tactics, and technologies appropriate to mid-level and lower-level elections.

Part I investigates campaign preliminaries, beginning with chapter 1, which provides a glimpse into the planning process. Chapter 2 looks at the contextual factors that might define a particular race. Chapter 3 examines opposition research—collecting and using derogatory information that might prove useful, either on offense or on defense.

Part II looks at strategic thinking. It begins with an overview of segment analysis in chapter 4, moving on to survey research in chapter 5, and voter targeting in chapter 6.

Part III examines voter contact, beginning with fundraising in chapter 7, moving to communications in chapters 8 (overall media strategy) and 9 (news coverage), and then to direct voter contact in chapter 10.

Part IV explores new kinds of campaigns (outside groups, judicial campaigns, and noncandidate campaigns) in chapter 11 and the future of electioneering in chapter 12.

The speed and dynamism of electioneering heighten the importance of historical understanding. This book draws heavily on the past and not just the latest, greatest campaign technologies. Important lessons can be drawn from the successes (and failures) of bygone contests.

Electioneering, for all its cutting-edge bluster, is inherently unadventurous. In the commercial world, strategists can roll out a new marketing technique with full knowledge that poor returns would mean a temporary, but recoverable, dip in sales. The all-or-nothing rules of American elections mean a new technique that loses few percentages points can spell disaster. A rational consultant might resist change and look to the successes and failures of others, learning about strategy and tactics vicariously through the retelling of war stories (see Burton and Shea 2003).

And yet, a critical transformation is under way. New-style campaigning has taken hold from the presidential level down to city-council contests. Political scientists have begun to understand the larger processes, even if the details are elusive. Gerald Pomper once remarked that, although Americans choose more than half a million public officials through the ballot, "elections are a mystery" (1974, 1). This book hopes to explain the operation of campaigns and to underscore the art and the science of professional electioneering.

# PART I

# CAMPAIGN PRELIMINARIES

# CHAPTER 1

# The Campaign Plan

Consultant Chapman Rackaway argues, "Most successful campaigns, as well as the competitive losing ones, have done an extensive amount of preparation that isn't detected by the naked eye" (Bowers and Daniels 2011, 18). Campaign manuals offer worksheets, strategies, and election calendars. One popular guidebook says, "[A] campaign plan lays out exactly what your team intends to accomplish daily from the first day of the race to the day after the election" (Shaw 2014, 341). Another cautions its readers, "Do not ever go into a campaign without some sort of plan" (Bike 1998, 176). Yet another warns, "As you read this Manual you will notice the relatively high costs and enormous amount of work involved. The immediate reaction generally is, 'Is all this really necessary to win?' The answer is an emphatic YES" (Guzzetta 2006, 133, emphasis omitted).

Smart campaigns plan ahead. John F. Kennedy and his advisers spent three years planning their 1960 presidential campaign. Sociologist William McPhee, whose contributions still inform political science, built a computerized algorithmic "people machine" in order "to predict how population changes would alter the electorate over a four-year presidential cycle" (Issenberg 2012b, 118). A daylong strategy session in October 1959, more than a year before voting got under way, focused on the campaign's "final assault plans" (White 1961, 53). In the morning, JFK ticked off strategy for each region and each state, getting into the details of local political factions. After lunch, with brother Bobby taking the lead, the agenda would shift to more practical matters, when "assignments were to be distributed and the nation quartered up by the Kennedy staff as if a political general staff were giving each of its combat commanders a specific front of operations" (56).

Quantitative methods have trooped into campaign planning. The winning presidential campaigns of George W. Bush profited from the expertise of a political scientist at the University of Texas, Daron R. Shaw, who applied his academic acumen to a supremely practical problem: winning a majority of electoral votes using data on past electoral contests. Shaw (2006) found, "Multivariate analysis of the 1988 through 1996 data demonstrate that the relative importance of a state is affected not only by its competitiveness and population but also by the cost of advertising in its media markets and the amount of recent effort expended there by the opposition" (46). States were ranked according to electoral value, and campaign resources were allocated to a set of target states and media markets laid down in the plan. For the 2012 race, Shaw took his skills to the presidential campaign of Texas governor Rick Perry (Issenberg 2012b).

A Kentucky political consultant notes, "In most cases my campaign plan is a working document. Rarely does everything remain constant from day one through election day, especially budgeting" (J. Emmons, pers. comm., 2009). With good planning, midcourse corrections can shim up a strong foundation, and strategists will not find themselves writing a new design from scratch or jerry-rigging the campaign operation to rescue sunk costs. While it may be true that plans are most effective when everything goes "according to plan"—and perhaps less so when the prearranged strategy goes haywire—one research team has observed, "[U]nexpected events make a campaign plan even more important, because it is too easy to diverge from one's path to election when responding in an ad hoc fashion to problems that may arise" (Klemanski, Dulio, and Switalski 2015, 34).

This chapter discusses the rationale for careful campaign planning, the basic elements of a campaign plan, and the challenges inherent in the planning process.

## The Need for Campaign Plans

Joseph Napolitan (1986) noted that campaign strategies must be suited to the candidates who use them. When a candidate is uncomfortable with the plan, blunders can follow. Candidates who are confused about the relationship between strategy and tactics might become hostile, second-guessing staff decisions after a consensus has been reached. A good campaign plan, it might be said, prevents an exasperated candidate from asking, at the worst possible moment, "Why am I doing this?"

The ideal plan will be so well understood, so meticulously documented, so deeply ingrained in campaign activities, that the reasons behind every event will be obvious. Core principles would be visible in the candidate's schedule, briefing book, and advertising buys. In Napolitan's mind, "one of the worst things that can happen is to have a campaign go off in several different directions simultaneously" (1986, 27). Consultants who believe they can deal with problems while the campaign is in motion might find themselves yearning for a reset button. Open assignments can become failed expectations; undefined schedules can become wasted time. Campaign operations involve details and deadlines, as well as turmoil. A campaign plan is meant to "bring order out of that chaos we call the democratic process" (Grey 2007, 90).

A campaign plan describes what is to be done, when it should be done, who should be doing it, and how the work will be completed (see Beaudry and Schaeffer 1986, 44). Good plans divide responsibility, integrate work, and present a step-by-step blueprint of the electoral cycle. With agendas and timetables in hand, everyone has a job to do. A plan must be flexible. It might change and may well require fundamental revision at some point, and yet the campaign plan remains an important tool for coordinating a diverse, concurrent, mutually dependent assortment of tasks.

"On a single page of paper," a consultant advised in the 1990s, "you must be able to succinctly match dollars, strategy, timeline, and cash flow" (Allen 1996, 51). Two decades on, the "paper" might exist as bits in the Cloud, but the core idea holds. Voter contact might demand two-thirds of the budget, and campaign organizations would also want to think about costs such as office space and supplies, computers and gasoline, voter lists and consultants who know how to turn those lists into votes, plus the price of pizza and T-shirts, and nail files imprinted with the candidate's name. Raising the money to pay for goods and services will itself incur costs. A "prospecting letter" intended to identify likely donors by asking for small sums of money requires a healthy investment in postage and stationery.

Canvassing the same neighborhood two different times with the same exact flyer is an expensive waste of resources. Each campaign function requires some level of harmonization with all the others.

Multiple staffers talking to multiple reporters threatens to send conflicting messages, leaving the campaign in the embarrassing position of explaining what it was really trying to say. Image tends to become reality and a discordant campaign risks appearing irresolute—too weak to govern.

Planning helps avert mixed messages. A "message of the week" might hammer home a single aspect of an overall theme each and every day from Monday through Sunday—the expectation being that repetition helps the message "break through." A plan might consider ways to ensure that campaign pronouncements do not overlap. If the campaign wants to follow an environmental track during a given week, all communication during this period should reinforce that singular message, and little should be said regarding consumer protection until "Consumer Week." Later, when radio spots are aimed at consumer-protection issues, the direct mail consultant should be sending consumer-oriented letters as the communications director is trying to get this message into the news cycle.

Since the planning document represents a strategic exercise, campaigns will want to figure out what the opposition might be contemplating. According to one professional, "There's nothing more pleasing, from the point of view of a strategist, than to work against an incumbent who runs the same campaign again and again" (Shea and Brooks 1995, 24). If the candidate's own record is vulnerable (no one is perfect), then strong responses to impending attacks should be drafted ahead of time. Consultant Mark Weaver has suggested that the job of a campaign is "to predict the counter-attack and be ready—because it will come" (ibid., 29). Like chess, electioneering is a game of anticipating and defeating opposition maneuvers before they come into play.

Finally, plans can help get the campaign going. Coordination can be fostered, and time and money can be saved, by establishing command authority and delegating staff responsibilities. A campaign staff might include a campaign manager, a finance director, a volunteer coordinator, a communications director, and deputies for some or all of these roles (see Figure 1.1). And a plan can inspire confidence among potential supporters and members of the news media. A well-organized candidate looks like a winner. "Sure losers" can be written off by journalists and influential politicos and may receive little help from donors. A strong campaign plan might show that the organization is serious; that it will conduct itself in an orderly, efficient, professional manner; that it will not waste resources or miss

Figure 1.1
Notional Campaign Organization

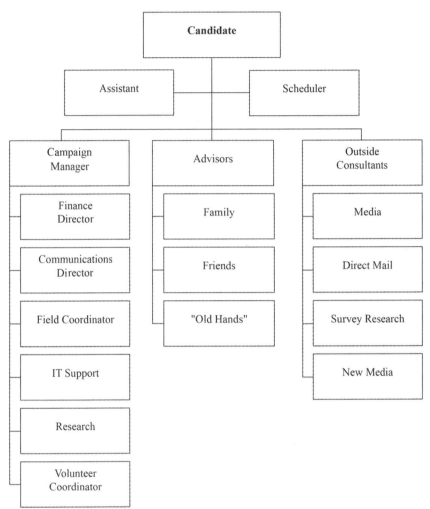

opportunities; and that it will not become an embarrassment. A candidate with a strong plan for victory might be worth watching.

## Elements of a Campaign Plan

No universal set of guidelines informs the development of a campaign plan, but the logic of electioneering suggests a few essential elements, including the following (which are detailed in later chapters).

- **District Profile.** A strategic portrait of a district would include physical geography, local industries, housing patterns, demographics, community organizations, partisanship, and other durable aspects of the political terrain. (See chapter 2.)
- **Candidate and Opposition Research.** A candidate's background, policy preferences, experience, committee posts, public (and not-so-public) statements, bill sponsorships, political appointments, and so forth can all have an impact on the campaign. The same holds true for the opposition. (See chapter 3.)
- **Segment Analysis.** A ward that has voted Republican in the past will likely vote Republican in the future. In the Digital Age, campaigns can readily move their analyses beyond geography, but an understanding of precinct analysis can help campaign strategists infer voter behavior from all sorts of political groupings. (See chapter 4.)
- **Polling.** If a campaign expects to hire a pollster, attention should be given to basic questions: What types of information will be sought? What sorts of questions should be asked? And how will the data be used? (See chapter 5.)
- **Voter Targeting.** Strategic considerations often dictate that campaigns court a narrow, persuadable slice of the electorate or a small group of supporters who might need some nudging into the voting booth. Finding these voters requires that a campaign figure out who might vote for the candidate, and why. (See chapter 6.)
- **Fundraising.** Just as a campaign must look for voters, it must seek the resources necessary to reach those voters, and contacting people in today's media environment is expensive. Campaigns need to raise money. (See chapter 7.)
- **Communications.** A strategic plan for campaign communications can be parceled into subsections—one for paid media, another for earned ("free") media—each subplan including electronic communication, print, and Internet strategies. (See chapters 8 and 9.)
- **Direct Contact.** Even as an increasing share of campaign spending is devoted to social media, campaign organizations carry on with traditional grassroots efforts, such as knocking on doors and putting up signs. (See chapter 10.)
- **Special Notes for Noncandidate Campaigns.** Recent court rulings, coupled with increasing emphasis on down-ballot issues, mean that campaign managers need to be well versed in the

expanding electoral environment, including the emergence of super PACs, judicial elections, and noncandidate ballot issues. (See chapter 11.)

## The Challenges of Planning

Integrating tactical elements into a unified schedule of action can be difficult. Budgets list financial income and outflow, and the idea that resources have to match expenditures provides a reasonable framework for assessing many aspects of the campaign process. With scarce resources—money, volunteer hours, candidate time, and so forth—income must equal outflow across domains. Somehow the whole operation needs to work together as a single unit; optimizing the sequence of events is a tricky business.

Campaign organizations have been urged to draw the electoral season on a flowchart. Starting with "a long roll of paper" (perhaps "butcher paper works best"), planners might attach colored sticky notes representing important events and functions (Shaw 2014, 342). Wall calendars and sticky notes are giving way to Cloud-based management software that produce Gantt charts, but the underlying rationale goes unchanged: Tasks must be divided into components, arrayed one after the next, and organized so that everything will be completed by the time the polls close on by Election Day. There is no "dog ate my homework" in political campaigning.

Campaigns should plan forward from the resources they have, or can reasonably expect to receive—why bother designing a million-dollar campaign unless the money is forthcoming?— and a political strategist might also want to think in reverse, starting with Election Day and moving backward to Day One (see Burton and Shea 2003, 6). Strategist Catherine Shaw urges, "[Y]ou know you will need to re-pair lawn signs the day after Halloween, so place a green Post-it reading 'Repair Lawn Signs' above November 1. Lawn signs usually go up one month before the election, so put that up next" (2014, 344). Binding it all together—assessing available resources and plausible outcomes, figuring out how to link means to ends—will likely turn into an ongoing design cycle that runs until the final moments of the contest.

With the advent of scheduling software, astute campaigns can automate the insertion of "pop-ups" into staff calendars. Reminders might be added for small items as well as large, such as making sure the candidate phones a key supporter on her birthday or buying airtime for a planned media hit. In the "heat of battle," a staffer can lose track of any number of items, but with foresight and care these mistakes might be held to a minimum.

Timing is important over the campaign season writ large. A strategist might contemplate a sequence that runs from (1) establishing name identification, that is, getting people to recognize the candidate by name; (2) persuasion, or bringing people to believe in the candidate; and (3) GOTV—"getting out the vote." Active partisans might know instantly whom they will support, and they may well cast a vote without prompting. For others, the decision-making process may take time, as the candidates come to awareness, as impressions are formed, and as a final determination is made—perhaps in the voting booth. A good campaign plan should probably attend to each of these phases.

Billboards (including programmable electronic billboards), bumper stickers, and yard signs serve almost no function other than establishing name recognition and perhaps affixing the party label to the candidate. There is room to question whether a campaign should push these materials out as early as possible—slowly building momentum as time goes by—or if a last-minute explosion might have greater impact (see Shaw 2014, 147–148). In some jurisdictions, the choice might be dictated by signage ordinances, such as one limiting the number of days that yard signs may be displayed prior to an election. Elsewhere, the fact that yard signs are vulnerable to late-campaign vandalism might force a decision to abandon their use altogether.

Political professionals want to control perceptions as they usher voters through the persuasion process. Campaign veteran Mary Matalin has called it "cardinal rule 101 of politics: Never let the other side define you" (Matalin and Carville 1995, 72). The corollary to rule 101 might well be: "Define the opponent early."

Early definition was central to Barack Obama's reelection plan. In spring of 2012, the Obama campaign painted Governor Mitt Romney as a wealthy, out-of-touch member of the corporate elite. Many voters learned about Romney's wealth and his purported "job killing" work with Bain Capital before they could learn about his political experience, policy positions, and personal life. Michael Feldman, former adviser to Vice President Al Gore, commented, "They . . . used the critical months between the end of the [Republican] primary and the general election to better define Mitt Romney than the Romney campaign did" (Mason 2012). Romney would struggle against this narrative for the remainder of the election, and arguably the early image of the

GOP (Grand Old Party—a common name used to refer to the Republican Party) candidate made later attacks on him seem more credible.

Defining candidates and opponents requires money and media. *Early* money allows a campaign to attract *more* money, and early money helps the campaign get a jump on the opposition when it goes looking to place its own media advertising. Operatives who fail to buy spots promptly can see the best ad times sold out from under them because local affiliates can deplete their stock of pre–Election Day ad slots if the opposition gets there first. A down-ballot race can lose out if an up-ballot race gets heated. Or a campaign might simply run out of cash while there is still time left (and GOTV to do) before the end of the election.

Even the best plan cannot eliminate uncertainty. In the same way an investment strategy will never take full account of future economic conditions (see Taleb 2010), a campaign plan relies on delicate guesswork about the political landscape that may or may not hold true. A campaign progressing through the final week of an election would not want to realize that most of the ballots had already been cast by mail. Errors of simple miscalculation are also possible. Sometimes the money does not come in; sometimes the volunteers do not show up; sometimes the stock market crashes in the closing weeks of a campaign cycle, as it did in September 2008, when operatives were sent scrambling to figure out how to communicate with voters who were watching their life savings evaporate as Election Day approached.

There is another reason campaign plans fail: The opposition is executing plans of its own. Many Americans worry that household budgets will be upset by unforeseen circumstances—layoffs, flat tires, and other bumps in the road resulting from the vagaries of an indifferent world. In politics, as in business and warfare, the world is not simply indifferent—it is hostile. Opposition forces are hard at work trying to figure out the candidate's next move so they can find the best place to lay a political trap. In a competitive enterprise, the unpredictability that bedevils forward planning and backward mapping is often the result of opposition attacks, and this fact bodes ill for many campaign plans. A truism of winner-take-all elections holds that only one campaign plan can survive a political duel.

## Conclusion

Thoughtful campaign plans hope to minimize doubt and waste. A plan seeks donor confidence, directs candidate energy, dampens the impact of opposition attacks, and tightens organizational focus on the endgame. If volunteers and staffers fixate on daily events, a team can wander "off message" and divert resources from mission-critical objectives. A solid plan can help keep everyone on task and on schedule, or at least it can help maintain big-picture perspective on routine electoral volatility.

Lacking omniscience, mistakes are made. "The best laid schemes o' Mice an' Men," Robert Burns intoned, "Gang aft agley"—that is, go awry—"An' lea'e us nought but grief an' pain / For promis'd joy!" If a campaign plan is not based on an accurate reading of past, present, and future events, of the candidate and the opponent, of the strengths and weaknesses of the sparring campaign organizations, and of the voting public, then even the most thoughtful preparations threaten to disappoint.

In 1991, those who designed George H.W. Bush's reelection effort assumed—quite reasonably—that the economy would pick up in short order, that there would be no real opponent in the GOP primaries, that the Bush White House and the Bush campaign would work co-operatively, and that the president would not need to hit the hustings in earnest until the Republican Convention. Life unfolded differently. The economy remained sluggish, conservative commentator-turned-candidate Pat Buchanan ran well in New Hampshire, coordination between the White House and the Bush campaign team was prob-lematic, and, because the president chose to spend time governing instead of campaigning, he fell so far behind Bill Clinton that recovery became all but impossible. Businessman Ross Perot jumping into the race, then out, then back in again, did not help President Bush. The Bush campaign plan, thoughtful though it may have been, did not match the unfolding reality.

A wise strategist knows that any plan might be no better than its assumptions, and assumptions can be wrong. While the value of a campaign plan is that it might keep an organization tightly focused through troubled times, sticking to a flawed plan extends the agony. Campaign strategists must decide when to cut the rope and when to hang on.

# CHAPTER 2

# The Context of the Race

American theologian Reinhold Niebuhr cautioned against worldly naïveté. Emotional support groups of all description would later soften his message, but the "Serenity Prayer," as it is now called, was originally expressed by Niebuhr in Old Testament prose, and it was meant in just that spirit. His prayer read: "God, give us grace to accept with serenity the things that cannot be changed, courage to change the things that should be changed, and the wisdom to distinguish between the two" (Sifton 1998). Niebuhr's prayer was intended to concentrate the mind on the rigors of differentiating the tractable from the intractable.

An ability to visualize the limits of practical possibility is an important part of political wisdom—the ability to look at a race, a district, or an opponent's popularity and then distinguish what can be changed from what cannot. Political scientists talk about "the fundamentals," meaning the features of the political terrain that are visible before the contest starts and that lie outside the control of a campaign organization. In some districts, the number of registered voters cannot be modified, while in others a strong voter registration drive can bring dramatic transformation. Partisan campaigns will be more effective in some areas than others. A discussion of political strategy is largely meaningless until the context is understood—until the things that cannot be changed are distinguished from the things that should be.

This chapter lists basic features of a political terrain: partisanship and turnout, the office being sought, voter expectations, the media environment, the salience of the contest at hand, the candidates' incumbency status, the structure of the ballot line, the type of election year, national conditions and perceptions, concurrent races, physical geography, demographics, the legal context, and other contextual factors.

## Features of the Terrain

Political consultants talk about the "landscape," "environment," and "political terrain." What office is in play? What do the demographics look like? Who else will be on the ballot? New-style politics begins with an understanding of campaign context.

### *Partisanship and Turnout*

Generally speaking, Democrats vote for Democrats and Republicans vote for Republicans—with those who mix their votes between the parties constituting the roll of persuadable voters. The idea that campaigns are won or lost in the middle of the electorate is premised on the existence of "persuadables" who (1) lack partisan commitments, or (2) agree with one party on some issues and with the other party on others. At a time when the parties held many conservative Democrats and liberal Republicans, this idea made sense. Voter behavior in recent years suggests Democrats and Republicans have become increasingly polarized, even "hyper-partisan." The widening gap between party adherents has been used to explain declining competitiveness among candidates in general elections (where party cues may dominate over policy cues) and rising competition of primary contests (where claims to the party mantle may be intense). Strategically, rising partisanship creates new hazards and opportunities that will be explored in chapter 6.

Likewise, people who have voted in the past tend to vote in the future. If a district is highly partisan, the real battles may take place in the primary election, not in the general. If the district is polarized, victory in the general election may depend on mobilizing partisans. Strategies for getting out the vote are discussed in chapter 10.

### *Office Sought*

Successful mayors can sometimes fail when they run for Congress. Congressional representatives are now and then defeated when they attempt a move to the Senate. The larger constituency may be quite different from the smaller districts inside it, and the difference might bring a loss. The electorate of a city might not look like that of the larger congressional district in which the city is located. In fact, voters may prefer candidates from one party for one level of government and another party for a different level (Burden and Kimball 2004) or candidates of one gender for one branch of government and another gender for a different branch (Dolan 2014).

### *Voter Expectations*

In matters as basic as tone, body language, and personal style, distinctions make a difference. Voters could well see prospective mayors, members of Congress, and senators quite differently. A loud tie and bombastic personality may be loved in city politicians and loathed in higher officials. The formality of an executive might seem pompous in a legislator. Voters might be looking for a Senate candidate who wears a dark suit but regard prospective county commissioners in business attire as haughty. A judicial candidate will usually want to sound nonpartisan—though expectations may be changing. Mayoral candidates at a public forum should know the details of local zoning laws and sewer problems, while a candidate for the House of Representatives standing before the very same audience will be forgiven if he or she does not know the nuances of recent tax levies. The congressional candidate will likely be expected to speak intelligently on issues of national importance—the federal deficit, for example.

A mold can even reward those who break it. Traditional wisdom holds that candidates for the U.S. Senate should remain stately, but one of the most talked-about ads from the 2014 campaign cycle featured pig castration. With a smile, the candidate explained,

> I'm Joni Ernst. I grew up castrating hogs on an Iowa farm. So when I get to Washington, I'll know how to cut pork. . . . My parents taught us to live within our means. It's time to force Washington to do the same—to cut wasteful spending, repeal ObamaCare, and balance the budget. I'm Joni Ernst and I approve this message because Washington's full of big spenders. Let's make 'em squeal.

And if gubernatorial candidates should wear dark suits, the rule was broken in 1998 when Minnesotans elected former professional wrestler Jesse "the Body" Ventura, whose television ads featured a seemingly naked Ventura posing as the model for Auguste Rodin's sculpture, *The Thinker*.

Not long ago, candidates typically wore business attire in public. Jackets might be doffed at barbecues and ice-cream socials, but for the most part, candidates should arrive at political events with greater formality. When a candidate is photographed with sleeves rolled up, the implication is obvious: "Let's get to work!" In some areas, this advice still holds, but in a time when the corporate world endorses "casual Fridays," formal business attire might connote self-importance. Campaign ads and brochures often show a candidate talking to citizens with a jacket draped over the shoulder. As more and more women have joined the ranks of the elected, their bright colors have been accepted, though in 2008, disparaging comments were sometimes directed at Hillary Clinton's wardrobe. In her "Squeal" ad, Joni Ernst's rural Midwestern style showed in a plaid shirt and a warm vest.

Experimental research has shown that people differ in their perception of candidates, depending on race (see Lerman and Sadin 2014), skin color (Weaver 2012), ethnicity (see McConnaughy et al. 2010), and gender (DiTonto, Hamilton, and Redlawsk 2014). Women, like racial and ethnic minorities, are handed the burden of figuring out how to "navigate" (Dittmar 2015; see also Jones 2014b) an electoral environment that was designed by, and continues to feel disproportionate influence from, white males who continue to be the majority of candidates and political staffers. Voters believe they "know" what a president, governor, or legislator looks like. Scholar Kelly Dittmar notes that Hillary Clinton in 2008 made the case for her candidacy in terms of strength and competence, not her gender. Dittmar's interviews with campaign strategists show that consultants are mindful of the strategic challenges facing (and opportunities presenting) women candidates. Evidently, "gender is a more common consideration for Democratic than Republican consultants, likely because of Democratic consultants' experience with female candidates and because of the alignment between gender stereotypes of women and the stereotypical expectations for their party" (2015, 35).

### Media Environment

The office being sought affects voter and media expectations. To gain positive press, a strategist should understand what reporters expect from candidates. For many voters, the lines separating local, state, and national issues are hazy, but to good reporters they are fairly clear: Federal candidates will be expected to be familiar with about national matters, state contestants should know about state issues, and local office seekers should understand community concerns.

In the fall of 2009, a special election to fill a House seat in the 23rd Congressional District of upstate New York drew wide media attention. Local GOP leaders had endorsed State Assembly woman Dede Scozzafava, while national conservatives like Rush Limbaugh and Sarah Palin endorsed political neophyte Doug Hoffman of the state's Conservative Party. As the race tightened, each candidate sought news media attention. Hoffman's editorial board meeting at the *Watertown Daily Times*, the largest newspaper in the district, backfired. As the editors described it, Hoffman "showed no grasp of the bread-and-butter issues pertinent to district residents" (*Watertown Daily Times* 2009). Hoffman lost to the Democrat by a razor-thin margin.

Presidential, Senate, gubernatorial, and U.S. House candidates might expect to see their commercials, speeches, and debate remarks double-checked, but state and local candidates are rarely evaluated by the mainstream news media. Reporters are overworked, underpaid, and have a great many demands on their time. Recent years have seen diminished local political reporting, which may mean reduced scrutiny from knowledgeable journalists who once covered the political beat (Fletcher and Young 2012). Then again, "ad watch" journalism, which emphasizes the disclosure of inaccuracies in campaign messages, has become a political force. Bloggers, who seem to be filling the space left by traditional journalists, cover state and local candidates and delight in publicizing factual gaffes, especially if the blog has a partisan bent.

### Contest Salience

Political novices can become frustrated that their campaigns do not make the news—or that the campaign may be of little interest to voters. This is natural. Candidates, party activists, volunteers, and professional consultants can become immersed in their campaigns and may believe others should be as well. Yet most voters prefer to think about their own spouses, children, bills, vacations, vaccinations, hobbies, cars, jobs, and other aspects of daily life. Political elections are of marginal concern to them. In the past few decades, the data from the American National Election Study indicate roughly one-third of those interviewed reported they did not care who won their congressional race, so few voters are concerned about county auditors.

Judge Lawrence Grey, a former elected appellate judge, dismisses the value of television: "You can . . . forget about any broadcast coverage of your campaign as a news event. . . . News divisions are operated as entertainment enterprises, and serious news is often not entertaining" (2007, 174). Statewide and large-city mayoral races receive a good deal of coverage but most congressional campaigns are given short shrift. Absent a controversy, colorful candidate, or cliffhanger, a race for city council, as well as county legislative, and state legislative, and local judicial races are usually ignored.

Down-ballot races demonstrate apathy among voters and donors. People who go to the polls almost always select a candidate for president, governor, and congressional representative, but many leave the ballot blank when they get to county commissioner. Lower-level offices can suffer drastic roll-off. The same is true in political fundraising. Individuals and organizations give money to candidates partly because they are aware of the campaign, and maybe excited by it. Presidents can raise hundreds of millions of dollars; county commissioners might raise thousands. If only a few people are familiar with the race, then only a few will contribute. Local candidates may have to rely on family, friends, a handful of associates willing to make a donation, and self-funding.

### Incumbency Status

Two-way electoral contests can be classified into three dyadic types: *uncontested, contested incumbency,* and *open seat.* An uncontested race has a single candidate and no challenger (so the winner is a foregone conclusion). Races in which an incumbent faces a challenger are usually won by the current officeholder. As much as people say they want to "throw the bums out," they tend to vote for "the devil they know." Most uncertain is an open-seat election. Two well-qualified candidates running against one another can make for stirring political drama.

Despite occasional twists of fate, incumbency is a valuable resource. Officeholders typically enjoy higher name recognition than challengers, deeper relations with the news media, more staff assistance, better finances, a broader base of volunteers, and stronger connections with parties and interest groups. Some incumbents cultivate support through e-mails, impromptu meetings, telephone town halls, and scores of receptions, dinners, parades, church services, and holi-day mailings. Incumbents generally have at least a measure of built-in appeal—they were already elected at least once—and they are a good bet for the future.

In 2014, a devastating year for Democrats, a meme crossed the Internet with a photo of the House Floor emblazoned with the words: "11% APPROVAL RATINGS; 96.4% RE-ELECTED" (Issa and Jacobson 2014). The numbers were slightly off, but only slightly. Survival rates may differ in state and local government elections—legislative, executive, and judicial—and yet overall the value of in-cumbency holds across political domains.

If an incumbent is free of scandals and bloopers, a challenger's odds are slim. Most challengers have comparatively little name rec-ognition. Political action committees and major donors hesitate to back challengers for fear of antagonizing incumbents (i.e., the person most likely to be making policy after the election). According to the Campaign Finance Institute (CFI), in 2012 there were 256 House races wherein the incumbents netted over 60 percent of the general election vote, and incumbents in these races garnered an average of $1.3 million, while their challengers raised an average of just over $154,000. The gap is smaller in competitive races, but when the in-cumbent netted less than 60 percent of the vote, the average chal-lenger raised less than half the amount collected by the incumbent (Campaign Finance Institute 2012a).

Generally speaking, the higher the profile of the race, the weaker the incumbency advantage. Presidents, governors, and U.S. senators benefit from greater media coverage, especially in the early stages of a race, but these carefully watched campaigns offer significant media coverage to the challenger as well. Yet, so strong is the incumbency effect that, when mixed with partisan advantage, the 2014 race saw the reelection of a married congressman who had been caught on camera passionately kissing a congressional staffer and another who was facing tax evasion charges.

### Ballot Line

The head-to-head contests of a typical general election, which pit nominees of the two major political parties against one another, rep-resent a portion of the elections held in the United States. A ballot line may include three or more candidates—minor-party entrants, independent candidates, and write-ins. Voters in Nevada can vote for "None of These Candidates." Some contests have a two-step process: If a candidate garners more than 50 percent, the election is over; if no candidate crosses the 50 percent mark, then the two top vote-getters are forced into a runoff. In the 2009 race for mayor of Atlanta, the leading candidate had 46 percent of the vote on Election Day, but since no contestant crossed the 50 percent threshold the race went into overtime, and the leader in the many-way general election wound up losing in the two-way runoff. Some jurisdictions offer a handful of "at-large" seats to the top vote-getters. Five candidates might vie for three seats, and the three candidates with the largest number of votes win those three seats.

Minor-party candidates rarely win general elections but often make a difference. They can erode a major-party base of support, undercut the intended message, and siphon off volunteers. Minor-party candidates often join the race because they are dissatisfied with the incumbent, a feeling that might be shared in the wider electorate. It is no accident that Jesse Ventura's win came at the expense of two well-known Minnesota officeholders. Challenging the system was the point of his campaign. In 2014, a Democratic nominee pulled his name from the Kansas ballot in (vain) hopes that an independent candidate for the U.S. Senate would have a better shot at defeating the incumbent Republican.

### Election Year

Campaign professionals distinguish three different kinds of campaign year: "on," "off," and "odd." An *on-year* election occurs when presidential candidates appear on the ballot (e.g., 2012 and 2016); *off-year* elections also occur every four years, in the even-numbered years between presidential contests (e.g., 2014 and 2018); *odd-year* elections occur in odd-numbered years (e.g., 2015 and 2017). An occasional "special" election for House or Senate will be held in an odd year to fill a prematurely vacated seat.

The number of people going to the polls varies by election-year type. Turnout is almost always highest during on-years, thanks to presidential electioneering, which boosts overall interest. The entire House of Representatives, one-third of the Senate, most state legislators, and many governors are elected during on-years. Generally speaking, off-years have lesser turnout. The vast majority of jurisdictions reserve odd-years for municipal offices.

Special elections and runoffs also suffer diminished turnout. "Specials" are often held on short notice when an office suddenly becomes vacant. In New York's 23rd Congressional District special election in 2009, just 34 percent of eligible voters went to the polls whereas 63 percent had voted in the 2008 election and 43 percent in 2006. High-intensity races can suffer diminished turnout when they depart from the regular calendar. The runoff for the U.S. Senate seat from Louisiana in 2014, which was driven by massive spending and other voter outreach, saw a drop in turnout of 15 percent as compared to the general election that preceded it a month earlier.

Political scientists have observed a cyclical phenomenon they call "surge and decline" (Campbell 1960; Cover 1985). In on-years, presidential victory is accompanied by co-partisan gains in the House and Senate. In midterm congressional elections, the president's party will lose seats. The party typically loses more in the second midterm election than in the first. There are exceptions. Democrats gained seats in the sixth year of Bill Clinton's term of office and Republicans did the same in the second year of George W. Bush's term. Surge and decline seemed to have run its course. But Republicans lost control of the House and Senate in the sixth year of Bush's presidency, Democrats solidified their gains with the election of Barack Obama, but the House went back to the GOP in the second year of Barack Obama's presidency and the Senate was lost to Republicans in year six.

### National Conditions and Perceptions

All politics may be local, as Tip O'Neill famously said, but local politics cannot escape national trends, moods, and obsessions. Each year, media outlets highlight some concerns and downplay others, as the "crime issue" demonstrates. The mismatch between crime statistics and public perceptions has been a persistent feature of the political landscape. From a legal historian in 1993:

> Throughout the country, newspapers, movies, and TV spread the word about crime and violence—a misleading word, perhaps, but a powerful one. Even people who live in quiet suburban enclaves, or rural backwaters, are aware of what they consider the crime problem. (Friedman 1993, 452)

Gallup surveys show public perceptions have not changed over the years (McCarthy 2014), while actual crime rates have steadily

declined. From a crass, strategic point of view, the difference between perception and reality may have little meaning. A candidate
for city prosecutor may be able to assume voters share a fear of crime
without commissioning a survey of local residents.

Other conditions and dispositions also translate into electoral
politics. In the 1970s, election scholar Edward Tufte (1975) built a
strong predictive model of congressional elections using presidential approval scores and shifts in economic conditions—factors that
House candidates are hard-pressed to control. Although scholars
have since produced more refined models, Tufte's point is well taken:
Voters reward or punish subnational candidates for national events.
Trends can be set in motion by tragedies, crises, and wars. Following the terrorist attacks of September 11, 2001, a federal candidate's
foreign policy experience and commitment to military power were
seen as key qualifications for office. The GOP gains in 2002, which
ran counter to surge-and-decline theory, owed partly to the rise of
security concerns prompted by 9/11.

But events are subject to interpretation. A Republican may trust an
economic recovery is a product of tax-cut policies, and a Democrat
may conclude that crime is not the most important item on the political agenda. Campaign professionals understand that public perceptions can be nudged—for better or worse—if prior beliefs are taken
into account. Whatever might be responsible for national tragedies,
the economy, or criminal behavior, these are the sorts of issues that
voters can feel in their bones. A campaign that wants to bring people
closer to the truth must begin with what voters believe, not what they
ought to believe.

### Concurrent Races

Popular presidents and governors may help (or hurt) friends down
the ballot. Faith in "coattails" is deeply embedded in electoral politics. The glow of one candidate, it is assumed, will reflect upon co-
partisans. As reasonable as the coattails theory may appear, direct
evidence for a strong effect eludes scholars.

The relationship between up-ballot and down-ballot candidacies can
make cause difficult to infer. Election scholar Gary Jacobson (1989)
suggests "strategic politicians" pay close attention to early polling data,
particularly relating to co-partisans. When colleagues are unpopular,
strategic politicians sit the race out. The nomination is left to lesser

candidates, who, with poor qualifications, little money, and low name recognition, tend to lose elections. When the party is in good favor with the electorate, stronger politicians enter the race. Because they have better qualifications, recognition, and financing, strategy-minded politicians are more likely to win elections. So, in some part, the observable correlation between down-ballot and up-ballot fortunes may be due to strategic decisions made by down-ballot aspirants.

While coattails may have little direct effect, they are not inconsequential, just nuanced (Stoll 2013). Close analysis of statewide results shows marginal benefits for down-ballot candidates (Meredith 2014). The perception that coattails exist may bring strong down-ballot contenders into the race when more prominent candidates lead the way. Better candidates bring increased financial support and heightened media coverage. If supporters believe a candidate will get a significant boost from higher-ups on the ticket, they may see things are going well and want to lend a hand. In other words, the coattails theory may be self-fulfilling.

### *Physical Geography*

Campaign tactics are molded partly by a district's physical layout. Door-to-door canvassing is feasible in suburban areas and may be more cost-effective than broadcast advertising. This kind of electioneering might be more difficult in the central business district insofar as high-rise apartment buildings (containing rich lodes of voters) often forbid entry. A sparsely populated countryside can dampen the enthusiasm of weary volunteers.

Some jurisdictions present interesting problems. While a candidate for a statewide seat in Rhode Island has more than a million souls packed into 1,000-square-mile area, a candidate in Wyoming has fewer than 600,000 residents scattered across almost 100,000 square miles. In a Quixotic run against a well-resourced incumbent, Democratic challenger Charlie Hardy ran against U.S. Senator Mike Enzi by traveling across Wyoming "in a 1970 Crown school bus that's painted blue, white, green and black and has Washington plates and Wyoming Cowboys plate holders." The *Casper Star Tribune* reported that the owner of the bus was Hardy's

> campaign manager, who is from Olympia, Washington, and purchased it about a year ago for social justice activism road

trips. Wilkinson and some friends replaced the seats. They built tables of plywood and bunks of mahogany they found in a Dumpster at a hardwood business. It seats about 30. It sleeps six comfortable. (Hancock 2014)

Evidently, 62 miles per hour was the maximum attainable speed. (The driving distance between Jackson Hole and Cheyenne is a lonely 450 miles.)

Some jurisdictions allow a candidate to bicycle from one end to the other while others are burdened by high mountains, thick forests, and wide bodies of water. Some districts encompass urban density, making the placement of campaign headquarters obvious; others are so fragmented that careful calculations must precede the placement of far-flung outposts.

### Demographics

Campaign professionals have long understood the power of demographic categories. Meaningful differences in partisanship and turnout can be drawn by race, income, profession, age, neighborhood choice, religiosity, and education. These differences shape the ways in which strategists segment, target, and message the electorate as a whole.

A snapshot of salient features of today's American political demography shows general differences with respect to partisan preferences:

- Women tend to vote Democratic and men tend toward the GOP (Pew Research Center 2012).
- Married people have been voting disproportionately Republican and unmarried people more Democratic (Connelly et al. 2014).
- Union members are more likely to be Democrats than Republicans (Connelly et al. 2014).
- Greater religiosity is associated with increased likelihood for supporting the GOP (Newport 2014).
- African Americans have been solidly Democratic for several decades (Kohut et al. 2012).
- White voters are increasingly Republican (Jones 2014a; Cohn 2014a) and white southerners have become solidly Republican (Cohn 2014b).
- Latinos are a rapidly growing segment of the electorate (Lopez et al. 2014).

- All else being equal, upscale voters tend to be Republican and downscale voters tend to be Democratic (Gelman et al. 2010; Gelman 2014b).
- Voters who live in cities are more Democratic than voters who live in rural areas (Connelly et al. 2014).
- Young people in today's electorate tend to be more Democratic (Connelly et al. 2014).

One lesson for a political strategist would be that a white, married male living in a small southern town would likely vote Republican; if this voter lived in a city as was unmarried, the picture is muddied, as will be discussed in chapter 6.

Separately, strategists should consider the propensity of voters to cast a ballot. As compared to the eligible population that votes, people who do not register or are unlikely to vote—a Pew Research Center report calls it the "Party of Nonvoters"—are younger, racially and ethnically mixed, and downscale (in terms of money and education). These nonvoters and unlikely voters tend not to identify with a political party, though they lean Democratic (Doherty, Keeter, and Weisel 2014).

### Legal Context

States and counties vary in the rules applied to electoral contests. Some states have mail-in ballots while others require in-person voting on Election Day. In many areas special considerations are made for overseas and military voters. Campaign finance laws are not uniform, especially in relation to corporate and union participation. Some jurisdictions have laws on signage or push polling. Voter ID laws are controversial, but for a campaign looking to turn out the vote the details of existing law are paramount. The consequences to a campaign organization for failing to understand its legal context can be severe.

### Conclusion

Political context takes many forms. What counts as "context" in one area may well be classified as "opportunity" in another.

Nearly all districts have strong institutional traditions, boasting labor unions, chambers of commerce, service clubs, or other such organizations. Politically active associations might provide endorsements and contributions, but the importance of an organization is not measured solely by formal political affiliations. Nonpolitical groups can be central to word-of-mouth communication. In some areas volunteer fire departments loom large, in size and stature, and while these organizations are officially nonpartisan, campaigns and elections might be a constant topic of conversation. The same can be true for senior centers, kids' sports leagues, and Meetup groups that have no overt link to politics.

Local politicians can help attract media attention, endorsements, contributor lists, advice, and volunteers. Activists can make helpful introductions. Some local party organizations focus on winning elections while others place greater emphasis on policy questions. In the latter, a candidate's ideological purity might be more important than his or her ability to court nonpartisan voters (Shea, Strachan, and Wolf 2012). In some states elected officials transfer campaign funds to other candidates.

That said, rivalries often divide political communities, and a candidate who inadvertently lines up on the wrong side of a feud can cause irreparable damage to his or her campaign. A political hero can be a powerful force. But not all politicians are viewed favorably. Some depart public life on a bad note, and photos associating a candidate with a political villain (who looked like a hero) can cause headaches. Endorsers do not always share their checkered pasts willingly, and campaign operatives who are lured into an endorsement may find that they have generated a viral video and public wrath.

Constituencies have unique social customs, political guidelines, and pet peeves. Scholar Daniel Elazar, in *The American Mosaic* (1993), drew attention to the importance of historical, democratic, and economic factors that combine to create political cultures. Voters in some communities are much more accustomed to hard-hitting, aggressive campaigning than are voters in other areas (Patterson and Shea, 2003). A city might accept the use of mild profanity on the stump, while its neighboring suburbs do not. Are political discussions allowed in church? It depends on the community, and the church. Is it polite to call people by their first names? Perhaps, but it would seem best to find out ahead of time. Who insists on being called "Doctor"? Or "Colonel"? Who has a fantastical sense of self-importance? Who was divorced recently? Who is a vegetarian? The details get complicated. In some locales, candidates will find Democratic taverns and Republican lounges, and out-of-town guests might be expected to stay at hotels with a long-standing (or newly established) connection to a party.

Local party organizations vary in the degree of assistance they provide to candidates. In some areas, parties are eager to help aspirants to public office, maybe offering endorsements during the primary season, while in others they are no help at all. Where party organizations are strong, a candidate might find a powerful leader at the helm. It could be the chair, though sometimes an influential veteran is really in charge—and sometimes it is an operative from the neighboring county machine. Party bosses can be pivotal players, leveraging money and volunteers as no one else can. Gatekeepers can also be cantankerous. In New Hampshire, it has been said, a Republican presidential candidate who wants to call on experienced volunteers must first "enlist a poobah, a warlord, a New Hampshire potentate," involving political machinations reminiscent of "the old Kremlin and the Soviet politburo" (Ferguson 1996, 44).

Local political machines are important, and so are tourism, culture, and recreation. Ski resorts and sports stadiums are large employers, and knowing what voters do in their spare time helps a candidate develop connections with voters. Communities across the country are proud of their mountains, deserts, redwoods, boat ramps, trolleys, coal mines, battlefields, soft-shell crabs, po'boys, salmon, native prairies, cattle ranches, hippie-filled history, social protests, operas, high school football victories, pumpkin festivals, debate teams, and historic natural disasters along with social and political turmoil. A candidate in western Pennsylvania who knows little about waterfowl might want to go on a hunting trip. A strategist hoping to recruit young Christians as volunteers might want to know a few TobyMac songs.

A campaign is about strategy, and strategizing involves looking at the terrain on which the campaign will operate: a party boss who will not budge, a district so large that the candidate has trouble keeping to schedule, a national economic trend over which the campaign has no control but under which it must labor, meager candidates at the top of the ticket, minor-party spoilers, an opponent who enjoys the benefits of incumbency, and so on. Strategists who do not accept "the things that cannot be changed" might find themselves at a profound disadvantage. The difference between amateurs and professionals in the world of political campaigning is partly measured by the degree to which they can understand the realities of the districts in which they are working.

# CHAPTER 3

# Opposition Research

Operatives for Democrat William Magee's 1990 campaign for New York's heavily Republican 111th State Assembly District knew their voters, and their adversary. Magee had compiled stacks of information on Republican Jack McCann. After 25 years in public life, McCann had amassed a long public record, and Magee's campaign team used that record to assemble a damaging profile of its opponent.

Magee took advantage of the upstate/downstate split in New York politics. New York is two states in one: The greater New York City area is "downstate," and everything north of Westchester County is "upstate." Downstate has traditionally been heavily Democratic and most members of the Assembly from that area were Democrats. Conversely, most upstate politicos were Republicans. Animosity between the two regions stretches back to early America. Upstate politicos would not want to be called a pawn of downstate interests, and vice versa.

Democrats had held the majority in the Assembly for decades. They controlled the legislative calendar, appropriations, committee assignments, office space, and pork-barrel allocations. Republicans were left to nip at the edges and stall the process. Parliamentary games were played out during each legislative term as the two sides postured, harassed, and embarrassed each other. Although Democrats had nearly complete control over the budget process, Republicans stonewalled by offering amendments. Republicans might suggest adding money to the budget for law enforcement, compelling Democrats, who had already struck a budget agreement with the state senate and the governor, to vote against the amendment. Republicans would then claim Democrats were "soft on crime."

One year, the Republicans pledged to vote as a team. A few of the Republicans were from downstate—Long Island, mostly—and these members, like the rest of the minority, offered amendments seeking funds for roads, bridges, rail stations, parking lots, ferry ports, and other projects helpful to downstate residents. McCann was a team player so he voted with his GOP colleagues, though his district sat 200 miles to the north. Here the Magee campaign found its line of attack: Why was McCann voting for downstate projects?

The campaign assembled a direct mail piece with a large picture of then New York City mayor Ed Koch on the outside and a caption asking, "What Do Ed Koch and Jack McCann Have in Common?" Upon opening the mailer, the reader learned, "They Both Work for New York City!" Below the headline was a list of downstate projects McCann had supported along with staggering price tags. At the bottom, the costs were summed up, and a final caption read, "At a time when our roads, bridges, and schools are falling apart, Jack McCann is pushing for more than $1 billion for New York City. Who is he working for, Ed Koch or us?" Newspapers picked up the story as did many television and radio news programs. The notion that McCann was a "pawn of downstate interests" quickly spread. McCann, forced to defend his votes, was distracted from touting his central accomplishments. This one early-campaign mailing helped turn a long-shot venture into a neck-and-neck race in which Magee eventually prevailed. In 2014, Magee won his thirteenth consecutive election to the Assembly.

This chapter discusses opposition research—called "oppo" in the trade, or simply "research"—through discussions of the history of opposition research, ethical issues in opposition research, counteropposition research, and types of profile data.

## Historical Perspectives

Opposition research has deep roots. During the presidential election of 1800, Federalist operatives dug up rumors that Thomas Jefferson might have had several slave mistresses and fathered a child with one of them. (Genetic testing later suggested the Federalists could have been right about the paternity issue.) Years later, in the election of 1884, opponents of Grover Cleveland repeated the gossip that Cleveland had fathered a child out of wedlock with a woman named Maria Halpin. Supporters of James G. Blaine chanted, "Ma, Ma, where's my Pa? Gone to the White House, ha, ha, ha." The Cleveland team retaliated by charging that Blaine had used his congressional office for financial gain, and supporters had their own version of the song: "Blaine, Blaine, Jay Gould Blaine! The Contentional Liar from the state of Maine." Cleveland won the election, and on Election Night, Cleveland's people shouted, "Hurrah for Maria, Hurrah for the Kid. I voted for Cleveland, and I'm damned glad I did!" (Johnson-Cartee and Copeland 1991, 6–7).

Opposition research has been conducted by college students, friends, partisans, and family members. During most of the 20th century, a paid professional would have been considered an extravagance. A consultant writing at the dawn of the Digital Age recalled the old days: "Prior to the popularization of the Internet, [a campaign's] examination of the public record had to be done on-site, by hand." A public record spanning 25 years "took five people six months to complete. In addition to being slow and time-consuming, the cost to the client was staggering" (Bovee 1998, 48). Today, many consulting firms specialize in research—an oppo book can cost tens of thousands of dollars—and the resources available to oppo professionals have increased immeasurably (Hruby 2012). In 2014 a politico estimated that "nearly $17 million has been spent on oppo-related costs by federal committees that regularly disclose their finances" (Vogel and Tau 2014).

In the late 1990s, opposition research meant an operative "sitting in front of a computer examining everything from newspaper articles, to property records, to civil and criminal court records" (Bovee 1998, 48). Ironically, the rise of computer technology began to turn oppo back to its amateur roots, but with a high-tech twist. Votes, contributions, and public statements can be located in moments by a volunteer with little experience in computer technology or political research. Oppo is semiautomated, thanks to Web-based applications that track movement on social media or candidates' Web sites. Users are immediately alerted if a change is made to an opponent's digital presence. As Jeff Martin, chair of the Minnesota Democratic-Farmer-Labor Party explains: "Say you make a mistake or say something wrong and you delete it. . . . It's too late, we already have it. It's opposition research in real time" (Bierschbach 2014).

Campaign organizations and their allies can bypass traditional reporting outlets by pushing messages through social media channels. American Bridge, a so-called super PAC (see chapter 11), sends operatives into the field to record Republican candidates (and their presumed gaffes) on video. Jeff Berkowitz explains, "[T]the fastest way to disseminate information is through social media, such as Twitter and Facebook." Further, "Twitter is better because it breaks news faster. You can push things around on Twitter. It's like wildfire. Twitter both provides information and also provides the dissemination mechanism. Campaigns are going to have to adapt to that" (Reid 2011).

The best-known clip in the history of opposition research did not come from a political organization. In a private event held for political donors in Boca Raton, a bartender recorded Mitt Romney answering a question about campaign strategy:

> There are 47 percent of the people who will vote for the president no matter what. All right, there are 47 percent who are with him, who are dependent upon government, who believe that they are victims, who believe the government has a responsibility to care for them, who believe that they are entitled to health care, to food, to housing, to you-name-it. That that's an entitlement. And the government should give it to them. And they will vote for this president no matter what. . . . These are people who pay no income tax. . . . [M]y job is not to worry about those people. I'll never convince them they should take personal responsibility and care for their lives.

The bartender leaked the video to *Mother Jones* writer David Corn, who released it to the world in September 2012 (Corn 2012), and the "47 percent" strategy dogged Romney until Election Day. That Romney later claimed he was misunderstood meant little to those who thought the quote fit a larger narrative.

## Ethical Issues in Opposition Research

Media consultant Bob Squier once said, "I love to do negatives. It is one of those opportunities in a campaign where you can take the truth and use it like a knife to slice right through the opponent" (Luntz 1988, 72). Gary Maloney, who has worked on Republican presidential and senatorial campaigns, says the most rewarding part of oppo is "finding the truth, and using it to elect honest men and women and to defeat liberals, evildoers and crooks" (*Campaigns and Elections* 2006a). Still, many voters say they do not like negative campaigning, and a handful of misguided research projects have shocked the political conscience. Voters' reactions suggest that ethical bounds seem to exist for the production and dissemination of opposition research, even if the lines are hazy and even if they have moved back and forth over the decades, and continue to evolve.

Opposition research seems most ethical when the candidate grants permission. In 1987, following rumors of extramarital affairs, presidential candidate and senator from Colorado, Gary Hart, challenged reporters, "Follow me around. I don't care. I'm serious. If anybody wants to put a tail on me, go ahead. They'll be very bored" (Dionne 1987). Unfortunately for Hart, reporters had indeed been following him around and it is doubtful they were bored, as evidence of an affair (despite denials) started with an anonymous tip and led to a revealing stakeout of Hart's D.C. home and reports of a cruise to Bimini on a yacht named "Monkey Business."

Reportage on Bill Clinton and Monica Lewinsky culminated in Clinton's impeachment by the House of Representatives and fostered commentary on journalistic values. Larry Sabato, Mark Stencel, and Robert Lichter (2000) offered a standard that distinguishes reportable from unreportable "news" according to the story's impact on public affairs. A candidate's personal life should become news only when it affects public business. Extramarital affairs might be out of bounds, but not if the relationship involves a lobbyist. That scenario would make the story legitimately reportable due to the "clear intersection between an official's public and private roles" (2000, 8).

Within a few years, this optimistic framework was tested by the Internet's entry into scandal stories. Blogging and social media diminished the gatekeeping authority of traditional journalism, as amateur sleuths could join the fray. In 2004, a lively, sometimes vicious, conversation surrounded questions as to (1) whether a young George W. Bush had fulfilled his obligations to the Texas National Guard and (2) whether journalists at CBS, which aired allegations that Bush missed Guard training dates, had met their journalistic responsibilities to check the facts. At CBS, doubts about the story resulted in a formal internal investigation; Internet-based commentary labored under no such formality.

In the Digital Age, the countervailing ethical force is not journalistic gatekeeping but simple backlash. In 2008, as Sarah Palin's family was drawn into the blogosphere, Barack Obama was adamant that personal attacks were wrong: "Let me be clear as possible. I think people's families are off-limits, and people's children are especially off-limits. . . . We don't go after people's families; we don't get them involved in the politics. It's not appropriate, and it's not relevant"

(Marquardt 2008). John McCain pushed back on rumors a supporter had "read" that Obama was "an Arab": "No, ma'am. He's a decent family man [and] citizen that I just happen to have disagreements with on fundamental issues and that's what this campaign's all about. He's not [an Arab]" (Martin and Parnes 2008). In 2014, an alleged effort to photograph a U.S. senator's bedridden wife—the exact rationale is elusive—was condemned from across the political spectrum (see Burns 2014a).

While standards set by the press and public are sometimes cryptic, political news has guidelines. Some journalists are seeking greater disclosure of oppo sourcing (Shapiro 2012). Even as recreational reporting in the form of blogs and online rumor mills bypass traditional journalism, trained reporters hold considerable sway insofar as the online community cites conventional reporting as authority— and uncited work can be dismissed by those not already wedded to a blogger's point of view. Journalistic standards holding that reportage must be true, reasonable, and fair continue to maintain some degree of influence.

### Truthfulness

Rumors are rampant in politics and on the Web, but most gossip is not reported in the traditional news media because the hearsay is unverifiable. Without verification, a gossip-based story violates key tenets of the profession, and reporters are on the lookout for claims that stretch the bounds of credulity.

During the 2008 Senate race in North Carolina, Elizabeth Dole's campaign aired television ads against her opponent, Kay Hagan, implying that Hagan's attendance at a fundraiser held in the home of a man who advocated political secularism showed Hagan herself was "godless." The ad included video footage of activists giving interviews about their political agenda, and it ended with an image of Hagan, accompanied by a voice that sounded like it might be Hagan's, stating, "There is no God" (Brown 2008). The *Charlotte Observer* made clear that Hagan "teaches Sunday school and is an elder at her Presbyterian church in Greensboro" (Zagaroli 2008b). One unintended consequence of the ad may have been a surge in money for Hagan, who took in a large number of donations after Dole's ad was publicized (Zagaroli 2008a).

Two subsets of the truthfulness standard hold that the information must have been gained from a legitimate source—one that is legal and appropriate—and that the information must be independently verifiable. Operatives should not hide in the bushes with a camera or present gossip as if it were fact, nor should they hire someone else to do the dirty work. Even if the campaign is dealing with legitimately gathered information, it must think about the verifiability problem. Clinton's 1992 campaign, which was given a foreign news report that Bush campaign signage was being produced in Brazil, was unable to get the American media to air the story because no one could verify that the Bush campaign actually knew its materials were manufactured abroad (*The War Room* 1993). The story could not be authenticated, and therefore, it could not be run. (If such a story were to emerge in more recent times, it surely would make the rounds on YouTube and wind up reported by journalists who feel pressured to report water-cooler conversations among voters.)

### Reasonableness

A campaign that is proffering a fact, document, or plotline that "explains everything" may be surprised to find that reporters are unwilling to chase the lead. Journalists are averse to flacking political ideologies and they receive a great many half-baked story ideas, especially from people who happen to have a vested interest in publicizing those ideas. If conclusions seem far-fetched, veer from accepted premises, or ring false to professional observers of political events, the story might feel "conspiratorial." Reporters tend to reject fringe notions such as those pressed by 9/11 "Truthers" and anti-Obama "Birthers" as the purveyors of these conspiracy theories lament the failure of the "mainstream media" to pay attention (see Weigel 2011). A journalist who runs with an improbable story can be accused of letting the "coverage get ahead of the facts" (Nyhan 2013)—of engaging in "mere speculation."

Journalistic standards of reasonableness curb stray remarks. When Jack Welch, former CEO of General Electric, insinuated that the Bureau of Labor Statistics might have fabricated job numbers to enhance Obama's prospects for victory, an ABC News.com blog referenced Welch, saying the unemployment rate "has raised suspicions that the White House might be cooking the books ahead of the election next month" (Ellin 2012). The comment seemed to stoke cynicism rather than illuminate events. It prompted immediate criticism (Nyhan 2012) and scholarly research into the effects of credible sources repeating conspiracy theories (Einstein and Glick 2013) followed by a post on the *Columbia Journalism Review* Web site: "Irresponsible coverage creates the potential for a vicious cycle in which conspiracy theories about an administration help generate scandals that, in turn, reinforce yet more conspiracy theories" (Nyhan 2013).

Time pressures imposed by Twitter and other rapid-fire outlets may be straining cool-headed reason, though rapid circulation is also forcing quick correction. A comment can take off on Twitter, get thrown around among journalists and politicos, then get corrected, and then disappear shortly after the first tweet was released, as when Mitt Romney made an off-hand comment some interpreted as a nod toward Birtherism. Analyst Sasha Issenberg commented, "These little stories catch fire on Twitter more quickly than they did with bloggers in 2008, but it also means that they burn out faster" (Ingram 2012). Instead of letting the coverage wander into make-believe, the efficient market of news reporting quickly brought the conversation to its natural state and few voter learned of Romney's aside.

### Fairness

The National Public Radio (NPR) "Ethics Handbook" states, "We make every effort to gather responses from those who are the subjects of criticism, unfavorable allegations or other negative assertions in our stories." Moreover, "In all our stories, especially matters of controversy, we strive to consider the strongest arguments we can find on all sides, seeking to deliver both nuance and clarity" (National Public Radio, n.d., "Fairness"). The handbook looks for reporting from various and competing perspectives on political issues. In a two-way general election, journalists from NPR and other mainstream news outlets can be expected to request comment from a Democrat and a Republican of equal stature.

A candidate who believes fervently in his or her chosen viewpoint may be unhappy with "false balance." The public editor of the *New York Times*, Margaret Sullivan, commented in late 2012 that "readers and media critics are calling for journalists to take more responsibility for what is true and what is not" (Sullivan 2012). New questions are being raised about reporters' handling of topics that go to politically charged scientific inquiry and constitutional interpretation, among other sensitive topics. Sullivan quotes the national editor of the *Times*, who asserted, "It's not our job to litigate it in the paper. . . . We need to state what each side says" (ibid.). Absent fundamental changes in American journalism, a candidate can expect to see reporters tacking back and forth in search of contrary remarks on any given topic.

## Counteropposition Research

A nearly universal precept—from philosophy to theology to military affairs—holds that one should reflect upon one's self before attacking others. Ignoring counteropposition research can put staff in the unenviable position of the McCain campaign after Alaska Governor Sarah Palin was nominated as vice president. The governor came off well in person but she was being pursued in her home state by allegations of misusing gubernatorial power for personal gain. Pundits wondered if the McCain operation had fully researched Palin's background before adding her to the ticket (see Balz 2008; Bumiller 2008; Heileman and Halperin 2010, 360–64). To the extent that oppo is a search for comparative advantage, the candidate should be known inside and out. After all, opponents conduct research too (see LaPotin 2011).

A candidate should probably know what the opposition might find ("Talk of the Nation" 2012). Unexplained absences need to be taken into account, along with defaulted loans, off-color comments, and difficult votes. Prospective candidates might develop a scrupulous account of past work experience, political affiliations, memberships, outside activities, and the like. Selections can be distributed as a one-page biography, but files of original (or nearly original) documents should be kept to answer investigative inquiries about the candidate's background. A verified fact can stop a rumor before it starts if it can be authenticated.

A good campaign team might want to assume, at least provisionally, that its candidate has imperfect memory and faulty candor. Simply listing biographical information can be tricky. Given the scrutiny that follows political candidates, exact titles and job descriptions should be recorded, but determining whether a candidate upholds the highest ethical standards can turn into an awkward journey. Pasts can be blurred; memories can be selective. Strengths and weaknesses are perhaps best learned through research. The candidate's writings, tax records, school transcripts, court cases, tax forms, investment forms, vehicle registrations, medical histories, and so forth might be readied for retrieval at a moment's notice. Layers of pride, shame, and forgetfulness can render self-portraiture quite uncomfortable.

## Types of Profile Data

The point of counteropposition research is to ready candidates to deflect incoming attacks, and the point of opposition research is to go on the offensive. Past comments are obvious fodder, as are plagiarized publications, but so are many other kinds of data. Research need not be thoroughly active—it might be as simple as watching for tweets about the opposition—but the strategist responsible for research will likely want to look for the kinds of data that drive political negatives. This information can be separated into four distinct categories: political, campaign finance, career, and personal. These categories can be seen in a variety of painful (for someone) lessons culled from recent history.

### *Political Information*

Candidates generate "facts" throughout their tenure in public office or while campaigning for that office, whether intended for public consumption or not. No matter how thoughtful, careful, and attentive an official might be, a candidate's record inevitably holds *something* that can be presented in a damaging way. Opposition researchers find words, deeds, and works that will anger or disappoint some members of the electorate.

*Voting Records.* Candidates running for Congress in 2008 made good use of opponents' voting records. With George W. Bush's popularity fading, many Americans sought new representation. Democrats were quick to say their Republican opponents had voted with the Bush administration, and Democratic challengers freely posted pro-Bush voting habits online. Barack Obama was campaigning as an agent of political change, noting John McCain's support for Bush, while McCain was highlighting Obama's "liberal" voting record. In 2010 and 2014, Republican challengers routinely linked Democratic incumbents with votes for President Obama's agenda.

Congress, like most city councils, county boards, and state legislatures, processes numerous measures through its system every session, and elected officials cast more votes than anyone can be expected to remember. Many bills are technical in nature and may be of little importance to the voters, but others are (or can be) hotly debated. Research teams might look into a wide range of votes, no matter how insignificant they might seem, spanning an official's entire public career—including floor votes and committee votes. Which votes matter? Campaigns sometimes consult lobbyists and staffers who might know how to describe a "bad vote" in plain language. Surveys and focus groups can also help strategists frame votes in unflattering terms.

*Absenteeism.* Missed votes suggest dereliction of duty. Absences due to family matters and health concerns will likely be excused, but one way to intimate that an official is not working for the people is to point out chronic absenteeism. In the 1984 U.S. Senate race in Kentucky, Republican challenger Mitch McConnell worked to unseat incumbent Democrat Dee Huddleston by highlighting the senator's missed votes. In a legendary television spot, bloodhounds frantically sought Huddleston—in his Washington office and back home in Kentucky—but Huddleston was nowhere to be found. Huddleston was "missing big votes on Social Security, the budget, defense, and even agriculture," according to the McConnell camp; instead he was collecting money for speeches in California and Puerto Rico. Democrat Harley O. Staggers was defeated in 1992 in part because he missed a key vote funding a new FBI center in his West Virginia district. Charges of absenteeism are a staple of modern campaigning, and in the Digital Age, researchers can go to good-government websites to find "missed votes" graphed and ranked against the absences of colleagues.

*Bill Sponsorships.* Some bills have a single sponsor; others have two or three; and a few popular measures see dozens of legislators "sign on." Members are not always careful in screening their colleagues' proposals and good ideas can sometimes go bad. First, if a legislator fails to sponsor bills important to the voters, he or she can be charged with neglect. Second, if a legislator sponsored a bill that never became law, he or she can be charged with ineffectiveness. Third, if a member cosponsors many bills, it might be fruitful to ask whether their combined weight would bust the budget. Finally, campaigns might examine the relationship between bill sponsorship and voting records. If a legislator votes against a measure similar to one she is sponsoring, she might be portrayed as a flip-flopper (see below).

*Committee and Leadership Assignments.* Legislative posts reflect on policy priorities. Some committees are more prestigious than others, some tackle problems relevant to the candidate's district, and some are neither prestigious nor helpful to the people back home. Leadership responsibilities speak to an official's effectiveness. Failure to move up the ladder might indicate a host of problems, ineptness and apathy among them. Another kind of difficulty was encountered by Mary Landrieu of Louisiana, who hoped to use her position as chair of the U.S. Senate's Energy and Natural Resources Committee to pass gas-friendly legislation—approval of the Keystone Pipeline—favored by most of her constituents, and to do so right before a runoff election. The legislation failed and Landrieu was soundly defeated in the immediate aftermath.

*Pork.* A mainstay of incumbency has long been the procurement of "pork barrel" projects. Each year, legislative budgets are larded with contracts, environmental remediation funds, new highways, and the like. These projects let public officials take credit for actions performed in the Capitol, the courthouse, or city hall. Officials report their successes in the media, leading voters to believe that they are represented by effective legislators. Sometimes a legislator will be punished for failing to take care of the district with its share of the community largess; the quest for high-grade pork can also be interpreted as a propensity toward profligate spending, a possible problem for a candidate running as a fiscal conservative. "Earmarked" funds are now restricted in federal legislation, and yet targeted tax-breaks, which some analysts call "tax expenditures," have a similar role in public policy and perhaps also in political campaigns.

*Public Office/Personal Gain.* Perhaps the only thing voters despise more than pork-barrel spending is the use of public resources for personal gain. Allegations against former Illinois governor Rod Blagojevich, who seemed to be selling his executive power to appoint Barack Obama's successor in the U.S. Senate, put old-style graft back in the national headlines. A 2008 Pennsylvania scandal known as "Bonusgate" centered on allegations that public funds were diverted to employees who worked on political campaigns—allegations that inevitably became part of the electoral debate. At the beginning of the 1990s, many members of Congress were confronted by angry voters over personal checks that were "bounced" in a shared account, which caught politicians who seemed to have overdrawn their funds. Although little, if any, taxpayer money was involved, the public viewed the "House Bank Scandal" through a different lens. Many of the "overdrawn" members lost their seats in the following election.

Wise campaigns pay attention to travel records. Elected officials often conduct business on the road, but official trips, often derided as "junkets," can be a rich source of public embarrassment. Members may have traveled with their spouses to conferences, seminars, study sessions, and the like—perhaps in exotic locales. But sunny beaches are not necessary. Senator Charles Schumer reportedly spent more than $140,000 in taxpayer-funded travel in half of a single fiscal year (Phillip 2009). Acting on a campaign promise to visit every county in New York State each year, Schumer chartered flights aboard small aircraft. In response to accusations that the senator could have flown commercial, a spokesperson defended Schumer's actions by saying he "takes outreach to his 19 million-plus constituents seriously, and his busy travel pace makes him one of the most accessible members of Congress" (ibid.). The story was played up on the official Web site of at least one Republican colleague in the Senate. Travel funded by outside sources is frequently reported in the press and rarely good news for the recipients (see Simon 2014).

*Gaffes.* Everyone makes mistakes, but candidates have opponents eager to publicize them. In 2014, Democrat Bruce Braley, running for Iowa's U.S. Senate seat, was recorded belittling farmers during a closed-door meeting with lawyers. Democratic incumbent Senator Mark Udall of Colorado confessed to being "brain dead, today" when asked to recount influential books and "the last song you listened to." Texas governor Rick Perry may never live down his failure in a 2011 debate to recall the three branches of government his presidency would eliminate. When a rival and the moderator were unable to hint the governor toward an answer, Perry said the words that came to mind: "Sorry. Oops."

Occupants of a new job classification, campaign *tracker*, actively look for gaffes. In 2006, Senator George Allen was followed by a volunteer carrying a video camera. At one rally, Allen referred to the tracker, an Indian American, as "macaca," a slur few Americans knew before Allen made it infamous. The clip was posted on YouTube and sparked national commentary. Allen's opponent, Jim Webb, closed the gap and ultimately defeated Allen in a victory that some attributed to the "macaca moment." Republicans would later send their own trackers into the field, hoping to record Democratic blunders (Lightman 2009). In 2014, Senate Majority Leader Harry Reid was forced to apologize after being caught on camera by a tracker, saying, "The Asian population is so productive. I don't think you're smarter than anybody else, but you have convinced a lot of us you are. One problem I've had today is keeping my Wongs straight" (Everett 2014).

Trackers have become more common (Terris 2014b), and some campaigns are tracking the trackers. From an e-mail inside a congressional campaign: "I've gone over how to ask a tracker to leave with all of you. . . . Let's make sure we implement it at every private event we have." The staff compiled a bevy of warning signs, including "young [person] at a saturday [*sic*] morning event—HUGE red flag." Photos of suspected trackers were made available to staff (Woodruff 2014).

*Flip-flops.* Candidates and elected officials sometimes contradict positions once taken in speeches, votes, or bill sponsorships. Holders of low-level posts often pledge to serve out their full term, only to pursue opportunities for higher office. Others are hung up by term-limit pledges made in earlier years. Opposition researchers can (and do) exploit ideological renewal, especially if the issue is a controversial one, such as abortion. Mitt Romney, while governor of Massachusetts, vowed to protect a woman's right to choose; with the 2008 presidential campaign in the offing he professed opposition to abortion (Romney 2005). Some abortion opponents were skeptical of Romney's newfound "conviction" (Goldfarb 2007). A 2012 Web site, mittromneysflipflops.com, gave instant access to source material and a link to a separate site offering "Obama's Biggest Flip-flops."

### Campaign Finance Information

U.S. Senate and congressional candidates submit regularly scheduled reports to the Federal Election Commission, listing individual contributors and political action committees that have given to the campaign. States have similar requirements. Opposition researchers scour these records for oddities. If four people with the same last name and address give the maximum allowable contribution and two of the contributors list their occupation as "student," a researcher might wonder if the head of household was funneling contributions through family members. Extremist groups or problematic individuals can be found on finance lists. During the 2008 presidential race the Clinton campaign highlighted Obama's acceptance of contributions from Tony Rezko, a Chicago businessman who had become the subject of scandal stories (Morain and Hamburger 2008). (Obama returned the contributions.) Digitalization means that a great deal of information given to official campaigns and reported to county, state, and federal agencies is now fully searchable on the Web.

Well-funded campaigns and wealthy candidates are sometimes accused of "buying" elections. Governor Rick Scott of Florida put $13 million into his winning run for reelection, and he took heat from his Democratic opponent, Charlie Crist: "Florida is not for sale, it's up to the people who decide who the next governor is going to be" (Dixon 2014). In 2009, New York mayor Michael Bloomberg financed a $100 million bid for reelection from his own pocket in pursuit of a victory that rarely seemed in doubt. The *New York Times* endorsed Bloomberg but opined that his avoidance of campaign spending limits "does everyone a disservice" (*New York Times* 2009). An Iowa congressional candidate who lost a self-financed bid to unseat Bruce Braley in 2006 attributed defeat to a variety of factors but noted that a candidate's personal investment in a campaign can hurt, speculating, "There's a tipping point" (Jacobs 2014b).

### Career Information

Public service is not the only way to amass a record. Prior business activities, higher education, and other career data, if exaggerated, can cause problems. Such information can be grouped into two broad subject-areas: résumé inflation and questionable business practices.

*Résumé Inflation.* Many people stretch the truth when they write their résumés but puffery is seldom tolerated in candidates for public office. In 2008, Darcy Burner, a Democratic candidate for the state of Washington's Eighth Congressional District, declared: "I loved economics so much that I got a degree in it from Harvard. Now everywhere I go in this district, the only thing people want to talk about is the economy." The problem was that Burner had earned, as she later said, "a degree in computer science with a special emphasis in economics" (Heffter 2008). The campaign soon became preoccupied with the issue and a spokesperson for her opponent, incumbent Republican Dave Reichert, blasted Burner's "outrageous" claims: "It calls into question everything that she has said to this point. It demonstrates an arrogance that she thinks she can say what she wants and that no one is going to learn the truth" (ibid.). Burner lost.

*Business Practices.* Business experience puts business records in play. Mitt Romney's campaign was hounded by charges that Bain Capital's success was due to job-killing corporate reorganization; businessman David Perdue, running for U.S. Senate in Georgia, was confronted with legal records in which he said he "spent most of my career" outsourcing jobs (Bresnahan and Raju 2014). Bankruptcies and lawsuits are research fodder. If past business practices seem to conflict with stated goals, an aspiring officeholder could land in the same trouble as congressional candidate and former doctor from Wisconsin, Steve Kagen, whom the National Republican Congressional

Committee painted as overly litigious. Kagen was "proposing No Patient Left Behind legislation" but he himself had "'left behind' and sued 80 former patients, many for unpaid medical costs" (Pescatore and Zusman 2007). Kagen won the seat by a slim margin. Sometimes business practices can lead to allegations of criminality, as was the case with New York congressman Michael Grimm, who was running a successful campaign while awaiting trial on a number of finance-related charges (and pled guilty shortly after reelection, before resigning).

### Personal Information

The current, hostile news environment can be traced back to a 1974 episode of drunk driving by Chairman Wilbur Mills of the powerful House Ways and Means Committee. In the 1960s, the private lives of politicians were largely considered out of bounds. Reporters would ignore personal indiscretions so long as there was no gross interference with a candidate's public duties. But with the onset of journalistic distrust that accompanied Vietnam and Watergate, a more skeptical approach came into vogue. Mills was pulled over for speeding at night without headlights, at which point a stripper jumped out of his car and into Washington's Tidal Basin. The race to investigate public officials and their private lives commenced.

Thirty-five years later, South Carolina governor Mark Sanford came under public scrutiny during a bewildering absence from his office. He had led staff to believe he was simply hiking along the Appalachian Trail, but it was ultimately revealed that Sanford had gone to Argentina to meet his mistress (Barr 2009). While the old style of journalism might have overlooked Sanford's indiscretion, the new style thrives on it. The previous year, Vito Fossella, a Republican congressman from New York City, was arrested and charged with drunk driving, his blood alcohol level at twice the legal limit. Fossella admitted he was on his way to visit a woman with whom he had been having an affair and confessed they were parents of a three-year-old daughter. After two weeks of "damaging and scandal-filled headlines," Fossella ended his bid for reelection (Hicks 2008).

Thereafter, voters saw the online antics of Democratic congressman Anthony Weiner, allegations of harassment aimed at GOP presidential candidate Herman Cain, and a long list of accusations against other politicians who stepped away from public office under the cloud of a sex scandal (although Sanford did return to political life in 2014 as a victorious congressional candidate).

Any legal or ethical tangle is subject to review. A simple divorce raises few eyebrows, but slow alimony payments or child support can draw attention. Court filings in family matters, if made public, can lead to embarrassing disclosures that raise the possibility that the candidate does not uphold the image that members of the voting public expect of their elected officials. Those who cannot handle the basic responsibilities of family life might seem to lack the "character" necessary for public office.

Although guilt by association is unsporting in many arenas, such charges are often leveled in politics. Sometimes the matter is a blend of personal and political association and sometimes the issue goes to ideology. Opponents of Barack Obama in 2008 tied the senator to a former member of a leftist group implicated in domestic bombings. The tenuous connection between Obama and Bill Ayers made its way into the presidential campaign by way of a *London Daily Mail* article written by a UK-based conservative (Dobbs 2008). In 2014, in Arizona, a columnist lamented opponents of a Maricopa County judicial candidate who was being attacked because his wife, a conservative activist, opposed abortion and same-sex marriage: "For the crime of being married to such a person, they wish to run Judge Herrod from the bench" (MacEachern 2014).

In past years, membership in clubs that excluded people on the basis of gender, race, creed, color, or religion haunted people who had not anticipated social change. Now the problem seems to be the power of pictures. Louisiana congressman Vance McAllister was dubbed the "kissing congressman" in 2014 after surveillance video surfaced showing the married congressman kissing a staffer. Congressman Charlie Rangel had the misfortune of being photographed asleep on the beach in 1999, and the photo was still popping up years later. Campaigning for California's 32nd District House seat, Emanuel Pleitez promoted his Facebook page as a way for prospective voters to learn about him and his candidacy. Unfortunately, photos on the site showed Pleitez drinking and partying. Opposition forces used the candidate's own photos in an attack mailer, depicting Pleitez as unfit for public office (Kapochunas 2009).

## Conclusion

Before the advent of online databasing, research was stored in heaps of paper. Government agencies provided "blue books" and "red books," describing organizational structures, rules and procedures, and official biographies; commercial "yellow books" offered much the same information, often in a more useful format. Government documents were available in research libraries and on microfilm. Local newspaper offices assisted researchers who wanted to look at back issues. A metal filing cabinet in the early 1980s might have bulged with stapled news clippings, finance reports, and notes on where to look for more paper.

In 1984, the Republican National Committee spent $1.1 million to create the Opposition Research Group. The group's first task was to collect detailed information about each of the eight Democratic presidential candidates. The team pulled together a mountain of facts, using more than 2,000 sources and 400,000 documents. Readers sifted through the material looking for direct quotes, statements attributed to the candidates, and comments about the candidates. The information was coded and entered into a database that grew to contain about 75,000 items and 45,000 quotes (Bayer and Rodota 1989). When Democrats nominated Walter Mondale, Republicans pounced. "Vice President Malaise" was a 200-page analysis of Mondale's record sent to party officials across the country, and when Mondale spoke, Republicans highlighted the candidate's weaknesses. Ronald Reagan later used the research to prepare for presidential debates. The project was viewed as the "secret weapon" of the race (ibid., 25).

The new problems go to completeness and organization. Web-based searching can give the impression of a thorough investigation, but unless the user knows what has been left out of the database, he or she cannot be sure what was overlooked. Political novices who grew up with online search engines might not understand how they can miss important information posted on the public Web, or that the search engines vary in their coverage, or that results for one user in one location may differ from those of another user in another location. And if a large volume of information has been gathered, it must be filed and stored in ways that make it strategically useful. Michael Gehrke, a former research director for the Democratic National Committee, the Clinton White House, and John Kerry's presidential campaign, pinpointed a problem with the evolution: "It used to be the main thing you were up against was time. . . . Now it's simply managing all the information you have access to and being able to wrap your head around it" (*Campaigns & Elections* 2006b).

One of the most important resources a campaign might tap is the knowledge of experienced operatives. Candidates defeated in previous cycles could be storing files in their basements and past party chairs might recall the details of ancient races. Aspiring candidates might call on local politicos who have been through the process before. Those who have seen challengers come and go might remember old scandals and how they played out. Strategists can listen to war stories if they want to know about the foibles of past candidates and to learn the sensibilities of the district. In some areas, a certain amount of scandal is written off as a cost of doing political business, while in others, absolute adherence to moral and ethical codes is paramount—and opposition research itself might be criticized (Hartford Courant 2014).

Thorough research can still demand legwork. Generally speaking, newer information from national and regional sources can be retrieved in digital form; older, local sources of information might be stored on paper. Libraries may keep past campaign literature. Local stations will not likely have saved radio and television campaign ads and it is more doubtful that broadcasters would provide tapes or transcripts. Local partisans, however, might collect them. Other resources for campaign ads could include a friendly professor, an eager volunteer, or a bitter rival of the opponent. Historical societies maintain clip files. With narrowing profit margins, newspapers have become far less accommodating to requests for old articles, but the stories may still be around. Operatives in the Digital Age continue to leaf through yellowed clippings, and the effort brings them in contact with librarians, lobbyists, and party activists, who know whereof they speak.

Opposition research shows the dual nature of technology in campaigns. The increasing availability of data means volunteers can run an opposition research program from home. College students have been learning the craft of research in class (Hruby 2012). At the same time, a subset of the campaign industry has taken up the specialization (Hamilton 2011). Its core rationale: In a competitive environment, merely possessing the data may not be enough. A professional researcher cautions, "If you want your campaign messaging and decision making to stand up to the scrutiny of experienced journalists and inquisitive voters, don't rely on unsophisticated quick hits" (Kingsley 2010).

# PART II

# STRATEGIC THINKING

# CHAPTER 4

# Segment Analysis

Ed Baum, a Republican challenger for city council in Athens, Ohio, faced a daunting challenge. Baum's small town was heavily Democratic, he had never held elective office, and he would be running in a multicandidate, multiwinner, citywide election. Six candidates were going after three at-large seats on the council. The top three vote-getters would take office; the rest would get nothing.

Baum was a college professor and Athens is a college town. The campus precincts are heavily Democratic, as are many of the suburbs. To win, Baum reasoned he would need not only to hold his Republicans but also to pick up some non-Republican voters. He needed to make sure his supporters knew exactly *how* to vote. Of the six candidates, there were two Republicans, but city residents were allowed to vote for three different candidates. If GOP supporters voted for their top three choices, at least one Democratic candidate would end up with some votes—possibly giving one of the Democrats enough votes to knock Baum from the third-place slot he was shooting for. Baum needed to prevent Democratic competitors from picking up left-over support from GOP voters, so Republicans needed to cast their ballots for only *two* candidates, not three—one vote for each of the two Republicans on the ballot.

To find Republican supporters, Baum looked at the voting behavior of the city's precincts over recent presidential elections. He ranked each precinct as Democratic, Republican, or mixed. There was little reason to push hard in solidly Democratic precincts or in the areas that already showed a strong Republican affiliation. Few persuadable voters could be found therein. But the mixed areas, which might go either way—this was where Baum felt he could spend his time effectively, where a knock on the door to say "hello" and drop off some literature might offer the greatest payoff. The approach seemed to work. Although Baum lost a couple of his targeted neighborhoods, victory on Election Day spoke to the value of careful electioneering.

Baum's arithmetic can be reproduced on the back of an envelope. Elaborate polling and computer-aided segmentation might offer more precise estimates—survey research and voter targeting will be covered in the next two chapters—but each approach begins with a general theory of inference.

This chapter discusses the logic of segmentation, basic political segments, and yield analysis.

## The Logic of Segmentation

Baum's calculation represents a cost-benefit analysis. Groups of voters were identified and ranked. A rate of return was computed, if informally, for each unit of effort invested against each vote expected on Election Day. Baum divided his city according to geography, but his technique is fundamental to any segmentation process. A campaign might carve its electorate by gender and income, or by race and ideology. Segments can be identified within populations and subgroups can be stitched together as segments of the larger population. Whether segmentation is based on electoral history, as in Baum's case, or on public opinion polls, informed guesswork, or the myriad data points in a comprehensive voter list, the task begins with some basic concepts.

Scholars and political professionals have long struggled with the question of why an individual votes for a particular candidate. Party politics are important, but other forces also exist: ideology, personal finance, imagery, a sense of identity, and so forth. Some voters might base their decisions on a witty campaign commercial, while others throw their support behind one candidate or another on the advice of friends, and still others reject a certain candidate because they assume that short people cannot possibly lead a nation. Political analysts will always be frustrated by the eccentricities of individual-level decisions. But intelligible patterns of behavior can be found in the big picture.

At the aggregate level, myriad individual actions combine into voting districts, states, and the nation as a whole. Personal idiosyncrasies blend into a larger mix. Some districts go Republican by roughly the same percentage year after year. Some states are more favorable than others to minor-party candidacies. While Americans are constantly moving from home to home—about 12 percent move to a new address each year (Fields and Kominski 2012)—the political predisposition of a given neighborhood tends to remain constant. The individuals change but the community remains the same. Although populations can demonstrate a fair amount of uniformity, the constancy is unlikely to be perfect, making way for analytic segmentation.

The logic of segmentation can be stated with three mutually reinforcing propositions.

First, *populations are heterogeneous*. Districts that appear uniform might contain a wide variety of concerns. A young, white, middle-class neighborhood with look-alike houses gives the impression of Milquetoast consistency. Residents probably share many interests, goals, and beliefs. But under the surface might dwell a fair amount of ideological diversity. Some people will be pro-life and others pro-choice. Some will be pro-gun and others pro–gun control. While American housing patterns tend to cluster on race, ethnicity, income, and lifestyle, most communities, no matter how similar in appearance, comprise dissimilar elements.

Second, *heterogeneity can be used to segment voters into distinct analytic groups*. The Census Bureau asks people to record their gender, race, age, marital status, and educational attainment, among other things. Because individuals can be categorized by these variables, populations can be segmented likewise. Ambiguities abound, many categories are not politically significant, and frequently the power of a variable will change over time, sometimes decreasing and sometimes increasing, but distinctions among subgroups can be informative. Before 1980, gender was not a strong factor in presidential elections, though in subsequent years it would become a powerful predictor of partisan preference. Women are now much more likely than men to vote Democratic. One trick to electoral research is figuring out which demographic and political categories will be significant in the upcoming election.

Third, *membership in a segment suggests shared concerns with others in that segment*. Many Americans believe they vote from their own interests and not those of a larger group, but a good analyst can make predictions about *individual*-level behavior on the basis of *aggregate*-level research. In a white, middle-class neighborhood, there might live a 32-year-old married white church-going male of English descent employed as a well-paid accountant. Chances are good that this person would be a dependable Republican. Not every member of his demographic group would have identical interests, nor would everyone agree on any one item—segment analysis is a business of probabilities, not certainties—but party preference correlates with wealth, gender, geography, marital status, race, and occupation.

Care must be taken in the selection of salient features to prevent politically distinguishable groups from getting thrown together or politically similar groups from being needlessly distinguished. The second failing may be the lesser of the two. If people in one neighborhood are examined separate from those in another neighbor with virtually the same interests, values, and behavior, little harm is done beyond some extra (and unnecessary) work recombining the segments. If two politically dissimilar groups are treated as one—if, that is, a diverse group like "Latinos" is viewed as a simple bloc that includes conservative Cuban exiles in Florida and more liberal (on economic policy) Mexican Americans in southern California—the strategist will either dilute or misdirect understanding of Latino politics.

Baum was able to use the logic of segmentation when he examined the geography of the City of Athens because he knew the community well.

1. The city is diverse, containing students, professors, administrators, white-collar professionals, and hourly employees.
2. Neighborhoods vary in their partisanship, with student precincts leaning heavily Democratic.
3. A voter in a mixed precinct might be more likely to be persuadable than a voter in a more reliably partisan precinct.

Large aggregations can therefore be *dis*aggregated into smaller segments, and the character of the segment as a whole can say something about its members. There is a danger in this logic, as will be noted later, but an analyst who lacks individual-level data might be able to make informed guesses from aggregate-level characteristics.

Aggregate figures describe groups, not individuals. The number of *base voters* in a district—that is, party loyalists who always vote a straight ticket—is almost surely smaller than the size of a district's *base vote share* (i.e., the portion of the electorate that the party can always count on). Some diehard Republicans occasionally vote Democratic, and vice versa, so a precinct that never dips below a 25 percent share might boast only 15 percent diehard supporters. Mathematically, a district could be populated entirely by swing voters—everyone switching his or her vote back and forth between the two major parties, maintaining no loyalty from year to year—and still have no swing *vote share* whatsoever (every election splitting 50–50).

Herein lies the danger of imputation: Individuals are not necessarily microcosms of the larger groups to which they belong. Baum had lived in his town long enough to know that its precincts were demographically cohesive and that the aggregate-level totals were meaningful at the level of individual analysis. But this knowledge came from experience, not raw precinct data. Another Republican candidate in another college town might have run similar calculations and developed comparable findings though several of the mixed neighborhoods in the district were filled not with moderate voters in the middle of the electorate but rather a prickly jumble of liberal students and conservative administrators. In the latter case, a mixed neighborhood might contain equal numbers of staunch liberals and staunch conservatives, with few persuadable voters in between.

Statisticians call this difficulty the *ecological inference problem.* One example: George W. Bush received strong support from low-income *states* in 2004, but John Kerry received support from low-income *voters* (Gelman et al. 2008; Gelman 2014a). Concluding from state-level data that poor people generally voted for Bush would be a serious mistake. Sophisticated techniques have been developed to manage the ecological inference problem (see King 1997). Still, groups and individuals are not identical; individuals do not necessarily reflect the groups to which they belong; and so imputation is always risky. The fact that a group may consistently vote for Democrats and Republicans on a 50–50 basis does not necessarily imply entrenched conflict—it might simply mean half of the electorate is slightly to the left and the other half is slightly to the right (Dimock et al. 2014).

## Basic Segments

A competitive election is illustrated in Figure 4.1, which represents a district that generally splits its vote equally between Democrats and Republicans (the "average party performance"). About 16 percent of the vote (the "toss-up vote") is at the center, and another 17 percent on each side (the "soft-partisan vote") can usually, but not always, be counted upon by each party. Some 25 percent of the electorate (the "base vote") supports the least appealing candidates of one party, and another 25 percent supports the worst candidates of the other party.

**Figure 4.1**
**Diagramming the Electorate**

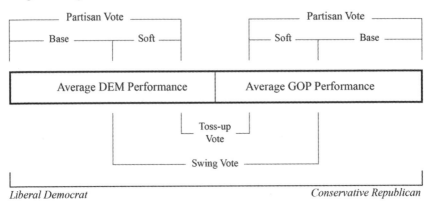

This model illustrates an important truth: Competitive elections can be decided by small groups of people. If a 25 percent share of the electorate always votes Democratic and another 25 percent always votes Republican, the remaining 50 percent share will decide the winner. Half of the electorate would be persuadable. If another 17 percent votes for barely acceptable Democratic candidates and yet another 17 percent votes for barely acceptable Republicans, then 84 percent of the electorate (the "partisan vote") may be deemed unmovable before the competition starts, leaving 16 percent at the center genuinely persuadable. Winning requires gaining a bare majority of these voters in the middle—just over 8 percent of the electorate. And because the effective turnout for down-ballot races is commonly less than 50 percent of those qualified, the key to victory might lie with slightly over 4 percent of eligible voters.

### Party Performance

A strategist running a persuasion campaign is charged with finding the (sometimes elusive) middle ground. The process can be demonstrated with a precinct analysis similar to Baum's research, using a measure of average party performance to find the midpoint of the electorate, along with base, swing, soft-partisan, partisan, and toss-up scores to section out the electorate.

*Average party performance* (APP) is the typical vote share a party receives when two evenly matched candidates meet head-to-head. It can be computed by selecting a set of competitive races and then taking the average vote share earned by the candidates of the two parties:

$$APP = Typical\ Vote\ Share$$

This average locates, for better or worse, a district's center of balance (see Figure 4.2).

While the arithmetic is simple, the required judgments are not. Presidential races may be used, but high-ballot contests might not parallel down-ballot races, either because the nature of the two offices is different or because presidential candidates operate with a distinct set of opportunities and resources. Barack Obama had a lot of money, fervent support, and a massive GOTV (get out the vote) operation in 2012; with none of those advantages, a candidate for county sheriff may want to avoid using Obama's victory as the basis for performance calculations. In some regions presidential candidates are less popular than state candidates of the same party. Reasoned debate can erupt over which candidates are quality candidates, which campaign operations were strong, and by extension, which set of competitors was "evenly matched." Calculating good estimates demands familiarity with local trends; otherwise, how can an analyst say what is meant by "typical"?

In politics, a "yellow dog Democrat" is someone who would vote Democratic if the party's candidate were a yellow dog. Some Republicans are "true blue" or "rock-ribbed." Although many voters reject party labels, some ostensible nonpartisans consistently vote for candidates of the same party in one election after the next. The same can be said for voting districts. The *base vote* corresponds to the worst performance that a party has shown over the past several election cycles:

$$Base\ Vote = Absolute\ Minimum\ Vote\ Share$$

**Figure 4.2**
**Average Party Performance**

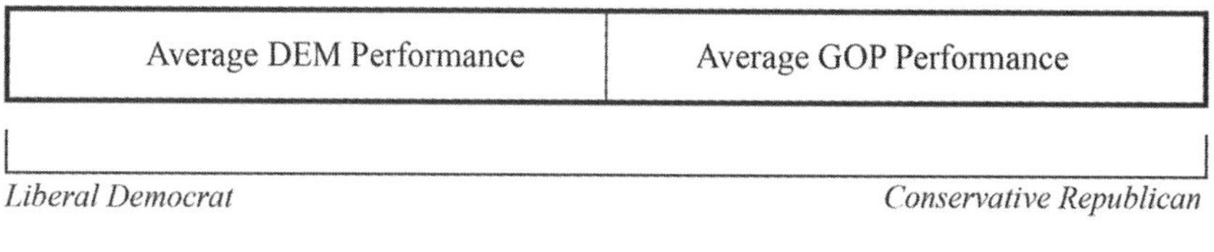

| Average DEM Performance | Average GOP Performance |
|---|---|

*Liberal Democrat*        *Conservative Republican*

**Figure 4.3**
**The Base Vote and the Swing Vote**

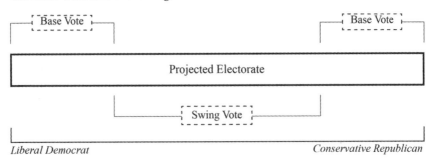

The base vote is easier to compute than average party performance—just find the worst-performing candidate in recent history (see Figure 4.3)—though an analyst must still be careful. An uncontested election, or a merely nominal battle, might prove misleading.

Setting aside the portion of the electorate that will vote for any of its party's candidates, no matter how bad, focuses attention on the more persuadable segments. The *swing vote* is the complement of the base vote for the Democrats and Republicans:

$$Swing\ Vote = Total\ Vote - (Base\ Vote_{Dem} + Base\ Vote_{GOP})$$

Political interest in the Latino community follows from its variability. While George W. Bush made a serious effort to court the Latino community, in the aggregate it has become more strongly Democratic (Lopez and Gonzalez-Barrera 2012). Exit polls since 1992 show support for Democrats, ranging from a high of 74 percent in 2006 to a low of 56 percent in 2004 (Connelly et al. 2014). For a strategist seeking groups to persuade, the Democratic bias is less meaningful than the variance between party support numbers. A swing of 20 percentage points between a presidential year and the following midterm suggests votes can be gained (or lost) with some combination of persuasion and mobilization. Interest in Latinos increases with growth in the voter-eligible population, with a voter-eligible population building from 7.5 million in 1986 to about 25.2 million in 2014 (Lopez et al. 2014).

Any effort to slice up the electorate is bound to be somewhat arbitrary, but reasonable distinctions can be made. The base vote was defined according to a party's absolute worst performance; the *soft-partisan vote* can be defined in accordance with *typically poor* performance. The soft-partisan vote might be characterized by an average worst performance over several election cycles, the performance of a few strong but losing campaigns, or some other measure of voter tendency that squares with political judgment. The idea is to subdivide the swing vote in a way that identifies the portion of the electorate that goes for less desirable candidates but shies away from the worst of the bunch. This can be computed for each party as follows:

$$Soft\ Partisan\ Vote = Typical\ Minimum\ Vote\ Share$$

The *partisan vote* can be computed as the sum of the base vote (the portion of the electorate that will vote for a party's absolute worst candidate) and the soft-partisan vote:

$$Swing\ Vote = (Base\ Vote + Soft\ Partisan\ Vote)$$

A good political analyst might refine the swing vote in ways that ensure strategic usefulness. The *toss-up vote* would be the remaining portion of the voting electorate—that is, the share that does not reside in either partisan vote:

$$Toss - up\ Vote = Total\ Vote - (APP_{Dem} + APP_{GOP})$$

While these metrics gauge the performance of partisan candidates over time, a *split-ticket factor* is similar to the swing factor as it looks for volatility within a single election. It measures the extent to which people divide their votes between the parties on a ballot form.

Figure 4.4
The Partisan Vote and the Soft-Partisan Vote

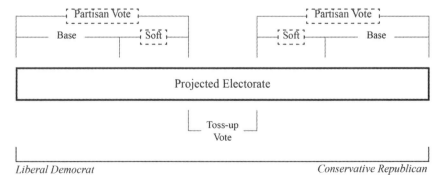

Liberal Democrat                    Conservative Republican

## Voter Participation

Not all elections are won at the center. While persuasion tries to bring swing voters onto the candidate's side, mobilization recognizes that many fairly reliable supporters need motivation to cast a vote. Focusing on supporter turnout is often called a *base mobilization strategy*, or simply a *base strategy*, when the effort does not concentrate exclusively on the most intransigent followers of the party line. Turnout is key.

The overall population of a district is easy to find, but a campaign professional is not interested in the size of the whole population so much as the size of the voting electorate. This figure might range between 30 and 70 percent of the eligible population, depending on the district, election year, and offices listed on the ballot. A county that holds 100,000 voting-age people might have 80,000 registered voters, of whom 50,000 typically cast ballots in a presidential year. While almost everyone who walks into a voting booth will select a candidate for president, "voter fatigue" sets in as people work down the ballot toward judges and county officials. Many constituents do not vote for down-ballot offices. The effect of this behavior is called *roll-off* or *fall-off*. The opposite of voter fatigue might be called "voter resilience."

Simply averaging the number of votes cast in recent elections can be problematic. If several recent contests are analyzed for a competitive two-way, open-seat race for the state assembly, an average over time might include years in which a president was elected and years without a presidential election, years when a U.S. senator was elected and years that did not include a Senate election. Turnout might go up and down in waves. Two methods of dampening these sorts of variations are (1) finding surrogate contests and (2) computing a *set* of averages.

Finding surrogate races is conceptually straightforward. The idea is to assume that several factors will influence the number of votes cast in the election and then to find one or more elections that roughly match those factors. Who else is on the ballot? Are voters going to be excited about the race? Does the contest fall on a presidential election year? Is the opponent an incumbent? If past is prologue, and if other elections have involved similar factors, it stands to reason that prior contests would offer a rough gauge of future events. Past elections might be averaged into a simple model of the upcoming campaign. So, if one surrogate election saw 50,000 votes and another brought in 46,000 votes, a strategist might reason that 48,000 votes would be cast in the race.

Although the math is easy, decisions about what to include in the analysis might not be. Finding a surrogate demands an accurate forecast as to which factors will matter in the impending election. As Yogi Berra decreed, "It's tough to make predictions, especially about the future." Furthermore, assessing the reasons for variation in past elections is not always easy. A spike in turnout might be attributable to aggressive GOTV operations, unique personalities, or some combination of demographic and social change. Again, smart people can disagree about the meaning of political history. When a prediction rests on a small sample of contests, analysts must use political judgment.

The second approach is to compute probabilities based on registration, turnout, and voter resilience. While regression procedures, machine learning algorithms, and other forms of analysis might provide better estimates by using a broader range of variables, a thumbnail sketch of turnout can be projected from the size of the eligible electorate, overall turnout, year type, and the office being sought.

A rough estimate of the *effective turnout* would be the size of the electorate multiplied by the percentage of the electorate registered to vote, by the percentage of registered voters expected to vote, and by the percentage of the voting electorate resilient enough to vote for offices down the ballot. That is:

$$Effective\ Turnout =$$
$$Total\ Electorate \times \%\ Registered \times \%\ Turnout \times \%\ Resilient$$

If the district consists of 100,000 eligible voters, 80 percent registration would reduce the number of possible voters to 80,000, and 75 percent turnout would reduce the voting electorate to 60,000— of which, at 30 percent average roll-off (i.e., 70 percent resiliency), 42,000 might cast a ballot for state representative.

As a group, African Americans are politically meaningful, not because they vary widely in their partisan preference but because they do not. Preference for Democrats since 1992 has ranged between 89 and 94 percent (with an outlying 83 percent in 1996). While the mobilization is generally steady among white voters, the proportion of voting African Americans to the overall population is apt to vary. If a Democrat can turn out a larger-than-usual proportion of the black vote then African Americans might turn the outcome of the election. One argument against voter ID laws is that implementation imposes a disproportionate impact on demographic groups that tend to vote for Democratic candidates.

Political judgment is involved in every step of the analysis. Is it better to work with surrogate elections or averages? How might the size of the electorate change over time? Where strong differences exist in roll-off between on-year and off-year elections, which is likely, the analyst might decide to stick with on-year elections. A district with low registration and a lot of people moving in and out might require that the analyst take preelection registration drives with an eye to past registration trends, looking at the typical increase (or decrease) of registrants between the beginning of the year and Election Day.

If 42,000 voters are expected to cast ballots for the legislative seat, the next question is, How much does that figure vary? Using surrogate races or averages in much the same way that the swing and toss-up votes were computed, an analyst can find high and low watermarks at the district level and voter resilience for particular offices. Finding volatility in turnout would assist a mobilization campaign for the same reasons that knowing partisan variability can help a strategist set up a persuasion campaign: It helps show how much the voters are willing to move.

The midpoint and volatility estimates described above involve two-way contests held on a regular Election Day. Multicandidate contests, special elections, and ballot initiatives can be more complicated, and less certain, than traditional two-way races, because firm precedent might be lacking. Special elections held for a single purpose at a unique moment in time might have no local precedent whatsoever, and ballot initiatives or referenda, particularly on issues that do not cut the electorate along party lines, require difficult assumptions. Creativity is obligatory, especially if precinct boundaries have recently been altered. The only consolation might be the fact that the opposition is facing the same analytic problems.

In any event, the number of votes necessary to win a two-way contest would be half the expected vote, plus one. If 42,000 votes will be cast for state representative, then 21,001 are needed to win. In practice, the breakpoint seldom cuts right at 50 percent. Some people vote for minor-party candidates and a few might write in their own names just to see if they will show up in news reports. Races can usually be won slightly under the halfway point. But it would be tough to defend a plan that aimed at a 49 percent plurality or a one-vote margin, since turnout and roll-off estimates are fragile. Wisdom dictates erring on the side of caution by working at the high end of the scale, and then perhaps adding a few votes to *that* figure. "Close" will not count on Election Day.

## Yield Analysis

Assuming that valid individual-level assumptions can be drawn from aggregate-level behavior, the next question is which segments to target. Ed Baum rated individual precincts according to party performance, and then segmented the full set of precincts into targeted and nontargeted precincts according to that performance. Precincts that appeared to be saturated with Republicans or Democrats were given less regard than those that were deemed mixed. In other races, a targeting effort might focus on turning out voters who are already committed to the candidate. The first approach is a persuasion campaign; the second is a mobilization campaign. Both types of campaign benefit from the use of model performance metrics and segment ranking.

### Performance Metrics

Most electoral strategies rely on persuasion as well as mobilization, and both sorts of campaign efforts ideally work to get the lowest cost per vote gained (CPVG), which can be defined as:

$$CPVG = \frac{Cost\ of\ Effort}{Number\ of\ Votes\ Gained}$$

If a $10,000 direct mail effort adds a hundred votes to a candidate's column from the undecided group, the CPVG would be $100; if 50 votes came in for the same effort, the CPVG would increase to $200. Bringing in a new voter who had not planned on voting is worth half as much as converting a voter who would have voted for the opponent. The number of votes to be gained is difficult to assess, so a campaign would be forgiven if it simply measured the cost per targeted voter (CPTV), the number of targeted voters reached per unit cost:

$$CPTV = \frac{Cost\ of\ Effort}{Number\ of\ Targeted\ Voters\ Reached}$$

Credit for developing this sort of calculation has been attributed to Bill Clinton's 1992 presidential campaign (Kurtz 1992a), and the notion has been fleshed out in the academic literature (see Green and Gerber 2008; Gerber and Green 2012; Green et al. 2013), but the logic of the cost-per-vote-gained estimate is implicit in virtually all thoughtful electioneering.

If campaign resources were infinite, a CPVG or CPTV computation would serve a mere accounting function: What was the final price of victory? But since resources are limited, CPVG and CPTV serve a planning function when they are combined with two additional measures: efficiency (the minimization of waste) and coverage (the maximization of outreach).

Efficiency is a function of success over effort. If a candidate meets with ten people, but only one of them was persuadable, the endeavor would not look terribly efficient. If, however, the candidate met with eight persuadable people out of ten, then time spent chatting with those voters would seem more efficient.

$$Efficiency = \frac{Number\ of\ Targeted\ Voters\ Contacted}{Number\ of\ Voters\ Contacted}$$

A candidate seeking high efficiency might look for precincts with a large swing vote, because the probability that any particular voter within those precincts would be undecided might be greater than in the precincts holding a small swing vote.

Veteran strategist Hal Malchow makes an important distinction between efficiency and coverage: "While efficiency measures what a campaign is getting for its money, coverage measures what it is leaving out" (2008, 9). Sending mail to a solitary, absolutely persuadable voter would be a highly efficient use of campaign money, but leaving the district's other 9,999 persuadable voters out of the loop would be a serious error. A sharp campaign thinks about coverage, a function of success over opportunity:

$$Coverage = \frac{Number\ of\ Targeted\ Voters\ Contacted}{Number\ of\ Targeted\ Voters\ Available}$$

Although a "no target left behind" strategy would be costly, perhaps too costly, increasing coverage at the expense of efficiency might be the only way to gather enough votes to win the election.

In the best possible world, a campaign would have 100 percent coverage and 100 percent efficiency, but perfection is all but impossible. Decisions must be made in every aspect of strategic planning. While there is no universal, ideal ratio combining efficiency and coverage, the distinction itself suggests one way to think about the problem. A two-way matrix can display false positives (e.g., calling a base voter persuadable) against false negatives (e.g., grouping a persuadable voter into the base). (A more sophisticated approach might analyze Receiver Operator Curves.) Campaigns with money to spare might pay attention to coverage, while those that are short on funds might decide to go with efficiency. Of course, a campaign that lacks money and needs to cover a lot of ground has serious work to do.

## Segment Ranking

The value of segment analysis is revealed as subgroups are rank-ordered. Ranking begins by estimating the size of the effective electorate and concludes with a set of targets that add up to victory. Strategists might want to rank precincts, counties, or towns according to their expected CPVG.

Table 4.1 illustrates a notional district containing 10,000 voters and assumes an intensive phone, mail, and door-to-door effort would cost $7.50 per voter. If the average party performance is 47 percent (4,700 votes can be expected), a candidate needs to pick up 301 more votes to win. Contacting everyone would run fully $75,000, a wasteful sum that suggests the need for targeting.

For simplicity, it can be assumed that the computed base vote of each precinct approximates the people who are listed as Republican or Democrat on the campaign's voter list; these, say, 6,984 base voters should probably not be contacted. Contacting all the others, the 3,016 swing voters, would cost less than $23,000, a savings of more than two-thirds over contacting each and every voter in the district.

Table 4.1 is subject to strategic assumptions: (1) the candidate's soft partisans will definitely vote for the candidate, (2) the toss-ups and the opposition's soft partisans remain open to persuasion (so they get counted as "persuadable"), and (3) contacting these open-minded citizens will cull newly supportive votes from 40 percent of these persuadables. If these assumptions hold true for Precinct 7, then reaching all 255 unaffiliated swing voters would hit 200 persuadables and cull 80 votes at a cost of $1,913, or $23.91 for each vote gained; by contrast, in Precinct 9 the cost per vote gained would be $37.00. Sorting the precincts according to CPVG lets analysts see an accumulation of votes and costs as they move down the two right-most columns. A cutoff can be established after Precinct 4. Contacting the unaffiliated voters in the seven highest-ranking precincts would, if

**Table 4.1**
**Ranking Precincts**

| Precinct | Voters | Swing | Target | Cull | Precinct Cost | CPVG | Accumulation | Total Cost |
|---|---|---|---|---|---|---|---|---|
| 7 | 848 | 255 | 200 | 80 | $1,913 | $23.91 | 80 | $1,913 |
| 11 | 679 | 205 | 160 | 64 | $1,538 | $24.03 | 144 | $3,451 |
| 14 | 765 | 231 | 175 | 70 | $1,733 | $24.76 | 214 | $5,184 |
| 1 | 699 | 211 | 153 | 61 | $1,583 | $25.95 | 275 | $6,767 |
| 2 | 663 | 200 | 140 | 56 | $1,500 | $26.79 | 331 | $8,267 |
| 13 | 581 | 176 | 120 | 48 | $1,320 | $27.50 | 379 | $9,587 |
| 4 | 628 | 189 | 125 | 50 | $1,418 | $28.36 | 429 | $11,005 |
| 8 | 633 | 191 | 123 | 49 | $1,433 | $29.24 | 478 | $12,438 |
| 10 | 816 | 246 | 158 | 63 | $1,845 | $29.29 | 541 | $14,283 |
| 3 | 643 | 194 | 120 | 48 | $1,455 | $30.31 | 589 | $15,738 |
| 6 | 654 | 197 | 120 | 48 | $1,478 | $30.79 | 637 | $17,216 |
| 5 | 621 | 187 | 115 | 46 | $1,403 | $30.50 | 683 | $18,619 |
| 12 | 544 | 164 | 98 | 39 | $1,230 | $31.54 | 722 | $19,849 |
| 15 | 737 | 222 | 130 | 52 | $1,665 | $32.02 | 774 | $21,514 |
| 9 | 489 | 148 | 75 | 30 | $1,110 | $37.00 | 804 | $22,624 |
| Total | 10,000 | 3,016 | 2,012 | 804 | $22,624 | | | |

*Assumptions:*

- Average party performance: 4,700
- Extra votes needed: 301
- Cull share: 40%
- Cost per targeted voter: $7.50

all these assumptions are accurate, yield 429 votes—meaning victory with a thick cushion—at a cost of $11,005, about 15 percent of the price of the districtwide contact plan.

Working through such calculations would force a campaign to examine many of the assumptions that go into its spending. If the campaign had many tens of thousands of dollars to spend, the preferred, and less risky, strategy would be to ignore the analysis and hit all the voters—and this is sometimes done—but if the campaign is working with limited resources, a need to prioritize is imposed by necessity and yield analysis is one tool it can use to make the cut.

A few lessons can be learned from this exercise. First, the battleground is often confined to a small portion of the electorate. Second, a persuasion campaign might benefit from high-energy voter mobilization efforts, involving registration and GOTV, in order to reduce the number of middle-ground votes needed to win and thereby to reduce the cost of reaching targeted precincts. Finally, precinct analysis alone may not suffice to narrow the targeting operation, and other techniques such as polling, microtargeting, and good political judgment can help reduce the wastefulness of mailing, phoning, and canvassing large numbers of voters.

## Conclusion

The payoff from segmentation and yield analysis might be a clean and simple set of numbers. But an analyst must bear in mind that the quality of the outcome depends on the quality of the input. Garbage in, garbage out. Weighting can correct for the geographic size of districts, or to favor contiguous precincts, or to insert hard-earned political wisdom into the equation. Findings can be adjusted in light of demographic, polling, volunteer lists, and other sources of politically meaningful information. Because politics goes beyond simple arithmetic—analysts need to know the social, economic, and political cultures of the district they are mapping—political wisdom is required not only under the hot lights of a news conference but also in the cold calculation of electoral data, as suggested in chapter 3 with the campaign of Bill Magee for New York Assembly.

Magee's district was, by all accounts, Republican. Nearly every local elected official in the district was Republican, and voter enrollment was roughly two-to-one Republican. Nonetheless, Magee, a Democrat, won the seat, defeating a 10-year Republican incumbent. The campaign team was facing a variety of difficulties, not the least of which was modest funding. Magee's operation needed to reach its coverage goals with extreme efficiency. A finely tuned targeting plan combining prior electoral history with polling data had to be devised.

Of the 105 election districts, roughly 25 were deemed solidly Republican. The Republican Party performance in these areas was more than 60 percent; few Democrats had won them. Despite criticism from the news media and local politicos for not covering these neighborhoods, the campaign directed no energy to heavily Republican sectors. The strategy team also sought out the few solidly Democratic areas available, finding about 20 of them, and because resources were tight, little effort was made there, either. If Magee could not count on solid Democrats, he was sunk anyway. Instead of cultivating base precincts, the campaign team was forced to assume Democratic voters in these districts were already in the bag and needed only to be reminded to vote.

Still under consideration were 60 election districts that might, by some optimistic measure, be labeled "swing." Yet the campaign did not have sufficient resources to work the voters in all these remaining electoral districts. A concerted effort had to be made to find districts with a high propensity toward persuadable voting and to rank-order these areas using a votes-needed-to-win estimate. Considering his base of support along with that of his opponent the question became, How many swing districts were needed in a target group if Magee was able to win them all with 52 percent? With 55 percent? 57 percent? 60 percent? In the end, roughly 40 election districts formed the core target group. If Magee could win more than half of these precincts by at least 55 percent and break even in others, he stood a chance.

The campaign worked hard to court voters in the targeted precincts, sticking to survey-tested issues and themes. The most appropriate way to reach these voters, given their dispersion across the district, was by fine-tuned direct mail, carefully planned literature drops, and neighborhood canvassing operations, augmented by ambitious telemarketing. In the end, Magee won the election by fewer than 500 votes. His base came through and he captured more than 55 percent in most of his targeted election districts. Magee's campaign had successfully tackled a serious shortage of financial resources and base voter support and had done so with a strong voter targeting plan.

# CHAPTER 5

# Survey Research

Richard Nixon wanted to remake the Republican Party in his own image. Following the turmoil of the civil rights movement and student unrest, Nixon reasoned, middle-class Democrats, especially Southerners, might want to join the GOP. The president saw opportunity in this disaffection and seized upon it. Planning began during the first year of Nixon's presidency. Seeking a new coalition and a new partisan divide, "White House polls tracked 'significant differences' based on party identification and ideology in trial heats, approval ratings, and concerning policy issues and other areas" (Jacobs 2005, 197). The idea was to locate disaffected voters within the Democratic ranks. Concentrating on ticket-splitters, a raft of survey analyses showed what might sway these unsteady voters, and strategies pulled from the data helped Nixon win reelection in 1972 (ibid., 197–199).

Some candidates might wonder if opinion polling is really necessary. Spending a lifetime in a district helps a leader figure out what residents are thinking, and an expensive poll might seem redundant. A "feel for the district" was essential to old-style political activism. Precinct captains would listen to voters and transmit their feelings up the pecking order. Knowledge was gained from newspaper reporters and civic leaders. Sometimes political assessments were based on campaign rallies and constituent letters. The quest for public opinion began long before scientific survey research was developed. New-style campaign operatives, however, believe they cannot rely exclusively on informal measures—if only because the old party hierarchies have broken down. While candidates and elected officials frequently say they ignore the opinion polls, few political professionals would want to run a campaign without survey research.

By 2008, political polls had become an integral part of presidential campaigning, as strategists, reporters, and armchair analysts obsessed over the numbers, watching Barack Obama and John McCain go up and down, speculating about the effect of Sarah Palin's nomination. Pundits fixated on the horse race, and pollsters explained why their favored techniques were truly on the cutting edge. After the election came to a close, analysts compared one survey to another and wondered about the future of political polling, an aspect of campaign management that has become technologically sophisticated and conceptually intricate.

In 2012, America was presented with the political theater that can emerge from the intersection of polls and outside data. On Fox News, after the network had called Ohio for President Obama, Rove claimed:

> I don't know what the outcome is gonna be, but you shouldn't, you gotta be careful about calling things when you've got something like 991 votes separating the two candidates and a quarter of the vote left to count. Even if they had made it on the basis of select precincts, I'd be very cautious about intruding in this process.

Rove was wrong, but not alone. Many Republicans had expected to fare much better in 2012, partly due to ill-fated attempts to "unskew" polls that, it later seemed, were not originally skewed.

During the midterm elections of 2014, America witnessed various pundits relying on different polling data to reach quite different conclusions. Fred Yang, who serves as the pollster for the *Wall Street Journal*/NBC News Poll along with Bill McInturff, believed that Democrats would maintain control of the Senate after other prognosticators had concluded that Republicans had a high probability of winning. Republicans won handily, beating pessimistic expectations of many Democratic analysts. Nate Silver later found that the average Senate poll conducted in the final three weeks of the campaign overestimated the performance for Democrats by almost four percentage points—leading to many pundits being surprised as results in tightly contested states began rolling in (Silver 2014; see also Cassidy 2014). And today, sites like PredictIT are adding new dynamics by allowing average citizens to research the possible value of prediction markets. Very different from polls, these sites let individuals place money on what they think will happen—and campaigns are taking notice.

As polling has become an essential fabric of modern campaigns, it has also become increasingly more complicated. This chapter discusses modern survey research by way of polling basics, assorted types of surveys, quality control, survey design, and data analysis.

## Polling Basics

Polls are expensive. If a campaign has its own list and is willing to use cookie-cutter questions and forgo deep analysis, a survey could run several thousand dollars. A comprehensive "benchmark poll," on the other hand, might cost $25,000 to $35,000, or more. Survey costs are a function of questionnaire design, interview length, the number of respondents contacted, and the depth of analysis offered by the analyst. Writing a complex questionnaire requires expertise and experience. Individual interviews consume time, and larger samples add to the cost.

Results from a benchmark poll can be unwelcome. A community leader planning to run for office might learn that popularity among peers does not necessarily translate into public fame. Low name recognition can be humbling. Political leaders with long records of public service might see low name recognition. In 1994, only 49 percent of voters in Georgia's 10th Congressional District could identify their own five-term incumbent—immediately after a hard-fought election season (Shea 1996, 402). But starting with low name recognition does not guarantee electoral defeat. Thom Tillis, who defeated North Carolina Democratic incumbent Kay Hagan for U.S. Senate in 2014, was known to just 28 percent of potential voters a year before his victory (Elon Poll 2014). Some candidates will be disheartened to read survey results showing broad segments of the public expressing preference for the opposition.

Another major use of polling is to identify issue preferences among voters. At the beginning of any campaign season, candidates might be thinking about a catalog of pressing issues, but the list must be pared down. Recalling the way he helped plan a 1991 Senate victory in Pennsylvania, James Carville wrote:

> [State Labor Secretary] Harris Wofford believes in a lot of things, but our researchers came up with three key issues that

the people of Pennsylvania cared about deeply: a middle-class tax cut, more affordable education, and health care. Wofford did too. That's what we ran on. (Matalin and Carville 1995, 74)

A generalized respect for human life, an essential belief in individual responsibility, and a firm sense that the public sector must care for the poor—these are deeply held values. A pro-choice position might be framed in terms of individual freedom; a flat-tax proposal might go to fundamental fairness. Campaigns need to understand voter convictions if they are going to frame policy issues appropriately.

Ideology, strength of social commitment, and partisan preference are all clues to the behavior of an electorate, and each can be tapped, in principle at least, by opinion surveys. At their best, political polls allow campaign managers to gauge the potential value of strategies and tactics. With an accurate analysis of the electorate's attitudes, a campaign organization can make informed decisions about message resonance, voter targeting, and the allocation of resources. As donors place their bets on favored candidates and journalists decide which office seekers deserve coverage, new-style campaigns gain recognition by showing—*scientifically*—that they have a shot at winning.

## Types of Surveys

Surveys commissioned by media outlets and interest groups are usually intended to write a story—not to strategize a campaign. Online aggregators, such as pollster.com, fivethirtyeight.com, realclearpolitics.com, PollTracker, Votamatic, and Frontloading HQ, help pundits follow the horse race, but these polls are general in nature and at any rate campaign operatives lack access to the raw data that lend strategic meaning to an opinion survey. And even if the raw data were made public, the questions asked by outside pollsters might not square with the questions that would have been asked by strategists. When the candidate's future and the consultant's fortunes are on the line, polls conducted by a survey firm that understands political research are much more valuable.

Surveys can be separated into five major categories: *feasibility tests, benchmark polls, in-cycle polls, qualitative research,* and pseudo-surveys called *push polls.*

## Feasibility Tests

Some candidates might want to dip their toes into the water before they start serious campaigning or pay the high price of a comprehensive survey. If the candidate is a prospective challenger, a plain and simple survey might determine if there is any chance of victory; if the candidate is an incumbent, the idea might be to find the likelihood of defeat. As such, the questions could be few, zeroing in on "name recognition for a candidate and the opponent, job approval for an incumbent, support for reelection of an incumbent, and an early matchup" (Stonecash 2008, 21).

## Benchmark Polls

A benchmark poll is a major survey designed for long-range planning. Several hundred respondents might be asked dozens of questions that assess name recognition, issue preferences, underlying attitudes, and prevailing levels of knowledge about campaign issues. Measures of partisanship, ideology, and religiosity might be gathered alongside standard demographic questions. The poll might also be used to test the relative value of campaign messages, including those that could expose vulnerabilities in the candidate's own record, with questions like: "If you knew that Mr. Lee had failed to vote in quite a few recent elections, would this fact make you more likely or less likely to vote for him, or would it make no difference?" Information gathered from the comprehensive benchmark can be used to design a basic campaign strategy and perhaps to recommend questions that will be asked in a follow-up or tracking poll, and in line with contemporary campaign strategy, the results can be used in microtargeting analyses.

## In-Cycle Polls

A follow-up poll is conducted after the benchmark is taken and after the campaign season gets under way. The idea is to uncover strategic mistakes and correct them while there is still time. Follow-ups are typically shorter than comprehensive benchmarks, and tracking polls are shorter still. Tracking polls follow a limited number of issues on a regular basis—weekly or daily—in order to keep an eye on voter trends. Key items might involve name recognition, candidate preference, issue support, and perhaps the effectiveness of campaign events and commercials.

A run of tracking polls allows a campaign to watch changes in the electorate. Samples might be drawn anew for each survey, or a single "panel" can be drawn once and reinterviewed throughout the campaign. The latter approach would be informative, though expensive, and care must be taken to ensure continued participation and to reduce the possibility that repeated interviews themselves wind up changing respondent attitudes. Another approach is the quick-response poll, using a new sample to identify the immediate effect of a campaign event. If the opponent launches a series of attack ads, a quick-response poll might determine their impact.

## *Qualitative Research*

In a focus group, a small pool of respondents chat about their opinions, beliefs, and attitudes for an extended period of time. A moderator pulls comments from the participants while a survey team records the conversation. Although the sample size is tiny, the depth of opinion offered in focus groups can capture subtleties that would be missed in a standardized poll. Although focus groups can appear informal, they must be carefully supervised in order to draw out useful information. Moderators must encourage shy members to speak up and prevent outspoken participants from dominating the conversation, and they have to ensure that the discussion does not become an exercise in mutually reinforcing "group-think" or needlessly divisive argumentation.

Close cousins of the focus group are "dial groups" and "mall intercepts." In a mall intercept, a researcher approaches a shopper, asks a few screening questions, and then escorts the respondent to a storefront office to ask substantive questions. Intercepts can be used to examine direct mail pieces, perhaps watching how people unfold an envelope and skim the enclosures. For television spots, a campaign might use a dial group, in which participants turn a control knob back and forth to indicate their changing level of satisfaction as they view the ads. Second-by-second analysis can pinpoint strengths and weaknesses in a campaign message, capturing problems with wording and sentence structure.

An alternative to the traditional focus-group is Web-based testing. Unlike a typical focus group, in which a small number of respondents get together in a room to chat, online focus groups engage in discussions over the Internet. Ads can be tested in a group or on an individual basis. Private firms offer demographically customizable online samples representative of larger populations. The disadvantage of online surveys is a loss of face-to-face nuance, but what might be gained in the large sample and the ability to run controlled experiments is a potential for increased confidence in the generalizability of results.

Other forms of qualitative research have emerged in recent election cycles. *Web scraping* pulls unstructured data from the Web to extract information for sentiment analysis. Ethnographic research goes to voters where they live—literally. By finding a representative voter and having that person invite friends into his or her home, a political ethnographer can watch how real political conversations unfold, with the added benefit of feedback from the respondent and friends who know what the respondent *really* thinks. The researcher might also ask permission to look around the home to see how the family lives and how it gets the news (in the same way that a commercial ethnographer might follow a shopper around the grocery store). Pollster Andrew Myers says, "Wherever possible, I've moved to the ethnographic approach since it tends to better simulate the real world and the flow of information within a respondent's personal network." The reason: "More and more in this cluttered media environment people rely on those within their personal network for information, and more often than not, these personal networks are important to how opinion is shaped and how people form opinions" (Myers, pers. comm.).

## Push Polls

Feasibility tests, benchmark polls, in-cycle polls, tracking polls, and qualitative research seek unbiased information about the electorate; push polls have an entirely different function. Often conducted during the final days of a campaign, push polls disguise voter persuasion as survey research. The term *poll* is inappropriate, actually, because the calls are not intended to collect data but rather to move support. The question might go to drunk driving or racial culture. Push polls came to public awareness during the 2000 presidential campaign when mysterious calls to South Carolina voters, operating under the guise of survey research, used a racially charged message against John McCain (Banks 2008). The practice has not seemed to abate in recent election cycles, even in the wake of widespread denunciation and state legislative efforts to curtail them.

Many legitimate surveys offer carefully phrased messages with an edge of negativity to gauge voter response: "Does this statement make it more likely or less likely that you would vote for Mr. Davis?" The intention is to find the right message. A push poll, as opposed to a push question on a genuine survey, lacks any intention to find anything, a distinction recognized by the American Association of Political Consultants (AAPC) when it condemned "advocacy calling" that:

1. Masquerades as survey research
2. Fails to clearly and accurately identify the sponsor of the call
3. Presents false or misleading information to the voter (American Association of Political Consultants, 1996).

"To our knowledge," the AAPC wrote, "there is no overlap whatsoever between legitimate polling firms and firms that conduct so-called 'push polls'" (ibid.).

Push polls in an advocacy effort and push questions in authentic survey research can be hard for nonexperts to distinguish, especially as the electorate has become sensitized to the problem of push polling. The American Association for Public Opinion Research (AAPOR) warns of suspicious calls: "One or only a few questions are asked, all about a single candidate or a single issue," or "the questions are uniformly strongly negative (or sometimes uniformly positive) descriptions of the candidate or issue" (American Association for Public Opinion Research 2007). But a respondent can hear the negative information contained in a push question and mistakenly believe the legitimate poll is intended for persuasion. A sincere questionnaire that is confused with a push poll can instantly create a public relations setback that the campaign might want to avoid.

## Quality Control

A "good" poll has minimal error. If 55 percent of the population would vote for a candidate on Election Day, then the poll should accurately represent that fact. But inference from a survey surely carries risk. Three types of error are particularly salient: *instrument error, sampling error,* and *nonobservation error. Total survey error* is a function of all these problems combined (see Weisberg 2005).

### Instrument Error

Wording and sequence are important. A classic study in opinion research demonstrated that public attitudes toward freedom of the press changed as the order of questions was altered (Schuman and Presser 1981, 28–29). The problem is that survey questions at the beginning of a call tend to "prime" respondents for later queries. The options provided to the respondent can also have an impact. If respondents are asked which of two candidates they prefer without offering the respondent a "no preference" option, the views of respondents who prefer neither might be lost; and yet, a pollster may *want* to force an answer, since the ballot voters will confront in the polling booth might contain only those two choices. Finally, the wording of questions has an impact on the content of answers. If a pollster tilts a question in search of a desired answer, money spent on the survey might well have been wasted. "Ask a bad question and you get useless answers" (Weisberg, Krosnick, and Bowen 1996, 101).

### Sampling Error

Any survey that polls a sample of individuals instead of the entire population is subject to sampling error, no matter how randomly the sample is drawn. One way to think about the problem: If a population consists of four people, two supporters and two opponents, a series of randomly drawn two-person tests will sometimes overestimate and sometimes underestimate the number of supporters. Increasing the size of the sample will reduce the range of probable error but will not eliminate it. The way to eliminate sampling error is to query every last member of the population—rarely a practical solution.

### Nonobservation Error

Unbiased samples are difficult to gather. One issue is survey *coverage,* the share of the target population reachable by the survey's intended method. Another is *response rate.* Combined, nonresponse error and coverage error are called "nonobservation error" because the cases were not "observed" by the researcher. Question-skipping is a form of nonobservation error called "item nonresponse."

Not everyone has a telephone, and not all those who have a telephone will publicly list their number—some because they value their privacy and some because they rely on a cell phone instead of a landline. Among those who have a landline phone, the phone number is often shared with others in the household. If family members typically differ in the rates at which they answer the phone—say, if women answer the phone more often than men—the sample might wind up lop-sided. Internet polling poses new challenges, since many participants may not be representative of the larger population.

Cell phones prompt a host of novel questions for survey researchers. In 2013, 39 percent of American adults had wireless service and not a landline phone; the next generation of voters was running at 47 percent (Blumberg and Luke 2014). The term of art is "cell-phone-only," or "CPO." The AAPOR has a task force charged to deal with this new fact of life (see AAPOR Standards Committee 2010). Because phone numbers have become portable—users are allowed to carry their numbers with them when they move from coast to coast—phone numbers are becoming detached from their original voting districts. Cell numbers are shorter lived, as people abandon their mobile numbers at a higher rate than landlines (ibid., 24). Further, response rates on calls made to cell phones are lower than calls to landlines, which are also in decline (ibid., 38).

Calling a cell phone invokes a different set of legal restrictions than calling landlines. These laws reflect the possible financial costs of answering a cell phone and the sense of privacy that people attach to a device they carry on their person. And since people can answer cell phones when they are surrounded by strangers, the respondent's physical location might affect answers. According to the AAPOR Standards Committee: "Questionnaires for cell phone surveys should be carefully evaluated so that if the question wording is sensitive the response categories may be able to be designed to protect the privacy of the information from someone who might overhear them" (AAPOR Standards Committee 2008, 25). Put another way, delicate answers to survey questions should not echo through a public restroom.

Representativeness is critical to survey research. If coverage varies by some politically meaningful factor, new problems arise. Samples picked out of a phone book are biased against people without telephones (who may be poorer than average), people with unlisted phone numbers (who may value privacy more than others), and people who rely on cell phones (who may be younger than most). Some evidence shows that CPO adults are more liberal than their landline-only counterparts (Keeter et al. 2007; Keeter et al. 2010). Segments of the population such as Latinos may entail unique considerations to avoid unique problems of bias and variance (Dutwin and Lopez 2014).

Among those who have any sort of phone, landline or cell, a growing percentage refuse to divulge personal opinions. If voters with some political preferences have a greater tendency to answer questions than voters with other preferences, the hoped-for randomness that follows "equal probability of selection" will be violated (though low response rates do not necessarily affect the final results if no systematic difference distinguish respondents and nonrespondents). After years of survey calls and telemarketing pitches, many people have simply stopped answering questions. By 2012, the contact rate dipped to slightly over 60 percent with the cooperation rate falling below 20 percent and the response rate below 10 percent (Shepard 2012). According to Pew researchers, "the response rate of a typical telephone survey was 36% in 1997 and is just 9% today" (Kohut et al. 2012).

## Survey Design

Face-to-face interviewing is an aging stereotype of campaign research; the process is rarely used in the Digital Age (except among high-quality academic research) because it is expensive, time consuming, sometimes physically dangerous to interviewers, and less than practical if voters live in gated communities, rural locales, or other places that are difficult to enter. Mail surveys, on the other hand, might reach out to broader sections of the electorate, but response rates to questionnaires can be exceedingly low and the polls take a long while to complete, though some media outlets and political professionals continue to use them in a throwback to earlier days. Internet-based polling can reduce costs, though many suspect that a Web survey suffers from the same self-selection biases as mail polls. Telephone contact continues to dominate political campaign polling. By whatever mode of contact, survey research depends on proper sampling, thoughtful questions, and competent administration.

## Sampling

One of the thorniest problems in survey research is the development of representative samples. A cautionary tale is the *Literary Digest* poll of 1936. For years, the *Digest* had accurately predicted the winner of presidential elections by sending letters to potential respondents drawn from subscriber lists and telephone books. On the basis of millions of mailings, the *Digest* predicted Alf Landon's victory in the 1936 election (*Literary Digest* 1936a; see also Bryson 1976). The results of the poll may have comforted Governor Landon, but the results of the actual election—in which Landon garnered less than 37 percent of the popular vote—were probably more satisfying to Franklin Delano Roosevelt. After the election, the *Literary Digest* issued a plea: "If any of the hundreds who have so kindly offered their suggestions can tell us how we could get voters to respond proportionally, and still keep the poll secret . . . then we wish these critics would step up and do so" (*Literary Digest* 1936b, 8).

To overcome nonrandom selection, pollsters have used "random digit dialing" (RDD). RDD generates telephone numbers based on area codes and local exchanges, not phone listings, so those with unlisted numbers might still be reached, helping to ensure a more random selection. More recently, political pollsters began returning to list-based approaches, but this time working with voter lists. Yale professors Donald Green and Alan Gerber (2006) made a strong case that registration-based sampling (RBS) is the superior technique because the sample starts with an information-rich data set—a conclusion reinforced by state-level empirical research on the 2004 presidential election showing RBS had higher completion rates (Mitofsky et al. 2005). Recent research goes to possible use of *un*representative samples (Baker et al. 2013; Wang et al. 2014).

Good sampling is intended to reduce the difference between the underlying reality and the reported results. In technical terms, bias is a systematic difference between the true population parameter (e.g., the actual number of people who support the candidate) and estimates of that support. If, factually speaking, the candidate has 50 percent support in the electorate, but polling shows 49 percent support from the sample, the results are slightly biased. (Evidence suggests that public polls have consistently shown a bias against the eventual winner [McGhee 2014].)

Even with a representative sample, researchers can expect that results will be "off" by dint of the fact that a sample, not the entire population, has been surveyed. As a matter of pure chance, a randomly drawn sample of 500 voters from a population of 100,000 will almost surely oversample or undersample supporters. If the difference between the candidate's measured support (say, 51 percent) and the opponent's (49 percent) is less than the three-point margin of error, journalists might call the race a "statistical dead heat" or "too close to call" (see Hill 2013).

When selecting a sample size, a consultant must determine how much error can be tolerated. The reason: Random sampling, by its very nature, is chancy, and sometimes randomly selected groups will be unrepresentative. Minimizing the odds of a "fluky" poll demands a large sample. A 5 percent margin of error at 95 percent confidence requires perhaps 384 respondents; a 3 percent margin at 99 percent confidence might require 1,843 respondents (see Table 5.1). Tighter boundaries and higher levels of confidence entail larger sample sizes, so campaign operatives are forced to choose between saving money and increasing accuracy. Splitting the sample into subsets might require "oversampling" certain groups to maintain a high level of confidence.

The practicalities of survey administration can create imbalances within a sample. If the survey is run in the afternoon, when many older respondents are at home, the survey may not include enough

Table 5.1
Margins of Error and Measures of Confidence

| Margin of Error (%) | 95% Confidence | 99% Confidence |
| --- | --- | --- |
| ±7 | 196 | 339 |
| ±6 | 267 | 461 |
| ±5 | 384 | 663 |
| ±4 | 600 | 1,037 |
| ±3 | 1,067 | 1,843 |
| ±2 | 2,401 | 4,147 |
| ±1 | 9,604 | 16,587 |

young people. If 250 males are interviewed, but demographic research shows 312 males were needed to build a representative sample, one solution is to give more weight to each male's response. Males at home during the day might have candidate preferences different from those of the men who are at work. The set of individuals whom a pollster can interview in the middle of a workday is not necessarily representative of all individuals in the district—a reason to make several attempts at reaching a voter who does not answer the phone. And if the pollster could reach everyone on the sample list, the fact that some people will decline the chance to be interviewed will produce a degree of nonresponse error. One way to manage this sort of nonobservation error is to weight individual cases according to known characteristics of the electorate such as its ethnic and geographic composition (see Peress 2010).

### Question Construction

Pollsters talk about "good" and "bad" questions. A good question is one that will be understood by almost every respondent. Clear language and bilingual interviewers can aid the process. The average citizen has little policy expertise, so questions about environmental issues might require discussion about the "loss of trees" rather than "deforestation." Likewise, a question's wording should not steer respondents toward any particular response. For example, the question "Do you believe in the constitutional right to keep and bear arms?" predisposes a respondent to answer "yes."

Professional pollsters spend a lot of time figuring out how to word questionnaires the right way. Colloquial phrases might tilt results. Slang means different things to different people and interpretation might vary by age, class, and ethnicity. Indefinite terms can also become problematic. What does "frequently" mean? How many is "several"? The word "voter" can be vague. If the interviewer asks, "Are you a voter?" and the reply is "yes," is the respondent indicating a ballot cast in every election, every general election, or every presidential election—or a one-time vote for a compelling candidate a decade ago? Also to be avoided are complex questions that ask about two things at once, as well as simple questions that assume facts not in evidence.

Distinctions can be made among various types of questions (see Backstrom and Hursh-Cesar 1981). An *information* question asks about facts relating directly to the respondent, such as standard demographic items (e.g., age, sex, race, income). A *knowledge* question goes to the wider domain of verifiable facts (e.g., the identity of the respondent's congressional representative). An *opinion* question asks for a judgment (e.g., the respondent's attitudes toward an issue or a candidate). A *self-perception* question relates directly to the respondent (e.g., whether the respondent considers him- or herself a Democrat).

Any of these four types of questions can be asked in an *open-response* or a *closed-response* format. An open-response question lets a person answer in his or her own words. Open-response formats, however, might require interviewers to know a great deal about the topic at hand. Asking "What do you believe is the most important problem facing America?" might bring a wide array of responses, and an ill-informed interviewer may well transcribe or interpret a complicated answer incorrectly. In the closed-response format, the respondent is asked to choose from a predetermined set of answers. Closed-response items are easier to record but may force respondents into judgments they would not otherwise make.

One important use of closed-format questions is respondent screening. Filter questions ensure the relevance of subsequent questions. A filter question might ask whether respondents intend to vote in the upcoming election. If the answer is "no," the survey might terminate. Why gather information from a nonvoter? Then again, a campaign might want to know what sorts of issues would prompt the voter to cast a ballot, which could be helpful to a get-out-the-vote effort.

After a respondent passes through the filter and is asked a few substantive questions, the polling agent might ask a sleeper or probe question. A probe seeks detail about a previous response. If the questioner had asked, "In politics, do you normally think of yourself as a Democrat, an independent, a Republican, or something else?" and the respondent replied "Democrat," a probe might go on to inquire, "Do you consider yourself a strong or weak Democrat?" Individuals who call themselves independents might be checked for the angle of their lean. Sleeper questions check the veracity of a respondent's answers to other questions. At some point in a questionnaire, the respondent might be asked whether he or she voted in the most recent election; later on, a sleeper question might ask about the location of the polling place.

### *Administration*

With a sample and a questionnaire in hand, the next step is to make contact with voters. Modern polling firms train callers to be professional. Written guidelines from Jeffrey M. Stonecash, a scholar who has worked for political campaigns, instruct callers to "follow the script at all times; deviations and attempts to elaborate/interpret questions ruin the validity of responses" (2008, 78). Dispassion is intended to wash out the caller's idiosyncrasies. "Interviewer effects" arise when something about the person asking questions winds up influencing the answers coming from the respondents. Beyond tone of voice or unconscious prompting, vocal characteristics associated with gender and race can alter the results (ibid., 76).

One way to manage interviewer effects while lowering the cost of survey research is to have a computer do the asking. Interactive voice response (IVR) systems work like the CATI software employed by live interviewers, except that the questions are asked by a computer and responses are entered directly to the database (which means the person answering the phone might not be known). In the same way that a bank's customer service line might guide a client through a variety of options, an IVR system asks questions and branches respondents to new queries based on received answers. If, as Stonecash notes, race and gender influence responses, the anonymity of an IVR system might reduce interviewer effects. The technology has become popular as an inexpensive alternative to live-caller surveys, though users must be aware of current legal restrictions on dialing mobile phones.

Yet another alternative is Internet polling. This form of administration carries built-in benefits, not the least of which is the instant delivery of media content. A respondent could watch a proposed commercial and comment on it without marching down to a research firm. Moreover, "the cost of transmission of information is very low; the speed of transmission is very high; and the data are immediately available to the analyst" (O'Muircheartaigh 2008, 306). While some advocates of Internet polling believe they can approximate demographic balance with quotas or weighting, detractors are not yet convinced (Baker et al. 2013; see also Gelman and Rothschild 2014). Nate Silver's analysis (2012) found that of the ten most accurate pollsters, five used live phone calls, four used Internet delivery, and one used robo calls (IVR). All had less than a two percentage point error with nine of the ten having a slight Republican bias. Of the ten least accurate pollsters examined by Silver, five used live phone, four used robo-dial, and one used the Internet. Perhaps the administration mechanism does not matter as much as the protocols selected within various administrations.

## Data Analysis

Assuming a poll was well constructed and well administered, its results speak to the values and opinions of a district's voters. Candidates may express interest about procedural matters about opinion surveys but might well be more interested in seeing the results. Tables 5.2 through 5.6 display the findings of a poll regarding a notional Senate race between Democrat Zhi Peng Lee, Republican Mark Wilson, and independent Joan Jones.

Table 5.2 shows that 452 individuals said they were "very interested" in the election, representing 43.1 percent of nonmissing cases. At the bottom of the grid is the number of respondents who answered "Don't know." These respondents were unable or unwilling to answer the question. The 13 individuals in this category constitute 1.2 percent of the sample. (A large number of "Don't know" responses can suggest either an ambivalent electorate or a bad question; an overabundance of missing cases—observations that are deemed invalid for one reason or another—might prompt an analyst to review aspects of the survey that might be responsible.)

**Table 5.2**
**Interest-Level Question**

In the election for the U.S. Senate, Democrat Zhi Peng Lee is running against Republican Mark Wilson and the independent Joan Jones. Would you say that you are very, somewhat, just a little, or not at all interested in this race? (1) Very (2) Somewhat (3) Little (4) Not at all (9) Don't know

|  | Observed Frequency | Percentage of Total | Percentage of Nonmissing Cases |
|---|---|---|---|
| Very | 452 | 42.60 | 43.13 |
| Somewhat | 360 | 33.93 | 34.35 |
| Little | 115 | 10.84 | 10.97 |
| Not at all | 121 | 11.40 | 11.55 |
| Don't know | 13 | 1.23 | — |

The poll shows a clear lead for Wilson. Table 5.3 reports candidate preference. The results indicate that Wilson is ahead with about 43 percent of the voters who expressed a preference, as compared to roughly 33 percent for Lee and nearly 4 percent for Jones. In Table 5.4 are results from a probe that was asked of all respondents who stated a preference. The CATI screen would have prompted interviewers to ask, "How certain are you to vote for [candidate's name]?" Roughly a third of the respondents said they were "somewhat" sure they would vote for their candidate on Election Day.

**Table 5.3**
**Candidate Preference Question**

If the election were held today, would you vote for Mr. Lee, Mr. Wilson, or Ms. Jones, or would you skip the race?
(1) Lee (2) Wilson (3) Jones (4) Skip (5) Undecided-IF VOLUNTEERED
(9) Don't know

|  | Observed Frequency | Percentage of Total | Percentage of Nonmissing Cases |
|---|---|---|---|
| Lee | 343 | 32.33 | 33.17 |
| Wilson | 447 | 42.13 | 43.23 |
| Jones | 39 | 3.68 | 3.77 |
| Skip | 109 | 10.27 | 10.54 |
| Undecided | 96 | 9.05 | 9.28 |
| Don't know | 27 | 2.54 | — |

**Table 5.4**
**Preference Probe**

How certain are you that you will vote for Mr. Lee? Very certain, somewhat certain, not at all certain, or don't know?
(1) Very certain (2) Somewhat (3) Not at all (9) Don't know

|  | Observed Frequency | Percentage of Total | Percentage of Nonmissing Cases |
|---|---|---|---|
| Missing | 232 | 21.87 | — |
| Very certain | 521 | 49.10 | 63.30 |
| Somewhat | 273 | 25.73 | 33.17 |
| Not at all | 29 | 2.73 | 3.52 |
| Don't know | 6 | 0.57 | — |

Table 5.5
Undecided Probe
Are you LEANING toward Mr. Lee, Mr. Wilson, or Ms. Jones?
(1) Lee (2) Wilson (3) Jones (4) Skip (5) Undecided (9) Don't know

|  | Observed Frequency | Percentage of Total | Percentage of Nonmissing Cases |
|---|---|---|---|
| Missing | 856 | 80.68 | — |
| Lee | 34 | 3.20 | 20.36 |
| Wilson | 27 | 2.54 | 16.17 |
| Jones | 4 | 0.38 | 2.40 |
| Undecided | 102 | 9.61 | 61.08 |
| Don't know | 38 | 3.58 | — |

Perhaps the most important category is that of the "undecided" voter. Table 5.5 shows preferences for those individuals who indicated that they had not yet made up their minds or intended to skip the race. Each was asked which way he or she leaned and the uncommitted were apportioned to their respective candidates. More than 80 percent of respondents had already expressed a preference in the initial vote-choice question and therefore were not asked this question. Of those who were, more were leaning toward Lee than the others, but most appeared to be truly undecided.

A cross-tabulation displays the frequency of responses to one item within the categories established by another. This sort of breakdown helps a campaign visualize the intersection of two variables. Table 5.6 shows candidate preference cross-tabulated by interest among voters who intended to cast a ballot in person. The column headed "Very" shows the number of individuals who said they were "very interested" in the race. In that column, cells for the individual candidates show Wilson leading Lee by about 54 to 35 points. In the second column are individuals who reported they were "somewhat interested" in the race. Here, the relevant cells in the "cross tabs" show Lee closing the gap to about 6 points. Among those individuals who said they are "a little interested," Lee appears to lead by a 4.5-point margin. A majority of those who said they were "not at all interested" in the race said they did not intend to vote.

Table 5.6
Cross-Tabulation of Interest Level by Vote Intention

| | Level of Interest in Campaign | | | | |
| | Very | Somewhat | Little | Not at all | Total |
|---|---|---|---|---|---|
| Lee | 158 (35.35%) | 124 (35.0%) | 43 (38.7%) | 17 (14.9%) | 342 (33.3%) |
| Wilson | 242 (54.1%) | 244 (40.7%) | 38 (34.2%) | 21 (18.4%) | 445 (43.4%) |
| Jones | 18 (4.0%) | 15 (4.2%) | 3 (2.7%) | 3 (2.6%) | 39 (3.8%) |
| Won't Vote | 3 (0.7%) | 35 (9.9%) | 11 (9.9%) | 59 (51.8%) | 108 (10.5%) |
| Undecided | 26 (5.8%) | 36 (10.2%) | 16 (14.4%) | 14 (12.3%) | 92 (9.0%) |
| Total | 447 (43.6%) | 354 (34.5%) | 111 (10.8%) | 114 (11.1%) | 1,026 (100.0%) |

## Conclusion

Campaign polls are usually run by professional polling firms, not in-house volunteer operations, where enthusiasm and inexperience might confound the results with irrelevant variables. But outsourcing carries its own set of risks. Polling firms, which might themselves contract out survey administration, may be using callers who differ in training and tenure. While almost anyone can be taught how to vocalize words on a CATI screen, few people are superb conversationalists. The method of payment can affect data quality. An hourly wage might reduce the incentive to submit bogus call reports, but it provides less motivation to complete the calls in a timely manner. Piecework payments might reward persistent employees but they might also credit sham call reports. Supervisors sometimes hook into interviews, call respondents back for confirmation, or allow clients to listen in on the process.

Not every used-car buyer is a mechanic, but an informed shopper can look under the hood for oil leaks and broken hoses. The same holds true for polling services. Knowing basic survey techniques and a range of analytic tools reduces the risk of a costly mistake. Consultants must be good consumers of survey data, aware of the many pitfalls of polling. There are, to be sure, scores of analytic techniques that pollsters can use to coax hidden findings from the data. Some firms build regression models or use more refined procedures, and survey data can be laid over demographic and electoral information. Advanced methods are employed to find the right place to position candidates in the electoral environment and to target voters for persuasion or mobilization.

## Note

A significant portion of this chapter is adapted from Jesse Marquette, "How to Become a Wise Consumer of Campaign Polling," in *Campaign Craft: The Strategies, Tactics, and Art of Political Campaign Management*, ed. Daniel M. Shea (Westport, CT: Praeger, 1996).

# CHAPTER 6

# Voter Targeting

In 1994, voters took power from the Democrats in the House of Representatives and the U.S. Senate and handed both legislative chambers to the Republicans. "Safe" Democratic candidates went down to defeat. Speaker of the House Tom Foley lost his congressional district to an attorney who had never before held elective office. It was a political bloodbath widely interpreted as a rejection of the Democratic Party in general and the Democratic president in particular. Many thought Bill Clinton could do little more than bide his time until his eventual downfall in 1996. Some thought a challenger would rise from within the Democratic ranks and beat the incumbent president in the primaries.

Two schools of thought circulated among the president's supporters. The first was liberal. Many of the losing Democrats were moderate or conservative and the Democrats who remained standing after 1994 were more partisan than their predecessors. The liberal view held that Clinton should concentrate on his Democratic base. The idea made sense: Why should the president cast himself as a Republican in Democratic clothing? Given the choice between a Republican and a Republican, the people will choose the Republican every time. The other school argued for centrism. The votes lost in 1994 fell from the center, not the left. To win in 1996, the middle ground had to be recaptured.

Consultant Dick Morris, who had advised Democrats and Republicans during his career, gave the centrist approach his own sly twist: Press simultaneously against the Democratic left and the Republican right, find the center, and rise above partisan conflict. Morris called his strategy "triangulation." In his words, "The president needed to take a position that not only blended the best of each party's views but also transcended them to constitute a third force in the debate." By following this path, Morris wrote, "either [Clinton] will be repudiated by the voters and slink back into the orthodox positions or he will attract support and, eventually, bring his party with him" (1999, 80–81). While the policies engendered by triangulation would later be called too moderate, too small, or too cynical, many have concluded the strategy was politically sound.

Thoughtful candidate positioning was sought in the old retail politics and gained importance with the rise of new-style campaigns. As mass-marketing becomes more customized, the focus is turning toward highly specific forms of communication, helping candidates and their consultants reach individual voters with personally tailored messages. Broad-based understanding of entire districts is being sliced by narrowly focused analytics that traffic in neighborhoods and individuals. A discussion of voter targeting is the culmination of campaign planning, candidate and opposition profiling, voter segmentation, and opinion research. Without a target, a campaign has no direction; without a theme, it has no rationale.

This chapter discusses six aspects of voter targeting: voter behavior, polarization, generalized approaches, specific strategies, campaign themes, and microtargeting.

## Voter Behavior

Among political scientists, broad theories of voter behavior go to sociology, social psychology, and rationality.

### Sociology

Early models of voter behavior are associated with Bureau of Applied Social Research at Columbia University. In the 1940s and 1950s, Columbia scholars examined the sociological factors in vote choice. They focused on groups (such as religious affiliations, workplace organizations, and social acquaintances), finding that group associations play a large role in individual decisions. In *The People's Choice* (1944), Paul Lazarsfeld, Bernard Berelson, and Hazel Gaudet surveyed voters over the course of the 1940 campaign season and found only a handful of respondents changing allegiance from one candidate to the other. Candidate selection seemed to be a function of social and economic groupings. This point was reiterated a few years later by

Berelson, Lazarsfeld, and McPhee in *Voting* (1954): Like "music, literature, recreational activities, dress, ethics, speech, [and] social behavior," the scholars wrote, political decisions "have their origin in ethnic, sectional, class, and family traditions" and "exhibit stability and resistance to change. . . . While both are responsive to changed conditions and unusual stimuli, they are relatively invulnerable to direct argumentation and vulnerable to indirect social influences" (310–311). Campaign persuasion, it seemed, had minimal effects.

If, as was true at the time, downscale Catholics voted for Democrats, an individual voter's "choice" could be predicted from religion and income. Persuasion is unlikely in the sociological model but it comes into play when a voter is "cross-pressured." Upscale Catholics would be pulled in two directions at once. When cross-pressured, voters had to decide among pressures; they did so by talking to people within their social circles. Voting choice might take time. If social alliances were aligned, as in the case of the downscale Catholic, no real decision was required and a voter knew early in the season for whom he or she would vote; the upscale voter, who was more conflicted, would have to listen to more information. Cross-pressured voters tended to vote late in the election or opt not to vote at all.

### Social Psychology

By the 1960s, the scholarly understanding of voter behavior was changing. Instead of focusing on the loose determinism of the Columbia School, scholars from the University of Michigan looked at development of preferences from historical context and early childhood learning to a voter's ultimate decision in the ballot booth. Party attachments develop early in life and typically go unchanged. Abundant evidence shows a voter's identification with a party is the single best predictor of a candidate choice, superseding demographic categories and issue preferences.

In *The American Voter* (1960), Angus Campbell, Phillip Converse, Warren Miller, and Donald Stokes argued that voting behavior worked its way through a "funnel of causality" that began with a voter's demographic position but proceeded through the development of party identification (largely inherited from parents) and later to candidate perceptions. Party identification is generally gained early in life and tends to screen out messages from the opposition, so short-term influences such as candidate imagery have meager impact on ballot-booth decisions. From this point of view, a campaign that believes it can persuade a mass of voters to defect from the opposition by talking about the issues will run up against decades of political socialization (see also Miller and Shanks 1996). The authors of *The American Voter, Revisited* have argued, "Once an individual has formed a party attachment, however embryonic, and whatever stage in life it happened, a self-reinforcing process of momentum takes over" (Lewis-Beck et al. 2008, 149–150).

Significant challenges to the Michigan School appeared in the 1970s as voter partisanship declined. Norman Nie, Sidney Verba, and John Petrocik, in *The Changing American Voter* (1979), saw a heightened role for issue voting. With issue salience growing and party identification falling, it was difficult to see how or why party affiliation would remain a driving force. In more recent years, a resurgence of partisanship (see below) may signal a revitalization of behavioral theories based on psychological attachment.

### Rationality

"Voters are not fools," declared V. O. Key (1966, 7), who reasoned that people look at recent history and decide whether the incumbents are worth keeping or if the voters should throw the bums out. A voter can make a rational decision to "stand pat" or to "switch." From Key's perspective, voters make policy choices even if they lack comprehensive knowledge of public policy. Morris Fiorina (1981) has argued that voters keep tabs on how the governing party seems to be doing, and Samuel Popkin (1991) has argued that uninformed voters are not necessarily irrational, just under-resourced in political knowledge.

Students of political science speak of "prospective" and "retrospective" evaluations. Prospective evaluations are anticipatory. A voter looks at a candidate—his or her qualifications, party label, personality, and campaign promises—and then guesses what kind of job the candidate will do. When Barack Obama promised to reform health care, he was asking voters to view his candidacy prospectively. Retrospective evaluations look in the opposite direction. Past actions are weighed in order to judge a candidate's future behavior. When Obama charged that John McCain consistently voted in line with George W. Bush, he was inviting citizens to think about the problems of the outgoing administration, a call to retrospective voting.

The most celebrated example of a campaign appeal to retrospection is Ronald Reagan's question to the American people in 1980, when the economy under Jimmy Carter was in deep trouble: "Are you better off than you were four years ago?" It was an attempt to convey the perils of the opponent by pointing to past performance. In essence, voters are confronted with a choice: Either look at each candidate's plans for the future (a speculative, time-consuming chore) or examine what has happened in the recent past (a quick, "factual" process). If backward-looking clues are unflattering, the evaluation of the candidate will be negative (see Fiorina 1981). The power of retrospection carries an obvious appeal, and as more and more candidates use negative advertising, voters might become accustomed to the attacks, depending on them for critical information even as they decry mean-spirited politics.

A nagging question is the content of voter rationality. Assuming a voter cannot compute all implications of all decisions (see Simon 1983), then rationality is bounded to what the voter sees at the time of the vote. John Zaller's "Receive-Accept-Sample" model (1992) has attentive voters hearing messages from political elites and then believing them to the extent those messages square with prior knowledge; finally, when the voter is called upon to make a statement or render a decision the stock of beliefs is sampled and something like a momentary average of those beliefs forms the basis of the action (see Lodge and Taber 2013).

## Polarization

Questions about voter targeting are tightly linked to the fall and rise of partisanship, insofar as the best predictor of vote propensity is a voter's party identification. In the 1970s and 1980s, a broad consensus of scholars saw partisanship in decline. While some continue to argue that the electorate is largely centrist—Morris Fiorina makes a strong case that a loud, partisan "political class" has taken over primary elections even as the broad electorate remains centrist—this view is being challenged.

Alan Abramowitz argues that polarization has become a defining characteristic of modern electoral politics. In *The Disappearing Center* (2010), Abramowitz shows a steady, powerful ideological realignment in the American electorate. The center points of the major parties have moved apart and left little overlap. As the electorate has become more polarized, with a smaller and smaller buffer zone, the stakes of winning and losing have increased, and as a consequence, the voting public has become more engaged in political debate.

The electorate has gradually become polarized and active—and more combative—over the past half century of partisan conflict. The Pew Research Center has found that while the gulf between the average policy positions of Democrats is widening so is political antipathy among voters. Partisans on each side are tending to dislike one another more, and the most active among these partisans are ideologically "pure" and fearful of the other side (Dimock et al. 2014). The American National Election Study shows similar polarization. Whereas in the 1990s about 50 percent reported they cared "very much" or "pretty much" who won their congressional district election, that number jumped to 70 percent in 2008.

Polarization can also be seen in media consumption. Research into viewing habits can be summed up in the notion that conservatives get their television news from Fox and liberals get it from MSNBC, with decreasing numbers watching middle-of-the-road news programs like CNN (Jamieson and Cappella 2008; Arceneaux, Johnson, and Murphy 2012; Levendusky 2013; Mitchell and Weisel 2014). A national survey shows liberals trusting *The Daily Show* more than Fox (Public Policy Polling 2013). Other surveys show that conservatives distrust science reporting that does not square with their prior ideological bearing (Leiserowitz et al. 2013; McKnight et al. 2013). If, as seems to be the case, voters are becoming more trustful of their own sources and more distrustful of other voters' sources, it is easy to see how and why partisans talk past one another, not even agreeing on "simple facts."

Jeffrey Stonecash (2014) finds that during the past few decades the American political system has undergone a slow but steady recalibration—a shift he calls "secular realignment." Unlike previous partisan realignments, where intense cross-cutting issues divided the electorate and reconfigured of voting patterns in a single election or two, the recent shake-up has happened slowly, but steadily, since the 1960s. This phenomenon can be seen in the 2014 midterm elections, as Republicans solidified their position in the American South. Whereas in the 1960s Southern governorships were dominated by Democrats—governor's mansions, state legislatures, U.S. House and Senate seats were occupied by members of Andrew Jackson's party—the end of 2014 saw that figure reduced nearly to zero. Survey analyst Guy Molyneux contends, "Some of it is about Obama; most of it is about the longer-term realignment of white voter preferences" (Cohn 2014a). Southern conservative Democrats are an endangered species and liberal Republicans are all but extinct.

One explanation of polarization is partisan gerrymandering. Whereas in the late 1990s about 90 congressional races were decided within a 10 percent margin, that figure dropped to about 50 in 2012 (DeSilver 2013). If state legislatures are shoring up majority representation by drawing district boundaries that help co-partisans—that is, if politicians are picking the voters who are most likely to pick those very same politicians—increased partisanship seems a likely result. But gerrymandering alone cannot explain the new partisanship. Voting blocs defined by fixed boundaries (e.g., towns, counties, and entire states) are also increasingly ideologically homogeneous.

Another reason for polarization may lie in geographic sorting. This idea was discussed by journalist Bill Bishop in *The Big Sort: Why the Clustering of Like-Minded America Is Tearing Us Apart* (2008). Bishop argued that partisanship extends beyond labels and issues into fundamental differences of lifestyle and outlook. People with similar hobbies, incomes, religious beliefs, sources of news, and lines of work tend to sort themselves into the same neighborhoods, and these neighborhoods tend to have partisan characteristics. Neighborhoods become politically homogeneous. Bishop observed the increasing number of "landslide counties," defined as counties in which the margin of victory in presidential elections exceeded 20 percent— a tripling from 20 percent in the 1970s to nearly half three decades later (6).

By 2004, Bishop writes, "nearly half of all voters lived in landslide counties" (1). In Bishop's view, "Pockets of like-minded citizens that have become so ideologically inbred that we don't know, can't understand, and can barely conceive of 'those people' who live just a few miles away" (40). Bishop found that women in Democratic landslide counties were strongly against the war in Iraq while Democratic women in Republican blowout counties were strongly supportive of the war; Democrats in Republican landslide districts were much more likely to attend church than were Democrats in Democratic landslide districts.

A scholarly treatment of this phenomenon has been offered by George Hawley (2013). Relying on individual-level survey data, he finds evidence to suggest the partisan and ideological composition of counties plays a role in shaping voting preferences. Local political context shapes voter attitudes. He writes, "Based on these results, we can be reasonably concerned that residential political balkanization is leading to a more extreme, polarized electorate" (2013, 36). Moderate voters become less so when they reside in ideologically charged communities as voters look to "fit" into their surrounding community and thereby snowballing the weight of partisanship (see also Motyl et al. 2014; Shea 2014, 309).

A shift of some type is apparent. A Pew Research Center survey of 10,000 Americans found that the gulf between the average policy positions of Democrats is distant from the average policy position of Republicans at any point in the last two decades. Party antipathy is at record high. Each side fears and dislikes the other. Those most active are ideologically "pure" and fearful of the other side. Among some of those who identify with a major political party, political intermarriage has become a problem: "Roughly equal percentages of Democrats (15%) and Republicans (17%) say they would be unhappy welcoming someone from the other party into their family" (Dimock et al. 2014).

## Approaches

The size and character of an electorate can vary from one community to the next. A sparsely populated area might supply a rich lode of swing votes while an urban center might offer a relative handful. In some precincts, Democrats never stand a chance, while in others, the Republican always suffers, and in still other areas, outcomes are in doubt. The approach a campaign takes to a given electorate—whom it will target and how it will gain the target votes—stems largely from the composition of the electorate it must persuade. A precinct or district with a strong party tradition demands one strategy; an area with a large toss-up vote calls for another. For campaign professionals, there are no immutable rules, only reasoned guidelines.

Targeting can begin with three distinct goals: *reinforcement, persuasion,* and *conversion.* Reinforcement is the task of making sure partisan voters stick with the candidate; persuasion brings toss-up voters on board; and conversion is the act of cajoling opposition voters to switch sides. In general terms, a campaign reinforces its own partisans, persuades the toss-ups, and converts the partisans of the opposition.

Voters are more easily reinforced or persuaded than converted. When the candidate is a member of a heavily favored party, the campaign might focus exclusively on reinforcement. The object is to get the partisan voters to show up at the polls or to mail in their ballots. In politically volatile areas, where neither candidate has an edge, persuasion might be the central strategy. If most voters are committed to the opponent's party or if a challenger faces a popular incumbent, conversion might be paramount. Early research, including opinion research, can say a lot about a district, and registration lists offer basic facts about individual voters, often including party affiliation. Combining this information into a larger portrait of the electorate can suggest a district's aggregate loyalty.

Figure 6.1 reflects a district that puts the Democrat in good stead. Democratic partisans comprise slightly under 50 percent of the vote, while Republican partisans are about 30 percent. Further, the Democratic base is about 50 percent larger than the Republican base. As such, a Democrat's goal might be to reinforce partisan supporters while persuading a small number of toss-up voters. Winning requires no converts, as many of the swing voters would be predisposed to vote Democratic anyway. A Democrat's best strategic position might lie among the soft Democratic partisans.

In 2014, African Americans were viewed as essential in Georgia, Louisiana, North Carolina, and Arkansas if Democrats were to retain the U.S. Senate. By looking at projections and demographic data, Cornell Belcher—a former pollster for President Obama—said there would be "crushing Democratic losses across the country" unless Democrats did more to get African Americans to the polls (Stolberg 2014). In the end, African Americans did not appear at the polls in these states at the same rates they had in 2008 or 2012.

**Figure 6.1**
**Strategizing a Partisan District: The Democratic Favorite**

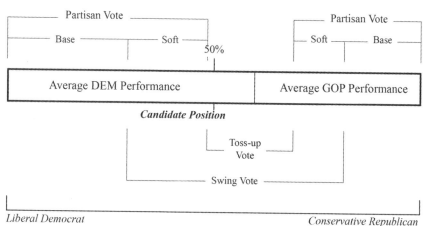

Figure 6.2
**Strategizing a Partisan District: The Republican Underdog**

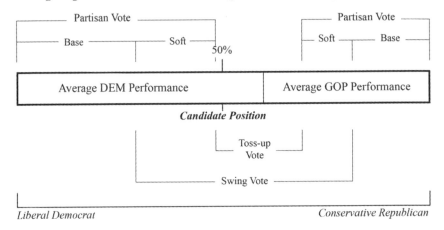

Some candidates enjoy the benefits of partisanship; others suffer. Looking at the district in Figure 6.2 from the Republican side, one finds a bleak landscape. A Republican campaign has little choice but to convert some Democratic partisans. Because the race is a long shot; it may be necessary to take Republican voters for granted, hoping they will stick with the GOP candidate. Reinforcement might take the form of a get-out-the-vote drive. Assuming some Republican partisans will be lost and a fair number of middle-ground voters will go Democratic, a number of Democratic soft-partisans must be converted. To accomplish the conversion, a Republican candidate might take a position at the center of the electorate, well to the left of the GOP base.

Low turnout and high creativity can help. Republican Dave Brat found a way to prevail against House Majority Leader Eric Cantor in a Virginia primary in 2014. Despite being outspent nearly ten-to-one, having no name recognition at the beginning, and running against the GOP establishment, Brat was able to utilize low turnout in the primary to help expose base-partisan dissatisfaction with the status quo. And Cantor's team failed to heed all warning signs: Brat supporters vastly outnumbered Cantor allies at local GOP meetings months before the contest (Sherman 2014).

Toss-up districts present a different set of problems. Figure 6.3 suggests a district with no clear bias. In one sense, the strategy is the same as it would be for an underdog: The candidate should find a position near the center. A basic strategy is to reinforce the partisans and persuade the toss-up voters.

**Figure 6.3**
**Strategizing a Toss-Up District**

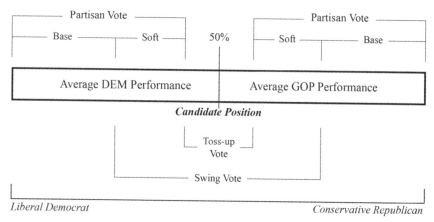

Few races have been more evenly matched than the 1998 Senate fight between Democrat Scotty Baesler and Republican Jim Bunning. The first was known in Kentucky from his college basketball days, the second from a career in professional baseball. Each was a sitting congressman in a state that split its votes between Democrats and Republicans. Bunning positioned himself as a moderate and then began running attack ads. According to political scientists who studied the race, Bunning "lay claim to the traditional Democratic issue of protecting Social Security" (Gross and Miller 2000, 189) and used this position as a strong foundation from which to commence a harsh advertising barrage against the Democrat.

Narrow targeting works. Candidates need to run hard, and smart. The folly of reaching broadly is twofold. First, political campaigns live on scarce resources. Time and money should be spent where they will do the most good, so campaigns have to be efficient. Second, covering areas offering little chance of success can do harm. If people who are predisposed to vote against a candidate start receiving literature and phone calls that denigrate their party and challenge their convictions, opposition interest can be piqued, and some otherwise lazy partisans might be activated to cast a vote (the wrong way).

## Strategies

A sense of how voters tick can suggest the correct approach to persuasion and mobilization. Political campaigns can be partisan (appealing to party identification), positional (taking stands that aim at a pivot point in the electorate), valence (associating a candidate with broadly popular sentiments), and wedge (splitting opposition constituencies).

## *Partisan*

Partisanship is more than just psychological identification; it drives behavior. If voters care about partisanship, and a district's partisan lean favors a candidate, middle-school arithmetic implies campaign outreach should emphasize the candidate's affiliation. If, however, the electorate tends to vote for the opponent's party, then it seems unlikely that stressing partisanship is a good idea.

Beyond persuasion, partisanship can mobilize. In 2004, the Bush campaign eked out a win by concentrating on its highly motivated base. A base strategy often relies on voter polarization. If half the electorate is Democratic and half is Republican and few people are persuadable, the key to victory might lie with getting one's own voters to show up in larger numbers. Karl Rove, who is often credited with developing the approach, has admitted that it is a "risky strategy," but the method has a strong rationale. An insider described the strategy this way: "Karl does not believe there's a true 'middle,'" because "everyone is a 'leaner,' and the leaners are affected by the actions of the base" (Kornblut 2004). By this line of reasoning, energizing the base increases the number of votes among natural supporters while at the same time gathering up a quantity of centrists who feel the effects of base enthusiasm.

Base energy is important, and sometimes a centrist approach fails. In 1998, in Ohio's Sixth Congressional District, Lieutenant Governor Nancy Hollister, a Republican, tried to draw moderate voters from incumbent Democrat Ted Strickland. The district had thrashed back and forth between the major parties since 1992, with 2 percent margins each time. Hollister was a quality candidate, but after a bruising primary with conservative GOP rivals, she was caught on the horns of a dilemma: Winning the district seemed to entail holding the center, even if holding the center meant risking the base. When Hollister's moderate campaign began, the right wing of the GOP might have had trouble understanding where the candidate stood on issues like abortion. A centrist message seemed to disenchant the conservative base (Burton and Shea

2003). In the end, Hollister lost the socially conservative district by 14 points.

## Positional

Many campaigns adopt an approach that squares with "median voter theory." This scholarly conjecture states that an electorate bulging with ideological centrists will entice candidates from both ends of the spectrum to run toward the center. In the middle lies the ideal point where some "pivotal voter" resides, and capturing *this* voter decides the election. This middle-of-the-road pivotal voter is the same person for both major party candidates. The logic of the model, which was detailed by Anthony Downs (1957), helps explain why both sides of the partisan divide so often chase voters at the center of the electorate. It should not be surprising that, in recent presidential elections, "battleground residents were *not* more likely to be contacted by only one party . . . instead, they were much more likely to be contacted by *both* parties" (Panagopoulos and Wielhouwer 2008).

A positional issue seeks a favorable division between the candidate and the opponent. If a candidate has a choice between two issues, one with a pivot point that gives a larger number of voters to the opposition while another has a pivot point that favors the candidate, the choice would seem clear. Candidates try to steer the discussion toward issues that they "own" (see Petrocik 1996). A Republican veteran of the war in Afghanistan may wish to emphasize national security issues; a Democrat who comes to the election from organized labor might want to make income inequality the subject of debate—if taking such a position can gather the pivotal voter into the fold on Election Day.

One difficulty with a simplistic interpretation of median voter theory is that it fails to recognize the power of base voters. Another is that it squeezes the electorate into a single ideological dimension. Life is more complicated. If a line is drawn between the extremes of left-wing liberalism and right-wing conservatism, where should a strategist place, say, a pro-growth opponent of capital gains taxes who believes women should have the right to choose an abortion? Or a blue-collar union member who believes in government-paid health care but wants to protect gun rights? These voters are pushed in different directions; they are "cross-pressured"—that is, two important factors run in different directions at once. A more realistic

**Figure 6.4**
**Ideological and Cross-Pressured Voters**

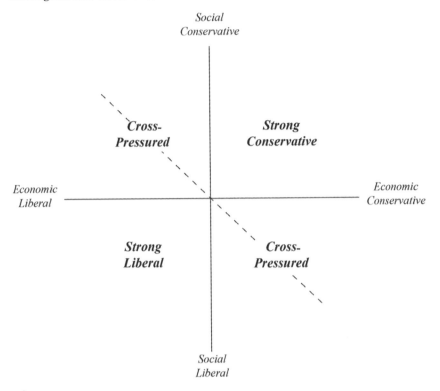

approach is to draw political space along two or more axes, perhaps beginning with social and economic values, as illustrated in Figure 6.4 (see also Fiorina, Abrams, and Pope 2006, 170–182). The main concept is the same as a one-dimensional analysis—find the center of balance between opposing forces—but the multidimensional model is more subtle, which is to say, more informative, and more complicated.

## Valence

Some issues do not fit an ideological continuum at all. Donald Stokes, an early critic of Downs, contrasted "position issues," which can be placed along a linear axis, with "valence issues," which cannot. A valence issue is one that has broad consensus, like opposition to crime or corruption. Voters dislike a corrupt politician, no matter which party the politician represents. In the 1950s, questions about corruption were raised along with questions about the economy and the Cold War:

> As the Republicans looked over the prospective issues for 1952, their problem was not whether to come out for or against Communistic subversion or prosperity or corruption in Washington. It was rather to put together a collection of issues of real or potential public concern whose positive and negative valences would aid the Republicans and embarrass the Democrats. (Stokes 1966, 173)

Base partisans find ways to validate or vilify candidates on the basis of ideology, but persuadable voters are more amenable to the power of valence issues (or they might not be considered so persuadable).

Subcategories of valence campaigns include informational campaigns and referendums. A local candidate for auditor who is facing token opposition may want simply to ensure that voters understand the candidate has done the job as expected. The campaign would want to inform voters, not to take a position or appeal to party. A referendum campaign—and here the term is used in reference to a messaging approach, not a stand-alone ballot question—seeks a yes-or-no answer to a larger question like the "Do you support the President." If the president is currently unpopular, voters are urged to cast ballots against supportive candidate. The Democratic U.S. Senate candidate challenging Mitch McConnell in Kentucky, where, in 2014, many voters opposed Barack Obama, found herself in an uncomfortable position when asked whether she had voted for Obama. After calling herself a "Clinton Democrat" she offered, "I respect the sanctity of the ballot box and I know that the members of this editorial board do as well." A *Washington Post* headline read, "40 painful seconds of Alison Lundergan Grimes refusing to say whether she voted for President Obama" (Bump 2014a).

### Wedge

Voters have party attachments *and* policy preferences, and they can become cross-pressured; but for D. Sunshine Hillygus and Todd G. Shields (2008), political cross-pressuring exists where there is an incongruence of policy preferences and party attachment. "The most persuadable voters in the electorate are those individuals with a foot in each candidate's camp," Hillygus and Shields write:

> This group of persuadable voters includes some political Independents who are closer to the Republican candidate on some issues and the Democratic candidate on other issues, but it is primarily composed of partisans who disagree with their party on a personally important policy issue. These are the "but otherwise" Democrats and Republicans, as in the voter who is "pro-life, but otherwise Democratic" or "opposed to the Iraq War, but otherwise Republican." These cross-pressured voters have a more difficult time deciding between the candidates, so they turn to campaign information to help decide between the competing considerations. (5)

Following this logic, a campaign would want to take advantage of the fact that many persuadable voters are highly interested in the election—but are stalling on their final answer because they are ambivalent or because some important policy preference is not squaring with their party's candidate. Hillygus and Shields find wide swaths of the electorate are in some sense persuadable, a conclusion that squares with the understanding held by some professionals (see Winston 2010).

The argument Hillygus and Shields put forward in *The Persuadable Voter* has profound implications for strategic targeting. The best issues, it seems, might be "wedge issues," which force members of the opponent's constituency to decide between loyalty and policy. *Wedge issues,* as the term is used here, refers not merely to divisive issues, but to issues that test the opposition's coalition. That is, wedge issues can be "aimed at pulling away voters from the other camp" (Hillygus and Shields 2008, 2). Because a two-party system inherently contains divergent policy preferences—voters do not constrain themselves simply to option "R" or option "D"—the reservoir of wedge issues is deep and the opportunity for voter persuasion is wide (ibid., 4). Using a mixed method analysis of the 2004 election, Hillygus and Shields estimated that much of the electorate was up for grabs.

## Campaign Themes

The idea behind voter segmentation, whether computer-driven or gut-level, is that voters can be distinguished by sets of characteristics that cluster in ways that do not follow simple traditional categories as partisanship, age, or income. American politics has seen competition for "soccer moms" and "NASCAR dads." In 2000, some Gore operatives scoffed at "Volvo drivers" who supported Bill Bradley. The 2004 cycle brought "security moms" to the forefront and in 2006 "mortgage moms" made a brief appearance, although they quickly gave way to "hockey moms" after Sarah Palin's enthusiastically received convention speech in 2008. And by 2012, "Wal-Mart moms" had become a key point of discussion.

While thumbnail categories jam diverse populations into pigeonholes, valid characterizations can enrich a strategist's understanding of a district, adding information beyond the left–right continuum. Formulating segments and clusters can help locate pockets of support that will respond to a campaign theme and move targeted voters.

A good campaign theme is a carefully crafted merger of what the voters want, what the candidate has to offer, and what the opponent brings to the table. Here lies the connection between candidate positioning, microtargeting, and the formulation of campaign themes: The candidate's position with respect to individual voters is given form and (perhaps) substance by a campaign theme and the issues that it represents.

Many campaign professionals believe it imperative for voters to hear the theme repeatedly: "If you stick to it, and say it often enough, you will define the criteria for the voters that they should use to make their choice" (Bradshaw 1995, 44). And imagination helps. Peter Hoekstra stunned the Washington establishment by knocking off the chair of the National Republican Congressional Committee, Guy Vander Jagt, in the 1992 Michigan Republican primary. On a shoestring budget, Hoekstra pounded home the idea that Vander Jagt was a career politician more interested in national affairs than in Michiganders. Hoekstra rode around in a 1966 Nash Rambler, a clever reminder of the year Vander Jagt was first elected. The sign on the car read, "Isn't it time for a change?" (Morris and Gamache 1994, 116). In 2002, a year after 9/11, Republicans unified around the idea that they could best protect the American people from terrorism; in 2006, Democrats highlighted a widespread perception of Republican failure on a variety of fronts. These approaches sought voters from different directions, but each seemed to work as intended. And in 2012, President Obama—against the wishes of many insiders—went all-in to link Mitt Romney with Bain Capital, which was accused of downsizing Americans out of their jobs.

If voters are moved by forces beyond such durable political anchors as party and incumbency, campaign themes would seem critical— and even if party and incumbency are important to a voter's decision, the voters might need some reminding. A theme, as consultant Joel Bradshaw notes,

> is the single, central idea that the campaign communicates to voters to sum up the candidate's connection with the voters and their concerns and the contrast between your candidate and the opponent. It answers the question, Why should your candidate be elected—to this office at this time? (1995, 42)

If the candidate comes from the majority party in a heavily partisan area, party-based appeals might work. If the candidate is an incumbent and voters prefer experience, then a record of accomplishment might provide the right theme. Voters rarely have time to assess candidate appeals on each and every issue; a well-constructed theme links voter concerns with the candidate's approach.

The Bush 2004 campaign found a strong theme in the charge that John Kerry was a "flip-flopper," voting first one way, then the other. Almost every day, Bush supporters used some variation on the idea: Kerry would "flip-flop," he was "flipping and flopping," he "flipped and flopped," and so forth. The term was used so often that it merited an exegesis by William Safire (2004). A young man wearing a giant sandal costume—a monster flip-flop, that is—was seen walking around Boston while the city hosted the Democratic Convention. In a post-9/11 world, when Americans were looking for resolute leadership, the charge of inconsistency seemed a strong line of attack.

A campaign's theme should be consistent with the candidate's past record. One function of opposition research is to locate discrepancies between a candidate's words and deeds, so a candidate whose chosen campaign theme is at odds with his or her past actions courts misfortune—along the lines of the "flip-flopper" charge leveled against Kerry. Also, the theme must be consistent with the views and actions of a candidate's supporters. Staffers and contributors who may once have worked on the other side of the candidate's current policy positions can become an unwanted part of a news story. Then again, if the staff and contributors are *too* consistent with the candidate's beliefs— if the candidate's platform is overly friendly to major donors—then conflicts of interest may be charged, legitimately or otherwise.

There is a redundancy to campaign themes. Strategist Catherine Shaw writes, "It's a story you tell over and over, a story you can tell in a few seconds: 'It's the economy'; 'This is about opportunity'; 'It's the small issues'; 'It's hope'; 'It's about community'" (2014, 48). These themes appear to be, at some level, interchangeable, but a smart strategist would need to figure out when to use which slogan. Which is the better theme: "This is about governing . . . and I've done it" or "The Change Will Do Us Good"? (Shaw 2014, 68). An operative would want to think about the candidates, the issues, and the electorate before making a hasty choice between the two ideas.

Generally speaking, themes are inclusive. They encompass diverse issues or a broad range of qualifications. It would perhaps be a mistake to sell a candidate as merely an "environmental leader," even when concerns about pollution are paramount and the candidate is well suited to deal with them. A better approach may well be to present a more general theme, something like "a candidate concerned about the future." A variety of issues, including environmentalism, can be fitted to this overarching message. Instead of being "tough on crime," a candidate might argue for "a secure community." Security can mean more cops on the beat and tougher sentences for convicted criminals as well as a better educational system, an adherence to traditional family values, pressure on terrorists, investment in housing and infrastructure, and so on. Broad themes can incorporate a variety of ideas, appealing to a wide range of voters.

Wedge issues, as noted above, work within the opponent's constituency. The name comes from a tactic in chess whereby a player forces an opponent to sacrifice a piece or to hold other pieces in a useless position to prevent the sacrifice. A liberal constituency that holds environmentalists *and* organized labor gives a Republican the chance to pit "jobs" voters against "environment" voters. A conservative constituency that holds pro-life and pro-choice elements is also vulnerable to wedge issues. Choosing a theme that splits the opponent's base can dampen enthusiasm among some of the opponent's supporters.

The office being sought might suggest a theme by itself. Candidates for executive posts—governors, county executives, or mayors—might wish to focus on leadership and competence. Candidates for legislative posts, on the other hand, might be expected to deliver ideological consistency. Scholars Judith Trent, Robert Friedenberg, and Robert Denton (2011, 107) argue that candidate status is an important element of communications strategy. An incumbent stressing "change" might be, in effect, asking for his or her own removal (though at least one Republican incumbent made this argument in 2008; see Shea and Medvic 2009) and then-Minority Leader of the U.S. Senate Mitch McConnell argued that change demanded reelection of the

72-year-old senator. Incumbents would seem on better ground if they highlight the need to "stay the course." Unlike challengers, incumbents can use the symbolic trappings of the office—strength, integrity, competence, and legitimacy; most incumbents try to show a "record of accomplishment." But incumbents have pasts from which they cannot hide, as opposition researchers well know.

Challengers enjoy more latitude—they often have a slim record—but the need for a powerful theme is heightened. They must convince voters to change old habits, and they often go on the attack (see Trent, Friedenberg, and Denton 2011, 112). As Barbara and Stephen Salmore argued, "Most challengers must simultaneously erode the favorable reputation of the incumbent and build a positive case for themselves" (1989, 128). Many consultants believe unseating an incumbent means *firing* an incumbent. Without a cutting edge, voters might have little reason to seek a change.

Whether designed for a challenger or an incumbent, a theme must be readily understood. In his successful 1990 bid for the Minnesota U.S. Senate seat, Paul Wellstone developed a straightforward theme: "A man of ordinary means"—a contrast to his opponent, who was ready to spend $6 million on the race. Eight years later, Minnesota voters made former professional wrestler Jesse Ventura their new governor, based largely on his defiance of traditional authority. The Ventura campaign theme was a "no-message" message. One analyst said, "Unlike the practiced politicians he was up against, he never stayed on message, deflecting the tough questions. That really set him apart." This is not to say there was no theme: An Independence Day T-shirt screamed, "Retaliate in '98" (Beiler 2000, 128).

Barack Obama's 2008 presidential campaign played on thematic power, as evidenced by the ubiquity of posters that underscored the candidate's likeness with the word "Hope." Such a theme can take many forms: "We are the ones we've been waiting for"; "Yes, we can!"; "The change we need"; "Change we can believe in" (see Pollard 2008). Even if some pundits were skeptical of the "silver-tongued freshman [who had] found a way to sell hope" (Krauthammer 2008), the very fact that Obama was criticized for his effective use of a campaign theme is a testament to its political wisdom.

John McCain had trouble settling on a singular message. One reporter counted six different narratives over the course of the presidential campaign: "The Heroic Fighters vs. the Quitters"; "Country-First Deal Maker vs. Nonpartisan Pretender"; "Leader vs. Celebrity"; "Team of Mavericks vs. Old-Style Washington"; "John

McCain [now] vs. John McCain [then]"; and "The Fighter (again) vs. the Tax-and-Spend Liberal" (Draper 2008). No theme stuck. McCain's shift from leader to maverick, which arrived with the unorthodox selection of Sarah Palin as his running mate—who was herself short on experience and seemed to enjoy the limelight—threatened to undermine the Republican's best attack on Obama: that the young senator was too immature for the White House.

## Microtargeting

Issues—whether partisan, positional, valence, or wedge—are bundled up in the minds of individual voters, and campaign operatives long to discover which issues will work politically and which will not. Polling, demographic research, electoral history, and a strong understanding of local politics all provide a good sense of a district. Strategists who want to broadcast a message far and wide could find inferences drawn from generalized sources of information perfectly appropriate to their needs. But sweeping analysis was better suited to the days of mass media campaigning than digital customization. With the rise of information technology, political campaigns have more opportunity to reach voters directly, and they are gaining the data and analytic tools they need to target those voters individually.

The emergence of microtargeting can be traced to low-tech direct mail. Richard Viguerie collected the names of people who donated to Barry Goldwater's 1964 presidential campaign and built a small empire on that foundation. Over time, targeting became much more ambitious and far more computer-intensive, merging preexisting data from outside the campaigns and voter identification generated by the parties and candidates themselves. More than simply collecting names, microtargeting can be said to operate by

> taking whatever individual-level information is available . . . and combining it with demographic and geographic marketing data about those individuals to build statistical models that predict the attitudes and behaviors of voters for whom that individual level behavior is not known. (Strasma n.d.)

In the early 1970s, the Claritas Corporation broke new ground with "geodemographic clusters." The underlying assumption was that people gather into "areas where the resources—physical, economic, and social—are compatible with their needs" (Robbin 1989, 109).

In other words, people choose their neighborhoods according to their lifestyles. These neighborhoods, in turn, have identifiable characteristics that can be used to draw inferences about the people living there. By examining 535 variables for the entire U.S. population, Claritas established dozens of distinct groupings that, it said, accounted for much of American diversity. Each cluster was given a nickname. One was called "Share Croppers" because it contained low-income, rural, poorly educated Southern whites. Other groups were labeled "God's Country," "Archie Bunker's Neighbors," and "Bohemian Mix." Each cluster was purported to comprise approximately like-minded individuals. Geodemographics thereby transformed a casual perception of neighborhood life into a sophisticated understanding of shared thinking.

Researcher Mark Atlas argued that geodemographic clusters did not live up to their billing. First, before-and-after evidence provided by the company, when reexamined, seemed to offer little evidence that the system changed electoral outcomes. Second, at a more conceptual level, Atlas wrote, "the forty Clusters derived from the entire nation's Census data may be very different from clusters that would be generated if each state's data had been clustered individually" (1989, 134). "The allocation of campaign resources," argued Atlas, "is too crucial a task to be undertaken when there is substantial uncertainty about the targeting procedure's validity both in theory and in practice" (135).

Voter constellations gained new importance a decade later. In 2000, Karl Rove, who came to presidential politics by way of the direct mail industry, believed the microtargeting techniques that had increased profits in the private sector could increase vote shares in politics (Wayne 2008). In the years leading up to the 2004 election, the GOP put roughly $20 million into a database it called the "Voter Vault" (Baldwin 2006). The Vault was packed with individual-level data and augmented by shoe-leather efforts to speak with voters one-on-one and by appeals to submit "church membership rolls, hunting-club registries, college-fraternity directories and P.T.A. membership rosters" (Gertner 2004). Ed Gillespie, who chaired the Republican Party, said the effort could be used for early persuasion, yet added, "[I]t's very, very important to us for people in the last 72 hours to e-mail their friends and knock on their doors and get Republicans to the polls" (Gertner 2004).

Parties and candidates have long maintained "house lists" of voters, contributors, and volunteers. Data might also be compiled from newspaper clippings, letters sent to the candidate, attendance at candidate forums and fundraising events, and rosters of prior campaign staff (Selnow 1994, 75). Lists might come from political parties, interest groups, and other campaigns. Some elected officials might keep a list of voters who have expressed an interest in one topic or another, though many jurisdictions forbid the political use of information acquired during official hours or in the conduct of official business. Furthermore, election laws and privacy statutes regulate the collection, storage, and use of some lists. As with all other aspects of a campaign, compliance with legal and ethical codes must be the top priority.

Using voter files as a starting point, a new-style campaign might look for ways to enhance voter records. For at least a quarter century, campaigns have been able to add data from state motor vehicle departments, fish and game commissions, and county assessors (see Beiler 1990, 33). A list of people with hunting licenses can show concentrations of hunters, and the appropriate political inferences can be made. In addition to direct, individual-level knowledge, assumptions about characteristics such as ethnicity can be imputed to the data records. But imputation is not foolproof. "Park" is commonly a Korean name, though many people with the last name Park have no Korean heritage. And distinctions within an ethnic group can be subtle. One researcher has found politically meaningful differences between Hispanic voters with Latin surnames and those without (Pineda 2007).

List production has become a professionalized industry. Vendors offer data sets, ranging from zip code sorts to club membership data to magazine subscription lists. Such lists might be rented directly from their owners or through a list broker. For campaigns that want to purchase the information outright, data firms build and maintain nationwide voter databases focused on party registration, probable ethnicity, gender, and so forth. Clients can customize data sets on-line with a keyboard, a mouse, and a credit card. These data can be supplemented with house lists and other demographic information to provide not simply a general understanding of the district but also a platform from which to launch targeted voter contact operations. Database companies provide speed and accuracy, and campaign managers can request voter lists, phone numbers, and entire mailing packages, transforming an onerous process that formerly relied on volunteers into an outsourced operation. Supported candidates can receive similar assistance from party organizations at various levels.

The implications of all this technology, and the power of their combined usage, are beginning to coalesce. Ken Mehlman, who managed the Bush 2004 campaign, was proud of his efforts:

> We did what Visa did. We acquired a lot of consumer data. What magazine do you subscribe to? Do you own a gun? How often do the folks go to church? Where do you send your kids to school? Are you married? Based on that, we were able to develop an exact kind of consumer model that corporate America does every day to predict how people vote—not based on where they live but how they live. That was critically important to our success. (Nagourney 2004)

Prospective Bush voters were said to be different from their counterparts on the Kerry side, not just in ideology but also in lifestyle. Mehlman explained: "[O]ur demographic studies and analysis showed us that a lot of young families get information not at the 7 o'clock news but at the 7 o'clock workout before they got home," so the Bush campaign began running ads on networks that narrowcast into physical fitness centers (Nagourney 2004).

Microtargeting has received praise for helping to lift Virginia Democrat Tim Kaine to the governor's mansion and Montana Democrat Jon Tester to the U.S. Senate (Weigel 2006; Wayne 2008). Private firms on both sides of the aisle are providing their own expertise, running complex calculations on powerful computers using software they buy off the shelf or write for themselves. GOP microtargeting pioneer Alexander Gage admired the Obama operation in the closing days of the 2008 election, saying, "The quality and the quantity of their ground game is measurably better than the Republican campaign of 2004 or the McCain campaign" (Wayne 2008).

Republican strategists soon set their sights on regaining their advantage in data collection and analysis. They began with a detailed survey of 10,000 voters, and continued to collect data from 1,000 voters in each of 20 states the midterm campaign. A sophisticated model was generated to predict likely voters—with the goal of out-mobilizing the Democrats. Brent Seaborn, one of the creators of the program, has said, "The political team, to their credit, totally bought into the system and used the numbers for everything" (O'Connor and Chinni 2014).

The challenge of microanalysis is largely computational, owing to the "curse of dimensionality." Each unit of complexity increases the number of possible models on an exponential basis. If a campaign wants to run cross-tabulations on a comprehensive benchmark survey, it might print cross-tabs for each possible two-, three-, and four-variable combination, beginning with (1) women, (2) Democrats, (3) Democrats who live in an urban precinct, and (3) Democrats who are persuaded by an environmental message, and then extending this form of analysis to all combinations of variables. The result could easily be a million cross-tabulations. Unfortunately, breaking down a data set with such granularity can deplete the cases available to fill the many individual cells. If each variable has several categories, a four-variable cross-tab can result in more than a thousand cells, which is a serious problem if the benchmark survey covered only four hundred respondents. This difficulty can be fixed by combining sparse cells into multicell groupings (e.g., rural women in one category, urban and suburban fused in another), except that including all possible *combinations* of cells in all possible cross-tabs can easily multiply the number of potential cells into the billions.

Mathematical techniques can work around the "curse of dimensionality," and segmenting political data often falls to professionals who know how to run machine learning algorithms such as decision trees. Roughly put, a decision-tree procedure figures out which variable creates the "best split" within a target variable—that is, which variable can be used to divide the data set into the strongest concentrations showing support for Williams, Lopez, and Smith, along with undecideds (see Figure 6.5). This variable is chosen as a splitting point (called a node), and the process starts with the full data set and continues until some stopping criteria (such as undersized groupings) is reached. To draw a notional case, the strongest split in an electorate might be among identified partisans, with Democrats going strongly for Williams and Republicans showing support for Smith. Among unaffiliated voters, the best split might be on domicile, between homeowners and renters, with a large number of undecideds among downscale voters, suggesting a highly attractive campaign target.

Decision-tree algorithms and other machine-learning procedures such as artificial neural networks fall outside the mainstream of statistical research and are subject to critique from traditional statisticians. Run enough tests and *some* kind of strong correlation will eventually be found, whether or not that correlation is meaningful. One critic of data mining in the field of economics showed how sheep populations can accurately "predict" stock market behavior

**Figure 6.5**
**Microtargeting Decision Tree**

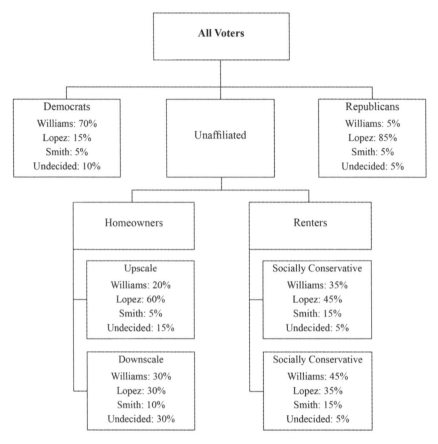

in the United States (Leinweber 2007): the same "stupid data miner tricks" can be performed in the service of political campaigns. Another problem is that, although it may or may not be true that "kale correlates to being a liberal, while a bacon orientation is tied more closely to conservatism" (Chemi 2014), excitement about the predictive nature of the bacon–kale divide should be suspended until the campaign can figure out how to operationalize this unique bit of political knowledge.

Analysts must pay attention to detail, or they might find themselves building a model that "overfits" the data, creating a complex diagram that has little meaning beyond the original sample. Hal Malchow, who has been using the Chi-squared Automatic Interaction

Detection (CHAID) algorithm to enhance voter contact since 1995, cautions that the technique "works best when you balance statistical measurements with a good dose of common sense" (2008, 96). Mathematical validation can trap some kinds of overfitting (see Burton 2010), and models can be checked with further research (perhaps by calling ostensible swing voters to see if they really are uncommitted). The sheer complexity of a microtargeting project reinforces the need for professionals.

## Conclusion

In commercial marketing, experts wax philosophical about "branding." A brand's identity is said to comprise the full range of attributes that consumers associate with a product or service. Many political professionals have come to use the language of brand management to describe what they do. A smart campaign uses principles of corporate branding as it maintains a basic palette of color combinations, messages, and a vocabulary filled with words that are friendly to the candidate's ideals, all under the rubric of a single theme. Like a corporate manager, a campaign professional wants to create a strong impression.

Caution is in order. Much of commercial advertising deals with mere perception; much of politics deals with harsh reality. While a retailer might deftly shift its targeting from one demographic category to another by ordering up a new advertising campaign, with different spokesmodels and a novel theme, a political candidate who attempts such a feat should beware of the pitfalls. Republican voters in 2008 had trouble warming up to Mitt Romney's newfound position on abortion. Romney said his views had "evolved" (Romney 2005), but many voters saw an ideological carpetbagger. The problem continued to dog Romney in 2012. Bill Clinton's "triangulation" never sat well with liberals, who felt abandoned, and conservatives believed the centrist move demonstrated once and for all that Clinton was little more than a slick politician.

In politics, consistency is a virtue. When Governor Arnold Schwarzenegger reworked his image from super-patriot to bipartisan moderate during the 2006 California gubernatorial contest, his advisers made clear that the effort was "not a rebranding" (Marinucci 2006). Analysis might show a tightly packed ideological grouping of likely voters, tempting a candidate to make a drastic shift in search of easy votes or perhaps to offer different messages to different groups, but in a time when a candidate's words are recorded and searchable, and when videos of old speeches can race across the district at Internet speed, consistency is of greater and greater value. The best strategy would seem to emerge from a theme that agrees with a candidate's own biography and the needs and desires of the district.

It is not enough to know where the voters reside and to develop a theme that might bring them to the candidate; a campaign must reach out to potential supporters. Voter contact is discussed in the next part of this book.

# PART III

# CONTACT

# CHAPTER 7

# Fundraising Strategies and Tactics

Mark Hanna, William McKinley's 1896 campaign manager, is said to have quipped, "There are two things that are important in politics. The first is money and I can't remember what the second one is" (Safire 2008). In truth, there are many "important things" in campaign politics, as Hanna, who built a large and effective organization, well understood. But campaigns do indeed require money. Volunteers, issues, good looks, and a winning personality can take a candidate only so far. The shortage of poorly funded, victorious challengers tends to prove the rule. While cause and effect are difficult to parse, campaign spending remains a strong factor in electoral success. During competitive cycles, candidates who spend the most win eight of ten Senate contests and nine of ten House races (Biersack 2012).

To the extent that money helps a candidate win, perhaps the power of campaign cash comes from the fact that money readily translates to other political resources. Old-style campaigns relied on endorsements and volunteers, but volunteers take time to organize and are sometimes unreliable. In the Digital Age, the endorsement of a key political figure can be helpful on its own—the publicity might do some good—but an endorsement carries more weight if it means a powerful name on a fundraising letter, access to donor lists, and money calls (see Spicer 2012). Given the volatility of campaign operations, liquid assets give added advantage. Money can be used to pay for phone vendors, media buys, and office technology.

A candidate thinking about a run for office should probably give serious attention to fundraising questions: How much will be needed? Where will it come from? And how will it be raised? (Borman 2014).

At the same time, because fundraising is often considered difficult and distasteful, aspiring politicos have been urged to dive into the "finance" side of elections (Sive 2013), as few people do it willingly and well. A strategy memo purportedly leaked from the campaign of U.S. Senate candidate Michelle Nunn called on the campaign "to prioritize fundraising above all else and to focus the candidate's time on it with relentless intensity" (Hohmann 2014a).

This chapter discusses money from a historical point of view, the role of campaign money, campaign finance law, individual and group donations, and fundraising tactics.

## Historical Perspectives

Barack Obama and Mitt Romney spent roughly $200 million of their combined $2.3 billion on the business of raising money (*Washington Post* 2012), but campaigns have never been cheap. George Washington's people, it has been said, gave away 160 gallons of rum, spiked punch, wine, beer, and cider to "391 voters and 'unnumbered hangers-on'" (Sydnor 1952) in his first bid for the Virginia House of Burgesses. During most of the 19th century, party organizations, rather than candidates, raised most of the money used in campaigns, and candidates were expected to contribute to the party. Those who received government jobs were also supposed to ante up. More money came from donors with a stake in the outcome of the election. When Mark Hanna raised millions of dollars, donated in large gifts by wealthy industrialists, to fund the "Front Porch" campaign of William McKinley in 1896, the Republican Party all but purchased the White House. In 1928, roughly 70 percent of the funds raised by the national parties came from contributions of $1,000 or greater, enough to buy a couple of Model T automobiles (Sorauf 1988, 3).

The political landscape shifted markedly during the 20th century. In the late 1960s outright corruption still existed in some areas—Vice President Spiro Agnew was forced to resign in 1974 after Justice Department officials happened across suspicious payments he was still receiving from his days as a Baltimore city official—but the major political parties were no longer at the center of the election process. Fundraising had become serious business by the 1980s; so serious, in fact, that retiring Congress members began to blame their departures on the burdens of fundraising. Illinois senator Paul Simon, who had to raise $8.4 million in his last reelection campaign in 1990, told *60 Minutes*, "When I first came here—man, when there was a

Democratic fundraising dinner, I was so eager to go. Now I drag myself. And it's probably a pretty good indication that this is a good time to step aside" (Simon 1995).

In 2012, House incumbents who won close races raised an average of about $3,000 per day over the course of a two-year election cycle; endangered incumbents had to raise a good deal more (Campaign Finance Institute 2012a). Money is being spent on a larger and larger electorate and the techniques employed cannot be supplied by volunteer labor. The rise of the baby boom generation; continued immigration; the inclusion of minorities in the electorate thanks to the Voting Rights Act of 1965; the addition of 18-, 19-, and 20-year-olds due to the 26th Amendment; and the overall growth in the size of the American population greatly widened the pool of voters. The number of votes cast for president in the 2012 election was more than double those cast in 1952. And survey research, direct mail, telemarketing, and computerized microtargeting, along with radio, video, Web site production, and social media design, content creation, and monitoring, have all driven up the cost of getting elected.

State and local races are not immune from this trend. When New Hampshirite Carl Johnson first ran for the state senate in 1990, he spent $300 on consultant advice. In 2004, this time as an incumbent, Johnson paid more than $10,000 to the Concord political consulting firm Elevare (Milne 2004, 1). "Consultants play a bigger and bigger role," explains Elevare's president. "It began statewide, races for governor, Senate, House. As we've seen of late, it's gradually working its way down the ballot. Large portions of candidates' expenses are now being paid to consultants" (ibid., 2). State legislative candidates in Wisconsin spent a combined total of about $4.8 million in 1994. By 2010, that figure had risen to $12.8 million (Wisconsin Democracy Campaign 2014).

## The Role of Money

Candidates might be mistaken that fortunes must be spent to win an electoral contest. But while the cost per vote gained may be difficult or impossible to ascertain, there is reason to think money makes a difference. In Virginia, in 2014, U.S. Senate challenger Ed Gillespie essentially ran out of money a few weeks before the election; donors and outside groups departed the field, leaving it open to incumbent Mark Warner, the run-away presumptive winner, who wound up with a narrow victory of a few thousand votes. Campaigns might be run efficiently with volunteers; then again money can hire an experienced professional. Enthusiasm goes a long way, but candidates who raise a lot of money are likely to be perceived as worthy contenders, and have the financial resources to execute their plans. A late bump in money might have changed Gillespie's fortunes.

Money raised early in the campaign cycle can scare off challengers. Building a war chest and hiring strong consultants can attract media attention, and stories about a solidly funded opponent might prompt potential adversaries to reconsider entry—a rationale that redounds to the favor of the well-funded candidate. The "scare-off" effect is especially helpful to incumbents. As Gary Jacobson has said, "The electoral value of incumbency lies not only in what it provides to the incumbent but also in how it affects the thinking of potential opponents" (2013, 42). As the electoral season gets under way, campaign organizations work furiously to raise large sums in the days before legally imposed reporting deadlines, hoping the media will run positive stories on fundraising prowess. Increasing polarization means that incumbents may want to scare off co-partisans intent on starting a primary contest (see Boatright 2013, 65).

The truth is, most incumbents win most of the time. Some 90 percent of House incumbent candidates were returned to office in 2012 (Center for Responsive Politics 2014b). Scholarly research has demonstrated that *challengers* gain vote share when *incumbents* spend a lot of money on campaign communications (Herrnson 2012). Presumably, a safe incumbent does not need to spend much money whereas an endangered incumbent has to fight hard.

Whether campaign spending is a cause or an effect of electoral competition, one thing is clear: Incumbents typically spend much more money than challengers. According to the Campaign Finance Institute, the average Senate incumbent in 2012 who won election with less than 60 percent of the two-party vote spent approximately $13 million and the average challenger just over $10 million. For incumbents who won with more than 60 percent of the vote, the disparity was more significant: $7 million to about $1.4 million (Campaign Finance Institute 2012c).

Roughly 45 percent of a House incumbent's war chest comes from political action committees (PACs), while approximately 15 percent of a House challenger's financing comes from these sources (Campaign Finance Institute 2012d). This inequality likely springs from the tactical reasoning of contributors: Because incumbents usually prevail, they seem to represent better investments. As noted years ago by a director of the Democratic Senatorial Campaign Committee, "Washington money, by and large, is smart money. Most [PACs] are not a bit interested in supporting people they don't think will win" (quoted in Luntz 1988, 178). David Vance, spokesman for the Campaign Legal Center, contends it is "risky to roll the dice" by giving to a challenger since it could alienate the likely winner of the race (Radelat 2014).

Other factors may also be in play. Incumbents usually have proven fundraising experience. After all, if they did not know how to raise money, they probably would not have been elected in the previous cycle. Once in office, incumbents maintain lists of reliable contributors, spend time learning from other candidates, and continue to refine their fundraising operations. It has long been understood that cash left over from previous campaigns help make the next effort credible from the start, attracting a good deal of "early money" from PACs and individuals, and discouraging challengers, leaving the oppositional field to less qualified contenders (see Maisel 1990, 125).

## Campaign Finance Law

The evolution of federal rules is important to strategists who want to grasp the complexity of a federal finance regime that is variously replicated, adapted, and rejected at the state and local levels. Regulations at the subnational levels vary—specific rules govern signage, disclosure, reporting, and so forth—and any responsible candidate would consult the appropriate regulatory body for specific information.

The foundations of contemporary campaign finance law were laid with the Federal Election Campaign Act (FECA) of 1971 as modified by the Supreme Court and amended several times during the 1970s. By 1980, federal law limited the amount of money that individuals could donate to political parties—though candidates could contribute unlimited funds to their own campaigns—and channeled corporate, union, and interest group donations through PACs. While corporations and unions may not donate directly to campaigns, they can pay overhead costs associated with raising federally regulated "hard money" donated to candidates. PACs are limited in how much they can give. Those that are not connected to an entity such as a union or corporation are called "nonconnected" PACs and must pay for the overhead from the funds they raise. Political parties could subsidize elections through "party-building" activities that would help their candidates across the board.

The archetype of a party-building activity was a registration drive combined with voter mobilization on Election Day. The money given to parties was called "soft money" and reform groups argued that it was being used in ways that had become indistinguishable from candidate support. Parties were running "issue ads" that seemed to promote a candidate even if they did not expressly advocate anyone's election or defeat. Some contended this soft-money loophole was being used as a backdoor for large sums that would otherwise have been prohibited under donation restrictions of the 1970s. The Bipartisan Campaign Reform Act of 2002, known by its acronym BCRA (pronounced BIK-ra) or as "McCain-Feingold" (in recognition of the law's key Senate advocates, Arizona Republican John McCain and Wisconsin Democrat Russ Feingold), was intended to outlaw "soft money." Under BCRA, any "campaign communication" that would run 30 days before a primary election or 60 days before a general election must be paid for with funds tightly regulated by the Federal Election Commission.

BCRA was immediately challenged by Republican senator Mitch McConnell of Kentucky and a host of reform opponents. The core of their argument was that the Act infringed on free speech, which, they said, was protected under the Supreme Court's ruling in *Buckley v. Valeo* (1976). *Buckley* equated campaign spending with political speech protected under the Constitution. Supporters of BCRA countered that speech accruing from those contributions was indirect and could be regulated without infringing on constitutional protection. In 2003, the Court ruled on *McConnell v. Federal Election Commission,* finding key provisions of BCRA constitutional—including the "electioneering communication" provision and a "soft money" ban.

Thereafter, the Supreme Court rolled back some BCRA restrictions. *Federal Election Commission v. Wisconsin Right to Life* (2007) held that an advertisement would be deemed "express advocacy"—and therefore subject to regulation—only if "the ad is susceptible of no reasonable interpretation other than as an appeal to vote for this or that candidate." In 2009, the Court heard the case of *Citizens United v. Federal Election Commission,* involving a documentary called *Hillary: The Movie,* produced by the conservative group Citizens United, a nonprofit corporation. A lower court had held that the film was a form of regulated electioneering, but Citizens United took the case to the Supreme Court, challenging the idea that it was a form of electioneering and arguing more fundamentally that political documentaries created by corporations are protected by the First Amendment and cannot constitutionally be regulated by BCRA. In January 2010, the Supreme Court announced that corporations did in fact possess free speech rights and could engage in express advocacy of candidates.

Days after the announcement, *Media Life Magazine,* in an article entitled "The Supremes' Gift to TV Stations: Big Bucks," advised readers to "[f]igure $450 to $500 million on top of the $3.5 billion already expected to be spent on advertising" in 2010 (Stern 2010). *McCutcheon v. Federal Election Commission* (2014) struck down the aggregate limits for individual donations across candidates.

Other changes that affect spending by outside groups are discussed in chapter 11.

## Individual and Group Donations

Whatever a candidate might think of the campaign finance regime applicable to the election, all the players must live under its rules. Candidates feel they have to raise money if they want to win, and to raise money, they need to understand why individuals and groups might give to political campaigns. In the days when Spiro Agnew collected payments from government contractors, political donations were easily understood. Campaign finance in the Digital Age is more complex. When CNN's Jack Cafferty asked why people donate, viewers responded with answers such as, "They are wishful thinkers, and they believe that if enough people think like they do then their candidate might have a shot" and "I would guess it's the same reason people sit in front of their televisions writing 'seed money' checks to televangelists. They aren't using their brains! They are expecting their donations will create 'miracles'" (Cafferty 2012).

### Individual Donors

Campaigns are not wholly financed by a few "fat cat" labor unions and corporate sponsors, as pundits often pontificate. They are largely funded by individual contributions. The number of citizens giving money to candidates has been growing, as has the overall weight of smaller-sized contributions. Campaign finance scholar Michael Malbin finds that today's campaigns are generally not financed by a small number of wealthy individuals but rather by a large number of average citizens; but then, notes Malbin,

> To take the most extreme example to date, Sheldon and Miriam Adelson made $92.8 million in disclosed contributions to political committees in 2011–2012. It would take about one million small donors (more than one-quarter the number of small donors to President Obama in 2012) to equal the financial value of this one couple's disclosed contributions. (Malbin 2013)

A political veteran put it this way: "Political fund-raisers ask rich people for money because that's where the money is" (Sive 2013).

Why would anyone give to a campaign? Many people give simply because they are asked. If requested to contribute, supporters need to make a decision, but without the "ask" a supportive voter might see no reason to give. Quite possibly, "the request for money activates some generalized, even vague, feeling of loyalty or sympathy, whether for the cause or the solicitor" (Sorauf 1988, 49). Perhaps contributors give to candidates out of a personal or professional connection to the candidate: "If a candidate cannot count on his closest allies for monetary support he may as well not run" (Klemanski and Dulio 2006, 52). Donors may believe they are helping someone who, if elected, will change the course of political history, or the part of history that goes to a single issue like gun ownership, abortion, or public health.

Dick Morris has argued that fundraising should be a result of long-term cultivation: "Fund solicitation has to be preceded by an extensive process of relationship building, by establishing trust, connection, and shared values" (2007b). Emotion is part of the game. One prominent GOP leader has advised fundraisers, "Ask yourself, who hates the incumbent, who wants to beat him as bad as I do. This starts the donor list process" (quoted in Shea and Brooks 1995, 25). A 2012 fundraising best-practices guide created by the fundraising consultancy Blackbaud builds on these sentiments by reminding fundraisers to

> consider why and how this audience typically chooses to support you. What is the driving concern that binds people to your cause? Which types of appeals are they most inclined to answer (legislative alerts, time-sensitive campaigns, end-of-year appeals)? What times that you interact with them are conducive

to inspiring action via mobile (for example, a walk or gala or volunteer day, when staff interact with individuals interested in learning more about your organization, or when your supporters are checking email on their smartphones)? (Andersen et al. 2012)

With electronic outreach, campaigns may choose to implement randomized experiments that compare "open rates" and donations on the bases of various combinations of message construction and style.

Passion and policy are powerful forces—but so is celebrity. As a class, politicians are disdained but as individuals many public officials are held in high esteem. Officialdom has its own strange magnetism. Most constituents would be amazed at the spectacle of a "photo line" in which individuals pay $1,000 and wait for a quick "grip-and-grin" snapshot with a Senate candidate. Few policy issues are discussed and supporters who try to take a moment of the candidate's time to point out a pet project are apt to be hurried off by staff. Some people want to be seen at fundraisers with successful candidates along with friends who regularly appear on television. The celebrity factor in politics explains the success of fundraising events that include popular figures from sports and entertainment. Perhaps for the same reason that some people give to the arts—the chance to participate in the allure and excitement of a well-known happening—many supporters choose to share in the experience of politics by writing a check.

### Interest Groups

Some of the incentives for individual campaign contributions apply to interest group contributions as well. The main difference is that interest groups are more likely to base their donations on strict policy grounds. Fundraiser Carl Silverberg has listed four reasons a PAC might give money to a candidate:

1. "The legislator voted with them on their issues."
2. "The legislator sits on a committee that has jurisdiction over the majority of the legislation the PAC has set out as its priorities for the year."
3. "There is a good following in the district."
4. "The corporation represented by the PAC has a good number of employees in the district." (2000, 62)

Interest groups want to elect officials sympathetic to their concerns, to have access to officeholders who handle their issues. Incumbents receive the vast majority of group contributions; funding losers confers no benefit. Some interest groups give money to both major political parties in order to ensure their voices will be heard.

There is little reason to believe interest groups are "buying" candidates in a straight quid pro quo. Rather, groups are said to contribute out of a desire for access—the hope that they will have the opportunity to present their case to the elected official. Senator Simon put the matter bluntly:

> I have never promised anyone a thing for a campaign contribution. But when I was in the Senate and got to my hotel room at midnight, there might be twenty phone calls waiting for me, nineteen from people whose names I did not recognize, the twentieth from someone who gave me a $1,000 contribution or raised money for me. . . . Which [call] do you think I will make? (1999, 306)

Researcher Richard Hall argues "interest groups dedicate most of their campaign contributions and lobbying efforts to legislators they already agree with, helping them make their case, and spend little time trying to persuade opponents" (Porter 2012).

According to Klemanski and Dulio, PACs are generally less active in state legislative races but they seem to be as strategic as the federal players. When local interest groups get involved they usually give to incumbents and likely winners, although if contributions are centered on the group's ideological concerns, challengers tend to fare somewhat better. As in national-level campaigns, interest groups might feel impelled to participate in the funding of candidates in both parties (Klemanski and Dulio 2006, 10–11).

Politicians might use their own PACs to gain influence for themselves. Such PACs have included then-Senator Hillary Rodham Clinton's Hill PAC, General Wesley Clark's WesPAC, Governor Sarah Palin's SarahPAC, and Governor Bobby Jindal's Stand Up to Washington PAC. In 2008, Illinois Republican Aaron Schock established a PAC called "GOP Generation Y Fund" while he was running for a seat in the House of Representatives. Nathan Gonzales of the *Rothenberg Political Report* said of Schock's efforts: "I don't know that there's a better way to curry favor with your colleagues than helping them win reelection" (D'Aprile 2008). Schock, who has since resigned from Congress amid questions about his use of public and political funds, won his race and became, at age 27, the first Member of Congress born in the 1980s.

## Fundraising Tactics

Fundraising expert Mary Sabin once summarized the key to successful fundraising:

> Work, work, and work. If you are not feeling anxiety and stress, you're not doing your job. . . . This isn't rocket science or brain surgery. [It] is working hard, staying at it, and concentrating on raising the money while feeling completely obsessed about it. (Shea and Brooks 1995, 25)

Campaigns offer ice-cream cones and personalized credit cards as part of their finance plans (Blanchfield 2006), but these gimmicks are generally add-ons to road-tested tactics—techniques that might emerge from a comprehensive money strategy. Part of doing good work is careful attention to planned objectives. Robert Kaplan is adamant on this point: "Fundraising for political campaigns is normally a chaotic process. Fundraising plans, Fundraising Committees, goals and deadlines bring order, structure and accountability to that process" (R. Kaplan, pers. comm., 2010).

One approach is to follow the logic of backward mapping: Figure out how much money will be needed to implement a winning campaign plan. By setting goals, the fundraising team has clear objective. Targets and deadlines are strong motivators. If the campaign strategy calls for a massive television buy in early spring, fundraising efforts should probably begin well in advance of the purchase. Traditional sources of money—party funds, local contributors, and PACs—may suffice, but if they do not, the candidate must think about alternatives: regional contributors, PACs that do not traditionally contribute to the candidate's party, and so forth.

One of the greatest financial obstacles that a campaign faces is obtaining "seed money," the funding needed up front before the campaign can move into high gear, including consultant fees and benchmark polling. Without early money, a campaign might find would-be contributors hesitant to give. Wealthy candidates can jump-start their campaigns by donating or loaning sums of money to their own organizations, signaling a concrete commitment. Pro-choice Democratic women often look to EMILY's List for seed money ("EMILY" stands for "Early Money Is Like Yeast"—it makes the dough rise). In 2014, EMILY's List was the second-highest spending "527" group (i.e., outside group that files under Section 527 of the Internal Revenue Code, as discussed in chapter 11), with total expenditures of $10.5 million (Center for Responsive Politics 2014a).

Campaigns might call on family, friends, colleagues, associates, partisans, PACs, habitual givers, adversaries of the opponent, and political parties at all levels. Many candidates group potential givers, or "prospects," into three general categories: small, medium, and large. These categories are relative, as a large contributor in a city council campaign might be considered small in a congressional race. Most candidates prefer that the public not believe they are relying on fat-cat donors. Former Republican senator Rudy Boschwitz, in his 1996 rematch against populist Democrat Paul Wellstone, went out of his way to let Minnesota voters know he was drawing large portions of his campaign money from "skinny cats" who gave less than $100.

In setting up a fundraising plan, campaigns may look to personal and interest group solicitation, direct mail, fundraising events, and digital outreach.

### Personal Solicitation

When GOP representative Rod Chandler of Washington decided to leave Congress in 1992, fellow Republican Jennifer Dunn saw her chance. Having run the Washington state Republican Party for 11 years, Dunn was able to organize a successful outreach program: "With the help of friends and volunteers, Dunn worked her way through the 5,000 names in her personal files, raising $492,444 from individuals and $168,373 from PACs" (Morris and Gamache 1994, 152). Fundraising consultant Nancy Bocskor counsels,

> [M]ake a list of 100 people you know that you can ask for an initial investment. Go through your Rolodex (yes, people still use them), your Christmas or holiday greetings list and your Facebook and LinkedIn contacts. Aim high—it's better to ask for $1,000 and negotiate than to ask for a minimal amount. (2013)

"Dialing for dollars" is an unpleasant way to spend an afternoon, or several months of afternoons—repetitive small talk and rejection generate disdain among candidates during "call time" (Lewis 2013)—but personal solicitations continue to generate campaign funds.

Some consultants look at the situation from the contributor's point of view: Why donate money to the campaign? Success often lies in the personal and professional interests of the prospect. Solicitors might detail precisely where the campaign is going and why the money is needed, offering polling information, campaign brochures, a summary of the candidate's policy stands, and a list of expenses the money would cover. Campaigns might find it worthwhile to provide prospective givers a short version of the campaign plan. The purpose of this approach would be to make prospects feel as though they are joining a tightly run, highly organized campaign that will put its money to good use.

Consultants might recommend separate fundraising efforts be established for each aspect of campaign operations. A donation to underwrite an ad buy shows a return for each campaign dollar. A telephone script for a typical request might read, "We're trying to raise $12,000 for some TV spots that have to be bought now for the November election. Would you be willing to make a pledge or send a gift to support our efforts?" (Shaw 2010, 128).

Among the hardest problems a professional fundraiser might confront is a candidate reluctant to ask for money. Kaplan has dubbed this phenomenon "fundraising fear" (2000, 64). Calls from the candidate are perhaps best, but telephone efforts from volunteers and professionals might also work. Although people seem increasingly annoyed with telephone pitches, the calls apparently still raise money. "Dollars for Democrats was the largest nonfederal fundraiser for the Democratic Party in 2006," writes scholar Ronald G. Shaiko, and "all of its money was raised via telemarketing" (2008, 111).

In a "pledge system," contributors are asked to donate at periodic intervals. This approach can increase the overall contribution. One technique involves contacting those who have given once to give again. Since the revolution in online fundraising during the 2004 elections—as campaign Web sites began to feature conspicuous "Donate Now" buttons—some campaigns offer the option for recurring donations on their Web sites. Obama supporters who made online donations in 2012 were given the option to have the same amount charged to their credit cards on a month-to-month basis. Locking small givers into a donation plan would seem to lessen the need to ask for money again (though it would seem to put a premium on thoughtful notes and trinkets).

The best mix of tactics may depend on the candidate and the consultant. Some candidates are comfortable asking for money, just as some consultants are more skilled in direct mail than PAC solicitation. Some prospects consider direct mail abhorrent, preferring the request be made personally while others think mail is convenient and phone calls are intrusive. Some will give online while others worry about sending their credit card number over the Internet.

### Interest Group Solicitation

If a candidate is on the wrong side of the policy fence, an interest group donation will probably be withheld. PACs that consistently give to the opponent and the opponent's party are poor prospects as well. But a campaign might find success in a "hook"—a bit of information that draws a PAC into the race. Campaigns can develop individualized arguments for each PAC on a targeted list, by offering biographies, district profiles, prominent consultants, leadership endorsements, and issue papers, possibly adding in campaign materials, poll results, and favorable news clippings. For "hot prospects," a candidate might hand-deliver the packet. Nonincumbents can increase their odds of receiving PAC backing "by taking a side on emotionally laden issues" (Herrnson 2012, p. 193). Candidates often host receptions on their own behalf, sometimes with the help of colleagues.

PACs send questionnaires wherein the slightest mistake can prevent a candidate from receiving funds, so political parties tutor candidates on proper completion of these forms. While "it is illegal for the parties to earmark checks they receive from individuals or PACs for specific candidates," Paul Herrnson writes that House and Senate campaign committees "help candidates in competitive contests raise money from individuals and PACs" and they "give candidates the knowledge and tools they need to obtain money from PACs" by "help[ing] candidates design 'PAC kits' they can use to introduce themselves to members of the PAC community" (2012, p. 119). Party leaders might also prod the news media to see certain races as competitive, and to cover them—leading perhaps to more PAC money. Overall, party committees can be a great help with fundraising, but to get party assistance, the committee must believe the candidate stands a good chance of winning.

### Direct Mail

Direct mail solicitation can be a powerful finance tool. Following Richard Viguerie's pioneering efforts for Republicans in the 1960s, George McGovern's successful direct mail fundraising in 1972 was followed by the rapid growth of Republican National Committee fundraising efforts in the late 1970s. The 1980s and 1990s saw an explosion in the number of direct mail professionals. Mail firms continue to flourish in the digital age because the process of sending direct mail has a complexity well beyond the familiar task of writing a letter and sending it off to a friend.

A direct mail fundraising effort might begin with a prospect list—a database of individuals who have shown "some characteristics or qualities thought likely to make them susceptible to a candidate's appeal for funds" (Sabato 1989, 88). Sabato was able to identify early on what consultant Kenneth Christensen would later suggest: "Potential donor lists are the foundation of the fundraising effort, period. These lists can mean the success or failure of your entire effort" (2009). Vendors offer voter lists appended with fields representing varieties of demographic categories and imputed voter preferences. Law restricts the use of some lists, so compliance procedures must be implemented.

A direct mail effort might accept early losses in expectation of future returns (see Sabato 1989). If a prospecting list contains 20,000 names and production costs (including postage and stuffing) run $1.00 per letter, the cost will be $20,000. Following this assumption, if the campaign receives a 5 percent response rate, or about 1,000 responses, and an average contribution of $19, the mail effort will return only $19,000, apparently a $1,000 loss. But there is another way to view the mailing: A list of 1,000 proven donors was purchased for $1,000, just $1.00 per name. Once this "house list" has been established, the cost of the next mailing can be much smaller (the list is a fraction of its original size), and the rate of return potentially much higher. A second appeal mailed to proven contributors would require a $1,000 outlay. If the response rate for this new mailing is 20 percent and the 200 repeat donors give an average of $50, for a $10,000 gross, the net is $9,000 for the second letter and $8,000 overall. This process can be repeated time and again.

One way to enhance a direct mail program for lower-level races might be to begin with a "suspect list." Rather than sending letters to a large group, the campaign looks for the individuals most likely to give. It may use a list of habitual party donors or the candidate's own business contacts. A candidate for county commissioner may draw up a list of personal friends. A statewide Democratic candidate might solicit all the registered Democrats in his or her hometown. Small lists can be created, personalized, and mailed in-house. Higher-end computational techniques can be used to improve prospect lists (Malchow 2008, 102–147).

Whether the campaign starts with a big list or a small one, writing a direct mail piece demands effort. "Dull is dull," noted consultant Ron Kanfer, so "the most successful direct mail programs are built around [a] compelling story" (1991, 22). Or, in the alternative, it might require little creativity. Templates and samples can be found on the Web and in commercial packages, and consultants are available to write the mailer for hire.

Because direct mail programs can be complex and risky (D'Aprile 2010), many candidates and consultants outsource the task. Professional firms can provide copy, layout, printing, lists, and postal know-how. But any investment can go bad. A mailing that costs more than it returns produces out-of-pocket expenses that some campaigns cannot absorb. Some doubt the value of direct mail fundraising. Dick Morris has suggested direct mail is antiquated and expensive (2007a). If other avenues for fundraising bring greater returns, direct mail fundraising, an inherently risky venture, might become riskier than it has been in the recent past. Mail sent too late in the campaign might well fail, since time passes while the mail travels to the donor, waits for a decision, and travels back to the campaign via the Postal Service (see Cornfield 2006; see also Burton and Shea 2003, 105).

### Fundraising Events

When the president, the vice president, governors, and members of the congressional leadership travel around the United States, they often stop in at candidate fundraising events. So do Hollywood stars and B-list celebrities. Fundraising events can be large-scale affairs, such as dinners, cocktail parties, concerts, or boat tours, or they can be small ones, along the lines of coffee klatches, ice-cream socials, and chicken barbecues. Done well, intimate gatherings can produce large sums of money, demonstrate to the news media and the general public that the campaign has momentum, reward past donors, and build a list of contributors.

Like direct mail, large-scale fundraisers are a gamble. Logistics can tie up a campaign team for weeks. Ticket sales may falter, and uncontrollable circumstances, including weather problems, can intrude on success. An event that flops causes financial headaches and suggests to the media, voters, and potential contributors that the campaign is struggling. Small-scale events do not court disaster in the same way, but they do risk tedium. Chitchat can be painfully boring. A smart campaign uses some imagination in its programming, perhaps holding auctions, wine-and-cheese receptions, cookouts, folk dances, and so on.

Successful event planners go out of their way to find interesting venues, but whether the event is on the waterfront or in a neighbor's backyard, the setting should have an air of success. Campaigns are cautioned that "perception is reality—especially in the event business. If you're having a small reception with 20 people, don't book a room that can hold 100" (Meredith 2000, 62). A good event staff will ensure that a room can be "cut" with draperies, movable walls, or greenery, in case the expected number of tickets is not sold. Lawrence Grey adds: "In planning any event, the cardinal rule is to keep it simple, and to keep the costs down. It does not do any good to sell $1,000 in tickets if it cost $900 to put on the event" (2007, 132).

### Digital Outreach

Internet fundraising in political campaigns has reached new heights. Morris attributes this to its small price tag: "By eliminating the transaction costs involved in direct mailing and phone solicitation, it's clear that online fund-raising produces bigger bottom lines more rapidly than any other method of campaign financing" (2008). When Howard Dean, former governor of Vermont, came into 2003 lacking adequate presidential campaign funds, few political observers took his candidacy seriously. But Dean broke records with his Internet fundraising. By one account, "Dean [rewrote] the playbook on how to organize, finance and mold a presidential campaign" (Drinkard and Lawrence 2004).

After Dean's success with Internet fundraising, John Kerry and George W. Bush each raised tens of millions of dollars online. Barack Obama's 2008 campaign for the presidency revolutionized the field: Over the course of 21 months, 3 million donors made a total of 6.5 million donations to Obama online, adding up to more than $500 million, and "[o]f those 6.5 million donations, 6 million were in increments of $100 or less. The average online donation was $80, and the average Obama donor gave more than once" (Vargas 2008). In 2012, online fundraising brought in $526 million (Tau 2013).

These figures were achieved using new strategies that include e-mail, text messaging, and social networks to motivate donors. Perhaps the biggest innovation in online fundraising to come out of the

2008 election cycle was the use of online social networks such as Facebook and Twitter. Obama and John McCain employed social networks to connect with supporters, and the Obama campaign made extensive use of these tools. Obama's organization maintained profiles on at least 15 social networks and created its own network called MyBarackObama.com, enabling more than 2 million supporters to sign up and connect with each other. Users were able to plan fundraising events and call supporters and donors (Vargas 2008). Anyone who chose to become a "fan" of Obama on Facebook or to "follow" Obama on Twitter received constant status updates reminding them to donate money to the campaign.

Online fundraising is spreading to state and local elections. As consultants Benjamin and Cheryl Katz have pointed out, "While presidential campaigns are often using some of the most exciting technology, these discussions miss the vast majority of online campaigns—those on congressional, state, and local levels" (2009). During the 2008 cycle, when Democrat Sean Tevis jumped into the race for Kansas state representative, he created an online cartoon strip featuring himself and his opponent in a bid to collect donations online. He netted some $95,000 in 12 days—well over his goal of a few thousand dollars (Varoga 2008).

San Francisco Mayor Gavin Newsom made extensive use of Twitter in 2009 during the primary races for the 2010 California gubernatorial election. He held "tweetraisers"—fundraising events over Twitter. The tweetraisers involved posting "updates" asking for donations (Thomas 2009). The idea was that supporters on Twitter would "re-tweet" the updates so others would see them and donate. Although Newsom was among the first to use Twitter as a fundraising device, his strategies clearly mirror the Obama campaign's efforts to promote fundraising through social networks, suggesting this strategy is quickly moving into state and local elections—although questions have been raised about the difficulty of providing disclaimers within the space limitations of a tweet (see American Association of Political Consultants 2009).

## Conclusion

Competition is the mother of invention. By 2012, with online fundraising fully entrenched in new-style campaigns and database systems integrating e-mail lists with voter files, curiosity turned to mobile devices. In 2008, as a GOTV technique toward the end of the campaign, the Obama organization sent text-message reminders to subscribers shortly before and on the day of the election, urging them to cast a vote. Why not raise money the same way? In 2012, Romney and Obama sought funding directly through text messages. Obama's text-messaging out-raised Romney by almost 500–1 (Lorber 2012). Because Internet fundraising is evolving quickly and because it demands a high level of technical expertise, many candidates lack the tools to build and maintain a successful online presence. Consulting firms have popped up to help.

Scholar James Campbell has argued that "While some claim that money does not buy elections . . . there can be no doubt that at some point it does. . . . The typical election to the House is not one in which the incumbent spends twice or even three times what his or her opponent spends [but rather] six to twelve times what the challenger spends" (Campbell 2003, 151–152). Following the 2012 election, journalist Philip Bump analyzed the effectiveness of campaign spending. What do candidates really get for all that fundraising? Is it really worth the trouble? Bump found that the size of a candidate's victory is closely correlated to the amount of money spent. This relationship holds for competitive and blow-out races. Also, of few incumbents who lost in 2012, most were outspent by their challengers. According to Bump (2013), "our shorthand for political success—more money, more votes—was validated in 2012." Malbin has put the matter as follows: "[Y]ou might be able to beat somebody with nobody, but you can't beat somebody with nothing" (Shea and Brooks, 1995).

# CHAPTER 8

# Strategic Communications

Dwight D. Eisenhower aired the first presidential campaign television commercial in 1952. Richard Nixon, who had paid scant attention to this evolving medium in 1960, made the first comprehensive use of television marketing when he ran for president in 1968. But the defining television presidency was Ronald Reagan's. A close adviser to Reagan figured out that the medium truly does shape the message and that "the message" is conveyed mostly by "the picture." Michael Deaver implemented a communications strategy that made imagery the primary focus of event planning. Deaver understood that "unless you can find a visual that explains your message you can't make it stick" (Deaver and Herskowitz 1987, 141). Because Reagan "knew exactly what he was and where he was going," Deaver wrote, the main task was to "draw the image around that, so that the public could see it clearly" (Hines 1992).

While scholars may have disparaged George H. W. Bush's visit to a New Jersey flag factory, thinking the message shallow, the event was reported faithfully by the news media. It was a powerful image: the vice president draped in patriotic symbolism. The imagery was honest in its own way. By appearing at a flag factory, Bush aligned himself with traditional patriotism while setting his beliefs apart from the civil libertarian views of his opponent, Massachusetts governor Michael Dukakis. The long-term dangers of symbolism, however, could be found in Bush's appearance at Boston Harbor, a polluted body of water that mocked Dukakis's environmental record. The assault on Dukakis was helpful in 1988 as Bush transformed himself into the "environmental candidate," but four years later, with a scanty record on environmental issues, this message came back to haunt the president. In 1992, many of those who called Bush the "environmental president" were derisive Democrats.

Casual observers may think political communication is all about money and message—and it *is* about these things—but it is also about much else. Communications professionals must know the fine points of television (broadcast and cable), radio, print, and digital media. They need to appreciate the tactical differences between paid media (advertising) and earned media (news coverage), how to buy one and how to attract the other. They must orchestrate the full range of available media as a coherent, strategic unit.

This chapter discusses the fundamentals of media strategy and differences among the various types of paid media. News coverage, which often runs afoul of campaign strategy, is examined more fully in chapter 9.

## Media Strategy

Political communication begins with the basics: What is the candidate trying to say about himself or herself, and about the opposition? Legendary Democratic strategist Paul Tulley has been credited with developing a simple way to frame the question. The device is called a "message box," or sometimes a "Tully Box." In essence, a two-by-two matrix contrasts the candidate's message with the opponents', the positives and the negatives. The four cells of the box illustrate:

1. What you say about you
2. What they say about you
3. What you say about them
4. What they say about them (Klemanski and Dulio 2006, 49–51; Pelosi 2012, 51, 75).

The message box "frames what's at stake in the debate, clarifies what you say, and helps you play defense" (Pelosi 2012, 50; see also Winston 2010). The basic idea is to draw clear comparisons between the candidate and the opposition in a way voters will understand, and it can be broadened to include all the positives and all the negatives on both sides of the electoral divide (see Figure 8.1).

A candidate's message must fit its medium. Marshall McLuhan (1964) popularized the idea that "the medium is the message" in his famous critique of modern culture. The written word, McLuhan argued, was surrendering its power to more compressed formats such

**Figure 8.1**
**Message Box**

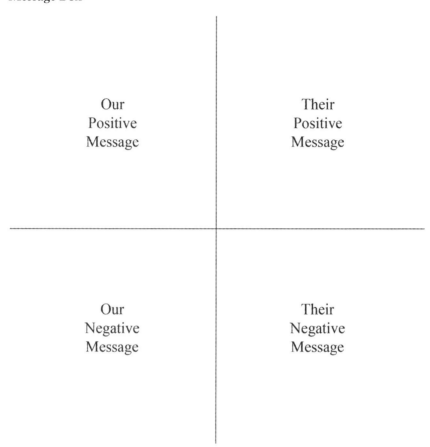

as television, and these modes of communication were creating new social arrangements. Print journalists say television offers less information, while television reporters might respond that a picture is worth a thousand words. If a medium somehow circumscribes the message it conveys, then political professionals should know how each one works and how various media can work together.

Coordination is critical. The overall image of the candidate is fashioned by the way in which various media are assembled. If the media do not interconnect, then voters may not know where the candidate stands, or they may conclude that the candidate does not stand for anything. To build a coherent image, a campaign must commit to consistency, efficiency and reach, proper timing, effective packaging, and a well-played expectations game.

## Consistency

Political campaigns are advised to seek "message discipline"—staying "on message," not wandering "off message." During the 2000 cycle, George W. Bush stayed focused on leadership. Whether the issue at hand was foreign policy, the domestic economy, or the need to change the nation's education system, *leadership* held center stage. Senator John McCain, Bush's main rival in the primaries, also projected a singular theme. For McCain, it was good government. By McCain's standard, nearly all the failings of the political system—high taxes, irrational public policies, and so forth—could be traced back to "special interests." The proof of McCain's political determination was his dogged fight on behalf of the then-unpassed McCain-Feingold reform bill. While pundits criticized Bush for his short experience and McCain for accepting funds that would have been disallowed under his own legislation, both campaigns hammered home their central messages. For 2008, Barack Obama pressed "Change"; for 2012 he hoped to move the country "Forward" while Mitt Romney wanted voters to "Believe in America."

Consistency can mean verbal and visual threads that bind a message across platforms. Joni Ernst's viral television ad—"I grew up castrating hogs on an Iowa farm"—was followed by an ad with Ernst standing in a lot filled with pigs to decry Washington politics: "Too many typical politicians, hogging, wasting, and full of [pause], well, let's just say, bad ideas." A Fox News commentator exalted, "She shines on the campaign trail. She's a joyous candidate." The Ernst campaign promptly posted the news clip on YouTube under the headline "Fox & Friends Talks Latest Ad, Says Joni is a 'Joyous Candidate.'" Conservatives across the country saw Web ads offering "Squeal" t-shirts in return for a campaign donation.

Consistency is not sufficient. Two of the most unswerving presidential candidates in recent decades have suffered the consequences of unshakable reliability—Senator Mark Udall of Colorado and publishing magnate Steve Forbes, son of the founder of *Forbes* magazine. Forbes pushed for a flat tax during his runs for the presidency in 1996 and 2000, arguing time and again that his scheme would be equitable for the taxpayers and profitable to the economy. The problem was that Forbes did not seem to talk about much else, and as he was using the same phrases over and over again, he was criticized as a "one-note-Johnny" (Tuttle 1996, 3). In 2014, Udall ran a reelection campaign centered on women's issues in an effort to draw clear dividing lines between himself and his opponent. His efforts were viewed by many as over the top—earning him the nickname "Mark Uterus" (Henderson 2014). A local reporter suggested his campaign should be housed in a gynecologist's office (L. Bartels 2014). Ultimately, Udall saw his lead with women diminish and he was defeated.

### Efficiency and Reach

New-style operatives work toward efficiency and reduce "waste" wherever appropriate. Consider the problem of a congressional candidate running in Chicago. Credibility might demand a candidate use television advertising—for some people, a campaign is not real until it shows up on TV—but Chicago stations hit a dozen or more congressional districts, some of them in Indiana and others in Wisconsin. Viewers who cannot vote for the candidate represent waste. The job of a media strategist is to optimize the number of times that *eligible* voters can be reached with a campaign pitch, either through traffic generation or through news coverage.

For electronic media, communications specialists think in terms of *reach* and *frequency*. Reach is the share of a target demographic that sees the campaign's ad. A campaign might want 30 percent of the market to see the ad, so it wants 30 percent reach. Frequency is the number of times that an individual might be reached. A *gross rating point* (GRP) represents 1 percent of a media market's total population reached by an ad; a GRP is reach multiplied by frequency, and it represents a basic unit of media purchasing. A message that plays three times on a program boasting 5 percent reach achieves 15 GRPs. An alternative approach is to count advertising "impressions"—that is, individual viewings—by increments of a thousand. Another approach is to narrow the focus to "targeted impressions." Hence, cost over reach can be measured in two ways: cost per point (CPP) and cost per mille (CPM), meaning "cost per thousand." Measured either by impressions or by share, an advertising effort can gauge its efficiency as a cost-benefit ratio.

Raw points and impressions are important, and demographics matter. ESPN's large viewership might not be the right network for a campaign that wants to reach woman voters. The Oxygen Network—with a demographic that skews toward women—might be a better buy.

If a network's demographic tends to represent strong *consumers*, a campaign that is looking for *voters* must compete with commercial marketers who want to reach the same audience and are willing to pay dearly for the option. MTV's viewership leans toward a youth-based demographic; if people of all ages watched MTV, its audience would be less valuable, even if the network attracted more viewers, because advertisers generally want to avoid scattershot targeting. During the 2012 presidential election, Barack Obama opted to run ads on shows like "The View" for women, "Late Night with Jimmy Fallon" for young people, along with ESPN for men and BET for African Americans (Rutenberg and Peters 2012).

Social media has also been important in recent election cycles. With sites like Facebook, Twitter, YouTube, and Instagram available for users—along with blogs—the potential for widened reach is great. Plus, these social media applications can track views, shares, and comments. As the viewing analytics advance for these platforms, so too does the ability for campaigns to track and integrate other demographic and preference information about users.

As a rule of thumb, a political campaign thinks not in terms of simple GRPs, but of the cost to reach voters who are persuadable. Everything outside the district is waste. A lot of the advertising that hits outside the targeted demographic is also waste. The more precisely a campaign can target persuadable, eligible voters, the more efficiently the campaign can spend its money.

## Timing

Part of the strategic calculus goes to proper timing. A challenger might introduce him- or herself to the public with a series of news interviews combined with a run of "establishment" ads (see Arbour 2014). Once a positive impression of the candidate is created, the campaign might build credibility with a series of "issue" ads, laying out the high points of a candidate's agenda. When the incumbent responds, the challenger might return fire with "attack" ads. Incumbents might follow a similar pattern, though they generally start off with better name recognition, so they may be able to bypass the establishment phase.

Ad buys and news coverage require advance planning. Reporters may decline an invitation to sit down with a candidate at a moment's notice; relationships are built over time. An opponent who enjoys a long-standing association with a reporter might be dropping subtle insinuations along the way. A challenger who waits too long before entering the race may find no way to erase the bad impression. With broadcast media, the problem is more acute.

Buying newspaper ads is a simple matter of phoning the advertising department and requesting display space. Broadcast media are limited resources. Only a fixed number of radio and television spots will be available during the electoral season. Although Web sites and social media are more readily available, unless campaigns trust followers to share relevant information within a personal network, paid advertising on the Web is also a limited resource. Because nearly every campaign wants to grab the ad slots and screen space that appear in the last few days of the cycle, a campaign that waits until the last minute might walk away empty-handed—another reason to raise money early.

### *Packaging*

An electorate that always votes Republican might need only be informed that a candidate is a member of the GOP. In this case, signs, radio ads, endorsements, television spots, social media, and Web ads should probably make the candidate's party affiliation explicit: "Wilson: Republican for U.S. Senate." Sometimes the cues are more subtle, and clever metaphors help make the case.

In the 1980s, few issues were more important than the standoff between the United States and the Soviet Union. Between Democrats and Republicans, the question was whether to build up, freeze, or draw down the nuclear arsenal. President Reagan stood with those who wanted to increase American nuclear superiority. The 1984 Reagan team needed a way to make its case. The campaign's "Bear" spot used footage of a bear wandering around his natural habitat along with simple language and a well-constructed metaphor:

> There is a bear in the woods. For some people the bear is easy to see. Others don't see it at all. Some people say the bear is tame. Others say it's vicious and dangerous. Since no one can really be sure who is right, isn't it smart to be as strong as the bear? If there is a bear.

When the bear encounters a man standing unafraid, and steps back, the message was unmistakable: "The best way to avoid a military confrontation with the Soviets was for America to be stronger than [its] Cold War rival" (Weaver 1996, 204).

Campaign ads can be divided into three general categories: positive, comparative, and negative. Advertising designed to establish a candidate's credentials and to lay out a policy agenda are usually positive. In a 1998 Georgia race, Republican Dylan Glenn was trying to become the first black Republican congressman from the South since Reconstruction. To introduce himself, he ran a biographical sketch: "From Georgia—for Georgia."

Comparative ads lay out differences between the candidates. In the 2006 Virginia race for U.S. Senate, Jim Webb responded to attacks by opponent George Allen with a spot that said, "Webb's plan cuts taxes for middle-class families and veterans; in fact, only one Senate candidate voted to make college more expensive: George Allen."

Comparatives can be distinguished from "attacks." In North Carolina in 2014, an ad called "Toughest Job" from Republican Thom Tillis against Democrat Kay Hagan clearly qualifies as an attack ad. It claimed: "It makes me so mad to see how the president's weakness has allowed the Islamic State to grow. And Senator Hagan? She just goes right along with him. . . . We can't let our kids die in vain. We have to change our senator." In 2004, former Beirut hostage Terry Anderson challenged incumbent Joy Padgett for a seat in an Ohio state Senate election. Padgett attacked Anderson with direct mail featuring a picture of her opponent next to an actual terrorist. The photograph was real, but "missing from Padgett's advertisement was any mention that the terrorist pictured with Anderson was the secretary general of Hezbollah, the group that abducted him in 1985. Anderson [had] confronted and interviewed the terrorist leader for a television documentary years after he was freed" (Simonich 2004).

A 2014 study by the Center for Public Integrity using data from Kantar Media/CMAG found, "In the 34 states with Senate seats up for grabs, candidates and political groups ran more than 1 million TV ads to influence those races"—about half of all ads run, though in North Carolina negative ads made up two-thirds of the ads (Kirk 2014). In Florida, an ad attacking gubernatorial candidate Charlie Crist drew a series of connections from the candidate to a donor, to the donor's investments to a strip club and to the evils of sex trafficking. One observer opined, "That's probably why people don't like politics very much" ("Morning Joe" 2014). The *Washington Post* headlined its story, "The newest ad in the Florida governor's race will make you thankful the election is almost over" (Fuller 2014).

Apart from a generalized public rejection, ham-fisted negativity can bring blowback. The reelection campaign in Alaska for Democratic

Senator Mark Begich was criticized from left and right for an appeal that looked uncomfortably close to the infamous "Willy Horton" ad (see Hohmann 2014b), a campaign commercial that attacked Michael Dukakis and was viewed by many to carry a racist appeal. An ad attacking Democratic governor Pat Quinn, who was running for re-election in Illinois, had pasted headlines and negative quotes over photos of the governor. The problem, according to the *Chicago Tribune*, was that the excerpts were not the whole truth: "In one case, the ad displays the words 'Quinn education cuts lead to teacher layoffs and larger class sizes'. . . . But the actual headline was 'Quinn, Rauner spar on education in 1st 2014 event' from a story about a joint appearance by the two candidates before the Illinois Education Association" (Pearson 2014). Adding people of color to a campaign flyer digitally to demonstrate the diversity of a candidate's support would seem ill-advised at a time when members of the public and the news media can browse stock images online (see McQuade 2014).

### *Expectations*

An important element of communications strategy is something political strategists call the "expectations game." News reporters thrive on drama, and if a front-running candidate wins a primary, there is not much news to report. If, however, a dark horse finishes a close second, then there *is* news—though not the kind of story that the first-place victor would have desired.

George W. Bush suffered from high expectations early in the 2000 campaign. Through most of 1999, Bush was the presumptive winner of the next year's primaries. He had nowhere to go but down. When Steve Forbes ran a little behind Bush in Iowa and John McCain won New Hampshire, media attention shifted to Forbes and McCain. Had the front-runner stumbled? Politically astute observers could probably see that neither Forbes nor McCain had sufficient resources for the long haul. Forbes had little organization outside of Iowa; McCain had some people beyond New Hampshire but nothing to rival Bush's national network of established Republicans and financial donors. Yet operatives for Bush's nationwide campaign were forced to reassure supporters about their candidate's long-term prospects.

The expectations game demonstrates the relativity of campaign information. The question is not, Did Bush win Iowa? Rather, the question is, Did Bush win Iowa *by the anticipated number of votes*? Critics may say the outcome is all that really counts, that too much attention is given to expectations. Still, the failure to meet expectations might signify an underlying problem. Although Forbes had little hope of eventual victory, his strength in Iowa exposed weakness in the Bush camp. Forbes's belief in a flat tax forced Bush to respond with his own tax-cut plan. Forbes's achievement *was* real news. The deeper meaning of the story is that political campaigns work in an environment where perception can become reality, so campaigns must do their best to control expectations.

Expectations can have serious consequences for front-runners, as Governor Howard Dean learned in 2004 and Senator Hillary Clinton learned in 2008. Dean generated high anticipation with an unconventional campaign filled with enthusiastic young people who wanted to believe. Anything but a solid win would likely have been questioned by political observers; he did badly in Iowa and New Hampshire. For years, Clinton had been treated as the presumptive Democratic nominee; but Iowa voters rejected her candidacy. Media coverage turned ominous. One prominent analyst wrote, "Clinton spent a lot of time and money in Iowa, and she had a terrific field staff. And she still got blown out of the water by Barack Obama" (Simon 2008). The succession of candidates who led the polls running up to 2012 seemed to follow a pattern of buoyant expectation, press scrutiny, or candidate blunder, then swift decline when the original expectations were betrayed. The sense of inevitability that had once fueled Clinton's campaign was replaced by stories of anxiety and reassessment.

A routine cycle drives the expectations game in competitive elections. At the beginning of a campaign, a challenger gives the impression that victory is possible, hoping to get at least minimal coverage. An incumbent seeks to show that victory is all but certain, hoping to scare off challengers. As Election Day nears, both sides claim the race is close. To make sure voters go to the polls, front-running candidates do not foreclose the possibility of a loss, telling supporters that they cannot sit out the election. An incumbent with a commanding lead might tell volunteers on Election Eve that the race is not yet won, that there is still plenty of work to do.

## Paid Media

Paid media allow campaigns to control their own message. Unlike news coverage, which inserts a reporter between the campaign and the voters, paid media allow campaign operatives to script the message, target the audience, and, for the most part, select the timing that best suits the campaign. The downside is that paid media, by definition, cost money. A campaign might be advised to spend 65 percent of its budget on voter contact (Arnold n.d.). Television ads can run tens of thousands of dollars, and a small display ad in a college newspaper can cost hundreds.

According to congressional scholar Paul Herrnson, challengers in the 2010 campaign cycle committed an average of less than $700,000 to campaign communications (2012, 261). Campaigns must be efficient in their targeting, gain the right amount of coverage, and choose the right media for their message. An analysis of 2012 presidential campaign spending by the *Washington Post* found that spending on advertising and mail accounted for roughly $1.3 billion of the $2.3 billion spent by the presidential campaigns (*Washington Post* 2012). Campaigns in the Digital Age have a wide variety of options, including television, radio, newspapers, and digital media.

## *Television*

Combining audio and visual imagery, TV absorbs its viewers in ways radio and print simply cannot. Joe McGinniss wrote that television was "something new, murky, undefined" and "the mystique which should fade grows stronger. We make celebrities not only of the men who cause events but of the men who read reports of them out loud" (1969, 28). Why? Because television imagery seems so "real": "the medium is the massage and the masseur gets the votes" (29).

Production costs can be high. Assembling a television spot might require the assistance of a producer, a videographer, assorted gaffers, and a postproduction house to edit the raw footage. An independent filmmaker has warned, "In the quick-turnaround, high-pressure world of media production, there are few situations where margins of error are smaller, time crunches more acute and smooth sailing more essential than in the production of political ads" (Arnold 1999, 62). In politics, where competition puts a premium on speed, television ads can be slow to produce, expensive to run, and resistant to real-time modifications—but it is a rare campaign that would turn down the opportunity to use TV ads if it has enough money.

Many candidates enjoy the benefits of discount rates when they buy television spots, though they should be aware that ad rates, even when discounted, can be expensive. A statewide buy can cost hundreds of dollars per point, and if the goal is to purchase hundreds or thousands of points, then the total expense will obviously consume a large portion of the campaign's budget. Smaller buys might start to look attractive, and a campaign manager may well consider sacrificing repetition to gain a broader reach (only to hear the media buyer urge that hitting a voter once or twice will not be enough for the message to "break through").

For federal elections, the paperwork associated with a buy is a reviewable public record. In the past, these data have been available at station facilities but are now moving online. Frequent checks of buy-orders serve as a distant early-warning system, because a campaign that buys early has tipped part of its hand. An additional reason to watch the opposition's ad buys in advance is to monitor broadcasters' compliance with the "Equal Time Rule" (technically, the "Equal Opportunities Rule"). Generally speaking, if a broadcaster sells time to one candidate, it must offer time to any other candidate in the race. Fee-based tracking services can report on television spots.

Another way to capture ads is by recruiting volunteers to watch for them. A campaign might send instructions to a corps of loyalists who are willing to note the time and station that the opposition (or supportive groups outside the campaign) is running spots. With digital recorders, volunteers might capture content, and with e-mail, a volunteer can deliver a television (or radio) spot to the campaign instantaneously. Supporters can also be organized to capture ads appearing on opposition Web sites and YouTube.

In the mid-1970s, broadcast was practically the only way to see a television program, but with the rise of cable and satellite television, broadcast has lost a significant share of the market. Videocassette recorders, digital video recorders, video games, and online programming further diminished the broadcast television audience. With more and more people recording their favorite shows for later viewing come increasing likelihoods that political spots will be "zapped." Nonetheless, broadcast television continues to be the mainstay of larger, new-style campaigns because a message can be sent to wide swaths of the electorate with a single ad buy. The need for broad reach has been accepted for decades. A media specialist in the 1990s was clear: "To be successful, we must obtain a market share of 50 percent plus one of the potential pool of political customers. This fact requires us to be mass-marketers. We want market share, not unit sales" (Hutchens 1996, 42). Especially for candidates seeking lower-income voters, broadcast remains an important medium.

While broadcast reaches the widest audience, cable has the capacity to target voters narrowly. For years, cable was gaining on all its competitors, but as the market approached saturation and as satellite and Internet video joined the fray, cable has leveled off. At the end of 2014, the broadcast industry group TVB estimated that satellite accounted for 33 percent of the market, over-the-air was almost 11 percent, and cable at about 57 percent (TVB, n.d.). In 2009, around 62 percent of American households were receiving cable programming, providing ad buyers with a whole new category of paid media.

On one hand, there is no difference between broadcast and cable advertising. Viewers watching a network television show transmitted via cable TV might not distinguish between ads run from the network and those inserted by the cable company. On the other hand, the ability to run ads in a single cable market provides a different set of opportunities. Cable companies have identifiable borders, and these boundaries might approximate those of electoral districts. If the boundaries are favorable, waste is minimized. Because cable offers dozens or hundreds of channels, "narrowcasting" becomes possible. The History Channel, A&E, BET, and MTV each seek a thin slice of the pie. Many candidates take advantage of Spanish-language networks to reach Latino voters.

A study by spot-cable firm NCC finds that specific targets can be reached by narrowing the geographic and demographic composition of a political audience while enhancing reach (Kay 2014). By reducing waste, a campaign would hope to increase its return on investment. The new dynamic of media buying requires that political professionals take into account the value of reaching a specialized audience against the cost of doing so. Future cable-buyers may be able to address different ads to different homes (Balaban 2014). Voters who leave the cable market and opt to watch video on tablets and handheld devices bring new challenges to media strategists.

### Radio

Radio lacks the visual element of television, but in some ways it offers the best of broadcast combined with the best of cable. Like broadcast, it reaches beyond paid subscribers, and like cable, it can be used for precision targeting. A talk radio station might attract more conservative voters than a pop station. Narrowcasting to selected talk shows can bring efficiency. And a radio strategy helps a campaign fly low, perhaps escaping the sort of "ad watch" scrutiny that could diminish the effect of negative advertising. And radio has a unique intimacy: "The images it conveys exist in the listener's minds" (Sweitzer and Heller 1996, 40).

While corporate ad production might grow out of extended concept meetings and audience pretesting, political campaigns can deploy radio in rapid response to unfolding events on a tight deadline with little money. A campaign might be inspired to make a radio ad in the morning, script the notion in a couple of hours, hand the script to the candidate for editing, drive the candidate to a studio to record the sound about midday, edit the ad immediately after recording, and deliver the spot to local radio stations by late afternoon.

> Radio's flexibility can be seen in a pair of ads that the Senate campaign of John Warner produced for the 1996 election. The *Washington Post* described Warner's predicament in the GOP primary: "He must drive up turnout dramatically. He hopes to do that with an aggressive media blitz aimed at mobilizing women, moderates, and especially Northern Virginians, while giving reason to doubt his rival's credentials as a true believer" (Baker 1996). In an apparent effort to tweak the demographics, Warner aired a radio commercial featuring a male voice assailing his Republican primary opponent for masquerading as a conservative. It ran just once before being taken off the air. A few days later, it resurfaced—but this time with a woman's voice. (ibid.)

## Newspapers

Once the chief means for transmitting partisan ideas on a mass scale, newspapers have lost a great deal of their once-dominant empire. Fewer people are reading the papers, and less money is spent advertising in them. While newspaper readership is aging and young people look to different sources, print ads remain part of new-style campaigning.

First, ad space is almost always available. Whereas television and radio are limited commodities (see Kang and Gold 2014), newspapers might be able to accommodate an end-of-campaign ad blitz by inserting a few more pages. Second, newspapers have responded to market pressures through customer segmentation. High-tech printing operations allow for geographic variation in advertising content whereby each suburb in a metropolitan area might receive its own set of display ads. Finally, a fear factor may be at play. Political operatives might believe failing to buy ad space can forfeit a rightful endorsement and might affect decisions about news reporting. The game can work both ways. Judge Lawrence Grey recommends that, if a paper never runs with a campaign's news release,

> threaten to cancel [campaign] ads and ask for your money back. . . . The editors will hate me for telling you this, but for a small newspaper on a tight budget, this is an effective technique for your campaign. (2007, 189)

Newspaper advertising may be a unique and valuable medium on its own terms. Among those who read newspapers, traditional hardcopy papers may seem to have the feel of authenticity, and associating with that feeling may reap a few votes. It should not be surprising that "newspaper readers vote at above-average rates" (Helliker 2007).

### Digital Media

In the late 1990s and early 2000s, as campaigns started to go online, consultants understood the main challenge was to drive traffic to campaign Web sites. Radio and television reached all the listeners and viewers who did not actively "zap" the ad; broadcast ads were "opt-out" media. Before people started spending much time on the Web, campaign sites were strictly "opt-in." Media consultant Mike Connell pointed out that the Web can serve as an extension of broadcast media. He noted that campaigns purchase:

> 30-second spots in which the candidate must explain to all the electorate who they are, what they have done, their vision for the future and why they are the best candidate. But put the campaign's Web site address on the advertisement and suddenly you've given the electorate access to complete, in-depth information on the candidate. (1999/2000, 58)

One bit of early creativity came from Donald Dunn, campaigning for Congress in 2000, who "ran a list of [Utah residents] who are owed money from their 1998 tax returns on his Web site." It proved to be a smart strategy: "The Dunn campaign . . . held a press conference announcing they would be posting the names, after which the Web site had nearly 20,000 hits" (Jalonick 2000, 62).

An early study of Internet electioneering showed that visitors spend the most time with "issue sections, candidate biographies and comparative sections" (Hockaday and Edlund 1999, 14). During the 2000 cycle, it became common to post news releases, calendars of upcoming events, and streaming video and audio, showcasing ads being run through more traditional media. More recently, the shift has been toward interaction and personalization, making a candidate's Web content feel unique to each individual voter.

According to the 2013 Digital Future Report from the University of Southern California's Annenberg School Center for the Digital Future, the portion of the American adult population who use the Internet is approaching 90 percent (Cole et al. 2013, 15). And the power of Internet outreach extends beyond candidate Web sites. Because candidates can buy ads linked to Web searches, they can be reasonably certain that their pitch is reaching voters who are somehow interested in the message and who are, to use the language of commercial marketing, in "buy mode": looking for reasons to support or oppose a candidate. Campaigns have purchased search ads tagged to their own names and to the names of their opponents. A voter leaning toward one candidate, hoping to learn a bit about her position on the economy, might see a link to the opposition's excoriation of her views on energy exploration. Recent campaign cycles witnessed an upsurge of videos posted on campaign Web sites and YouTube.

The depth and sophistication of campaign Web sites have increased dramatically since the 1990s (see Gulati and Williams 2007). It is difficult to imagine a serious campaign effort that does not incorporate Web technology. Web sites in the 2008 cycle contained candidate blogs, rich graphics and Flash media content, photo galleries, volunteer sign-ups, invitations to house parties, gear sales, sample text for letters to friends and to editors, and up-to-the-minute news releases. A witty tactic from the liberal group MoveOn.org, which was a strong player in 2008, allowed visitors to create a customized video designed to exhort friends to vote: a fake news broadcast blaming Obama's one-vote loss on whomever the sender chose to fill in the blank. A friend of Michael Jones could order up a well-produced campaign ad in which a fake newspaper appears on the screen, saying, "Nonvoter Identified: Michael Jones; Investigation of Tallies Leads to Culprit," along with fake newscasters talking about the gaffe, protesters forming in the street, and a church sign reading, "All God's children welcome—except Michael Jones."

While campaign Web sites have become rich with features, campaigns are selective about which features they offer. Apparently, campaigns in noncompetitive races are more likely to let voters sound off on their campaign Web sites whereas close races tend to avoid unsupervised remarks (Druckman, Kifer, and Parkin 2007). Competitive campaigns have a strong interest in controlling the message whereas long shots might be more willing to risk untoward comments in an effort to engage voters.

Campaigns are more and more turning to Web-based ads (Barnard and Kreiss 2013). As with traditional advertising, strategists can either take it upon themselves to buy ads on YouTube, search engines, political blogs, music streaming services, and elsewhere, or they can seek the help of a professional. "Promoted" tweets can reinforce "organic" tweets. New-media advertising has its own guidelines and its own metrics based on click-through, completion, and viewability. For political marketers, a key benefit over broadcast is an opportunity to reach narrow groups. The audience for a politically liberal or conservative blog can readily be inferred from its content and commentary. Web advertising networks offer well-specified audiences, some of which might line up with a campaign's targeted demographics.

## Conclusion

Direct evidence of paid media persuasion effects in a competitive environment is mixed. A postelection analysis by Daron Shaw (2006), who advised the Bush campaigns of 2000 and 2004, estimated that 1,000 GRPs for five weeks bought roughly half of a percent in vote share (136). Another study indicated that "about 3.3% [of respondents] said changing their vote, based on online information, was 'somewhat likely,' and 3.7% said it was 'very likely'" (Acohido 2008); other evidence is less optimistic (Brockman and Green 2014). For 2012, John Sides and Lynn Vavreck (2013) estimate that media persuasion can move polls a few percentage points, and yet the effect is usually short-lived due partly to the competitive nature of the environment, a finding that squares with experimental research showing how persuasion can be overtaken by preexisting partisanship as the campaign comes to a close (L.M. Bartels 2014). If decay follows persuasion the effort to influence voters might demand tactical persistence, and aggregate preferences may in fact shift and hold in presidential battleground states (Panagopoulos 2012).

Lacking direct evidence, strategists are left with a political wager similar to Pascal's: If they campaign their hardest, they might win; if they do not campaign hard, they will surely lose. With paid media, at least, the strategist has some measure of control, even if campaign charges are followed by countercharges as operatives seek to push the other side off message. "Free" media, by comparison, is less controllable and may require more hard work.

# CHAPTER 9

# Earned Media

Advertising consumes cash, whereas news coverage, though ostensibly free, nevertheless consumes the precious time of the candidate, staff, and consultants. A congressional candidate in a large city must work hard to win a profile piece in a wide-circulation daily paper; the paper might eventually decide to run a story, but many of the candidate's new admirers will be in the suburbs and exurbs. Perhaps gaining an interview with the city's business journal would be a more efficient use of time. Or, the best investment could well be a neighborhood weekly having the potential of reaching the campaign's targeted voters.

Paid media outlets allow control over timing, audience, and message, but campaigns do not have unlimited funds, and while news coverage is not truly free, it does have the benefit of low financial cost and heightened credibility. The message is sent through an independent conduit, which might seem more neutral or more ideologically correct. It resides in a context—on the television news, in the newspaper, during a radio news segment, or on an online blog—where its audience is thinking about politics. News media reach people where and when they are in the market for political information.

Political consultants call this sort of outreach *earned* media rather than *free* media in order to emphasize the work that goes into the quest for coverage. "A cheaply produced press release can sometimes lead to enormous media attention," writes media scholar Joseph Graf, "whereas paid media can have trouble breaking through the morass of advertising we encounter every day" (2008, 53). Breaking through is difficult. The only office that is guaranteed regular news coverage is the presidency—even front-running candidates for the office complain they are ignored. Reporters, for their part, object that politicians attempt to "manage" the news. While pundits grumble that candidates offer nothing more than "sound bites," the news media continue to run snappy political phrases as genuine, hard-hitting news.

Positive coverage is never assured. Over the course of the 2012 Republican presidential primary cycle, five different candidates held the lead in rapid succession (Romney, Perry, Cain, Gingrich, Romney, Santorum, then Romney), and some dropped down just as quickly as they emerged (Cain and Perry)—the news media and eager voters finding a face that looked fresh until they get a close-up view (Burton 2014; Miller 2013a; Sides and Vavreck 2013). In 2008, Alaska governor Sarah Palin was an instant superstar, until she stumbled over questions about foreign policy ("As Putin rears his head and comes into the airspace of the United States of America, where do they go? It's Alaska" [Palin 2008a]) and which newspapers and magazines she might read ("I've read most of them, again with a great appreciation for the press, for the media" [Palin 2008b]). Palin never fully recovered. More than one amateur pundit quoted a line from the film *Primary Colors*: "The media giveth . . . and go f*#* yourself" (connor17 2008). To candidates, consultants, and campaign staffers, the news media are a blessing and a curse, an opportunity and a danger—a basic need that looms as a constant threat.

This chapter explains earned media by discussing the development of news reporting, newsworthiness, today's "news," and the tactics campaigns might bring into play as they compete for coverage.

## Development of "The News"

A *Gazette* or *Intelligencer* of early America looked nothing like today's *New York Times*. Lacking a drive for objective, dispassionate reporting, published accounts of current events were unabashedly partisan (Dinkin 1989, 7–9). Publishers aligned themselves with one side of politics or the other, and they did so according to the whims of the parties that helped fund them. In the first half of the 1800s, publishers came to understand that people might be willing to pay for the news, and the "penny press" was born. For one cent, readers could get the news of the day along with feature stories. A larger readership meant higher profits, so there was little reason to restrict a paper's viewpoint to one particular party. Thereafter, publishers found they could make more money if space was sold for advertising. With the rise of profit-driven "yellow journalism" in the late 1800s—which gave front-page coverage to crime, scandal, and tragedy—newspapers became big business, and they were beginning to look like today's publications.

Broadcast news became popular in the first half of the 20th century. Unlike print outlets, which cover news in depth, radio distilled all the day's news into a few brief moments. Radio news was belittled for its superficiality but it gained credibility through serious journalists like Edward R. Murrow, whose voice gave Americans urgent reports from the Battle of Britain. After World War II, a number of radio reporters, including Murrow, moved to television, which also suffered under time constraints. The high cost of television production meant that viewers had limited options: Three broadcast networks alone seemed to decide what constituted "the news."

Dominance by the Big Three broadcasters was undermined in the 1980s by Cable News Network and thereafter by a collection of niche cable outlets such as CNBC (for financial news) and Fox News, which later rose to greater prominence as a conservative alternative to the "mainstream media." In response, MSNBC changed its format to provide a liberal alternative to Fox. Fragmentation and politicization in television news was following the trend of radio news and opinion-making, which was in the 1990s increasingly populated by politically charged commentary (mostly from the conservative side of the ideological spectrum). By the 2010s, the shift from broadcasting to narrowcasting was made clear by declining viewerships for the traditional "evening news" and a tendency of viewers to choose their news outlets according to their political preferences.

Declining readership has pressured newspapers into moving away from traditional print toward online delivery, alternative formats, and closure. Smaller papers like the *Ann Arbor (Michigan) News*, which stopped publishing a hard copy after nearly 180 years, are falling prey to a new business reality (see Pérez-Peña 2009). (Earlier, traditional news sources had begun repurposing their content to online sites while CNN and other national networks produced massive amounts of news content.) Home delivery is falling off. In the critical swing state of Ohio, the *Columbus Dispatch* has moved to smaller print "subtabloid" format and the news content was moving to a form its editor said would be on the order of a "daily news magazine" (Hartman 2012). In 2010, 151 newspapers closed and an additional 152 followed suit in 2011 (Mendolera 2012). Meanwhile, the rise of news-aggregators such as the *Drudge Report* and the *Huffington Post* has shifted much of the electorate toward the Web.

A 2014 study found that Americans follow the news on a wide variety of media. The most frequently utilized outlets include television

(87 percent), laptops/computers (69 percent), radio (65 percent), and print newspapers or magazines (61 percent; American Press Institute 2014). In 2013, a Digital Future Report from the University of Southern California's Annenberg School found that 79 percent of adult users said the Internet is an important source of information (for news and other information), higher than television (66 percent) or newspapers (45 percent; Cole et al. 2013). With this increase in relevancy, however, has come the invention of "clickbait"—headlines that grab attention and drive traffic (and therefore advertising revenue) to stories that lack news value.

Internet blogs and aggregators that focus on political topics are becoming an important part of the political landscape. From breitbart.com for conservatives to motherjones.com for liberals, any stance can find a home from which to present the arguments of their choosing, deeply fragmenting what is meant by "the news." Part of their influence stems from their deep, though narrow, credibility. A reader of RedState.com is likely to be on that site out of an interest in its particular brand of conservative politics. The same goes for the left moderate HuffingtonPost.com, TheRoot.com for a black political perspective, voxxi.com for a focus on a Latino viewpoint, ChristianPost.com for Christian conservatism, Wonkette.com for a liberal woman's point of view, and advocate.com for an LGBT outlook. Partisans looking for talking points may come across these sites as they search the Web because people tend to search for information that will confirm their political views, not challenge them (Knobloch-Westerwick et al. 2014).

Political discussions generated online are sometimes picked up by mainstream outlets. Journalists Mark Halperin and John Harris saw early in the days of blogging that the influence of Matt Drudge and his Drudge Report "derives only in part from the colossal number of people who visit his site. . . . His [real] power comes from his ability to shape the perceptions of other news media—Old and New alike" (2006, 54). If a community-based blog or news site picks up on a campaign event, there is a good chance that the traditional media will also move on it. Campaign organizations have begun to strike up relationships with bloggers and have also started generating their own news content.

## Today's News

In much the same way that broader sales freed newspapers from their partisan roots, the Associated Press (AP), a national wire service, released the press from its earlier geographic parochialism. The AP was formed in the mid-19th century as a cooperative that pooled the resources of New York newspapers. Instead of having dozens of reporters arrive at the same news site, the publishing community could propagate stories written by a single, local journalist. As the AP spread across the United States, reporting on the Civil War and other domestic news, regional perspectives gave way to a more national point of view. A backlash against yellow journalism reinforced the idea that "objectivity" should be the guiding principle of news reporting. Progressives in the early 1900s hailed the arrival of "muckraking" journalism, which exposed government corruption and corporate greed. Focusing on journalistic responsibility, muckrakers paved the way for professional standards that distinguished facts from analysis and editorializing. An ethical framework that would have seemed foreign to the early partisan press was taking hold.

The predispositions of journalistic "objectivity" have fluctuated over the past hundred years. In the middle decades of the 20th century, politicians were often treated with kid gloves. Many journalists accepted whatever they were told, and they rarely scrutinized the private lives of candidates. Larry Sabato labeled this era a time of "lapdog" journalism (1991, 25). During the 1960s and 1970s, the industry entered a period of "investigative journalism." Shocked by revelations of government misinformation, reporters covering the Vietnam War and the Nixon administration no longer presupposed the sincerity of politicians. Their colleagues began digging for political dirt, leading to an era of "watchdog" or "attack-dog" journalism. The idea that George H. W. Bush was so out of touch with the American people that he could be shocked by the workings of a grocery store scanner made for great copy; the reality was probably quite different. One reporter who was on the scene when the surprise was alleged to have happened called the whole matter "completely insignificant as a news event" (see Kurtz 1992b). And yet, the original version of the story, which invited a cartoonish picture of a sitting president, continues to circulate.

By the late 1980s, Frank Luntz could say, "[T]he mechanics of campaigning have become a better story than the campaign itself" (1988, 33). Interest in the horse race—who is running ahead and who is coming up from behind, the internal workings of campaign operations—makes the process of electioneering newsworthy. Journalists have focused on Bill Clinton's rapid-response operation, George W. Bush's speaking style, and Barack Obama's data analytics.

As the campaign season rushes to a close, a daily dose of polling and punditry almost appears mandatory, as news analysts compete for attention using electronic graphics, predictive analytics, embedded reporters, and special contributors who have earned their credentials not in journalism but in politics.

For many Americans, "the news" has meant "television news." Seeming to lack depth, television news was open to attack by the likes of Marshall McLuhan and Daniel Boorstin. Boorstin wrote: "Our national politics has become a competition for images or between images, rather than between ideals. The domination of campaigning simply dramatizes this fact" (1964, 249). The news media, Boorstin thought, were full of participants in trivial performance, having allowed themselves to become mesmerized by "pseudo-events."

By necessity, the news media pick and choose which facts are going to be reported. To say that a paper contains "All the News That's Fit to Print" merely begs the question, What counts as "the news" and who decides what's "fit to print"? It is too simplistic to proclaim that reporters are generally liberal while editors and publishers are conservative, that news organizations are nothing more than profit-seeking enterprises, or that reporters always base their stories on personal opinion. Political reporting is complicated and difficult, and the world of journalism has arguably become *more* complicated and *more* difficult to manage as bloggers and other online commentators have joined the conversation.

Journalists chafe at the idea that their profession is anything less than objective, but objectivity is an elusive ideal, and news is a business. Media outlets that go out of business can no longer inform the public, so news content must hold consumer interest. Television is good for pictures, though it tends to blur complexity; detailed information works better in text. Most reporters work hard to separate political partisanship from news coverage, and they are acutely aware of journalistic ethics, but they are forced to make decisions on the credibility of their sources and the relative importance of the events they cover. Are politicians, as a class, believable sources of information? In the early 1960s, the answer was assumed to be yes, but no longer. Does money influence policy? Perhaps, and this notion has become a basic motif for campaign coverage.

## Communications Tactics

Campaign stories must be fresh and should relate to public affairs in a way that affects readers, listeners, and viewers, but their publication is subject to two sometimes countervailing principles. First, journalism is a profession. Reporters are trained to uphold standards that have matured over a couple of centuries, complete with heroes like Bob Woodward and Carl Bernstein, who literally changed history with their reporting on the Watergate break-in and its cover-up. Journalists have a strong sense of newsworthiness. Second, reportage is constrained by cost-benefit calculations. Traditional news outlets need "good stories" if they are to "sell papers." Bloggers who earn money from "click-throughs" might want to deploy red meat and clickbait. On the cost side of the cost-benefit analysis, stories should be inexpensive to produce. One that would require a television crew to lug equipment over a mountain pass is unlikely to get covered.

Campaigns that fail to recognize the tenets of journalism and the business of news may earn less positive coverage. That is, campaigns would do well to think about the news from the reporter's point of view, which includes an appreciation of authenticity with respect to newsworthiness and conscientiousness regarding the reporter's time and attention (suggesting that strategists avoid the mistakes of Wendy Davis's gubernatorial campaign in Texas, which, in a two-week period sent a reporter to the wrong location and then gave a wrong address for campaign headquarters [Mann 2014]). But then, Congressman Michael Grimm was reelected after threatening, on camera, to throw a reporter off a balcony in the Capitol Building for asking some unwelcome questions (Edelman and Straw 2014).

This chapter discusses news releases, backgrounding, news conferences, media events, debates, editorial board meetings, opinion outlets like cable talk shows, and social media.

## News Releases

Perhaps the most important tool for selling a local candidate is the news release. Releases announce candidate statements and upcoming events, spin breaking news, highlight endorsements, and provide background facts that help reporters make sense of the race. The difficulty is that media outlets receive myriad news releases from businesses, civic groups, government offices, crackpots, and rival campaign organizations. A major paper might receive hundreds of news releases daily. Some are selected for follow-up but most are not.

A basic rule holds that one should make the text newsworthy and informative; few editors or producers want to run boring stories. To make life easy for reporters, campaigns provide everything needed to write a positive story. Many find that the best approach is to draft the release exactly the way the campaign would wish the news to appear in the paper. Communications directors have long employed the same notation reporters use, adding, for example, a "###" or a "-30-" to indicate the end of the release (see Hewitt 1999, 57). A political Web site vendor advises grabby facts, "maximum of 300 words—and be sure to proofread them before submission!"—and the firm offers "Campaign Letter Templates" to help operatives "[c]reate professional, powerful political press releases" (Daley n.d.).

Imitating journalistic style can help fit a story into the mind-set of a reporter, editor, or broadcast producer, and some smaller newspapers might run the "story" word for word. Thinking like a reporter, a communications director might include at least one quote from the candidate or campaign official. Quite commonly, the quote will be in the form of a "zinger"—a pithy remark with a powerful message. News releases might stand a better chance of publication if they contain a headline, a strong lead sentence, and photographs, particularly when they are written in the journalist's "inverted-pyramid" format, with the most important information at the top and less important information farther down.

Radio, editorial pages, Sunday morning magazines, and political bloggers each have their own manner of speaking, which might be adopted in a release. The name and telephone number of a contact person are usually shown at the top of each release. Some stories are "embargoed" for later publication; "For Immediate Release" indicates that the story can be run upon receipt. Communications directors also include links to online documentation. Tweets, of course, are limited in character length and consequently often make a clear point before linking to another Web page that provides greater detail.

As to the rate of sending news releases, opinions can be divided. Some believe "the more the better," arguing that a campaign can never tell when an outlet will have a slow news day. Favorable news stories sometimes stem from releases that were not expected to be picked up. Frequent releases also keep the election at the forefront of an editor's mind and let reporters know what is happening. But daily releases run the risk of being ignored. Reporters and editors who receive a stack of releases from the same campaign might tire of them and assume, perhaps rightly, that the releases contain nothing but fluff. The most important releases may get rejected with the rest. At any rate, minor announcements can simply be added to the campaign Web site along with a Twitter alert.

The video analog to a news release is the "feed." A historic use of feeds was the distribution of the GOP's "Contract with America" signing in 1994. According to Barrie Tron, who built the event, "We produced a multicamera live broadcast" that was distributed to news departments around the country (1995/1996, 51). Tron wrote that the "signal was distributed live, via satellite . . . to every television station around the country. The feed was free and produced as if we were feeding our own network" (ibid.). The whole event, from start to finish, was offered to the media because "news directors want the most options—especially in the midst of a campaign" (ibid.). Plus, "an audio bridge fed the audio portion of the program, [accessible] via telephone and made available free of charge to radio stations" (ibid.). The hard work that went into setting up a massive, tightly choreographed event on the Capitol steps paid off with nationwide coverage.

Video and audio can also be fed on a smaller scale. In the 1990s, many high-profile campaigns used "Satellite media tours" to reach a large number of stations in a short period of time. From a single studio, a candidate could be interviewed by one television reporter after another (Ouzounian 1997, 51). As the Internet gained bandwidth, video could be sent to news outlets as digital files posted on the campaign's Web site or, later still, social media sites. YouTube, launched in 2005, quickly saw the posting of user-generated political ads. Candidates began announcing their runs on YouTube (Shea and Reece 2008). When Obama announced he was running for president, the posting of his announcement on YouTube was a newsworthy event in itself. YouTube gave the story better legs and more exposure. An increasing number of small-town campaign events are posted online in the search for coverage by mainstream media outlets. Posting of newly released campaign ads on a YouTube channel is common practice.

### Backgrounding

A campaign might get its message out with nonattributed "backgrounders." Reporters shy from anonymous sources but often report information from campaigns without direct attribution. (Political bloggers are less cautious.) The messages might appear as informational data, or as "leaks." Many so-called leaks are given to reporters by authorized parties who strike a deal to remain anonymous (see Devine 2008). The use of nonattributed sourcing is controversial among journalists, and some outlets try to maintain standards on the practice (see National Public Radio n.d., "Anonymous sources").

## News Conferences

If the news release may be called a campaign's workhorse, the news conference is the campaign's show horse. News conferences bring reporters into a controlled environment to see and hear the candidate. They allow for personal explanations of complex issues or dramatic campaign developments, and they give reporters the chance to ask questions. Although the odds of coverage are poor for run-of-the-mill political items, many candidates use news conferences to announce their candidacies. News conferences are also employed to level attacks, defend against opponents' charges, introduce new rounds of campaign commercials, announce important endorsements, highlight fundraising activities, introduce celebrity supporters, and so forth.

In deciding whether to cover a news conference, assignment editors must weigh the merits of getting the story firsthand against the price of sending a reporter into the field. This balancing act suggests that the topic of the news conference should be exceptionally important and that the news conference itself must be logistically straightforward. Even when these conditions are met, most candidates still have a hard time getting coverage. If reporters choose to cover a candidate's news conference at all, their story may not carry the message that a campaign has in mind. A pointless news conference will be scorned by the media and might be the last one that reporters cover: "If you call a press conference and it ain't news, they might not cover you again" (Shirley 1997, 23). The campaign might be written off or, worse yet, ridiculed. After all, the campaign wasted the reporters' scarce time; *someone* will have to pay.

If the campaign chooses to proceed with a news conference, notice is sent to each outlet, outlining the importance of the issue, where and when the news conference will be held, and the name and telephone number of the contact person. Campaigns may then follow up with e-mails, telephone calls, or personal visits. Prodding may tip the scales. Pushing too hard can have the opposite effect.

Preparation is crucial. In new-style campaigns, close attention is paid to the backdrop behind the candidate. Good visuals are a boon to the campaign and the media—a powerful shot helps convey the right message while giving an incentive for media outlets to run the story. Well-organized campaigns help the shoot go as smoothly as possible. A "mult box" can let several television and radio stations plug into the candidate's microphone simultaneously. Good angles are established in consultation with camera operators, and the distance between the press riser and satellite trucks will be paced off beforehand. If the campaign wishes to make the 6:00 P.M. news, the event might be held at 3:00 P.M., leaving plenty of time for editing; the same logic applies to newspaper deadlines. Smart campaigns pay attention to parking and electrical power; seating; room for recording equipment, lights, and cameras; and the menu for a complimentary lunch.

## Media Events

The struggle for attention has led candidates to walk across states, do blue-collar jobs, sleep among the homeless, clean up neighborhoods, visit toxic waste sites, meet with senior citizens, greet workers at factory gates, and climb into hot-air balloons. In 2004, John Kerry went on a goose-hunting expedition in Ohio. It seems no coincidence that a candidate holding a low rating with the National Rifle Association would choose to go hunting in a swing state where gun rights were important to many voters (Romano 2004). One of the most memorable political media events in recent history came when Barack Obama delivered a speech to 200,000 people in Berlin on a visit to Germany during the 2008 campaign (Issenberg 2008). The dramatic setting and monumental turnout conveyed the sense that Obama was popular overseas and adept at handling international affairs.

The challenge of earned media is message control. While supporters probably thought Obama's speech in Berlin and Kerry's hunt in Ohio were perfectly good ideas, some believed otherwise. The image of Kerry in camouflage was used to portray the senator from Massachusetts as a phony politician trying to hide his patrician background (Hurt 2004), and the popularity of Obama, as evidenced by adoring European crowds, was cited as proof that the Democrat was a celebrity, not a leader, and the imagery was used in opposition advertising.

There is an art to event construction. All the rules for political staging apply: There must be enough chairs to seat the attendees but not so many that the event looks poorly attended. The lighting must be bright enough to distinguish the candidate from the background but not so powerful that the candidate starts to sweat. Unlike a news conference, the idea behind a news event is that the action itself is the message. When things go right, the result is a great picture and positive coverage. When things go wrong, the message can be disastrous. During the 1996 presidential race, Bob Dole fell through the railings of his stage at a campaign stop, a mishap that reflected on the competence of the Dole campaign and "led to questions about the senator's age and physical health" (Sockowitz 2008). Good advance staffers check every detail of event staging. It is not beneath an operative's dignity to jump up and down on a riser checking for squeaky joints and weak spots. And they might carry "the absolutely essential tools of the trade: Sharpies, a roll of duct tape and lots of index cards" (ibid.).

Michael Deaver, master of "the picture" for Ronald Reagan, thought the image must convey the message before a single word is spoken. "I am sure the purists, who want their news unfiltered and their heroes unrehearsed, gag on the word *visuals*," he wrote, "but in the Television Age, [an event] hasn't happened, or at least it hasn't registered, if people can't see what you see" (Deaver and Herskowitz 1987, 141). Matthew Bennett, who served as trip director for Vice President Al Gore, said in 2000 that visuals are important because "we can't control the decisions made by the writer or editor about what will be covered" (M. Bennett, pers. comm. 2000); if Gore wanted to talk about policy but all the media wanted to run was a "horse race story," the advance team could at least convey the intended message visually.

### Debates

For many local and minor-party candidates, a debate might be a rare opportunity to earn media coverage. Reportage on debates is generally balanced, meaning that each candidate gets about the same amount of attention. Unlike high-profile presidential or gubernatorial debates, there are few winners or losers at the local level; not enough people see them to make a difference. Debates can help poorly funded candidates get their names out—which is precisely why front-runners are often reluctant to debate. There is no reason to give a lagging opponent this kind of exposure. Nevertheless, most high-level candidates are expected to discuss the issues in the presence of their opponents. Approximately nine out of ten House and Senate candidates debate their opponents (Herrnson 2012, 242).

Candidates who want to maximize news coverage might gear their remarks more to the news media than to the audience at home. Many people who attend debates personally or watch debates on television have already made up their minds, but influential reporters and editorial boards pay close attention. Clear, brief, and novel statements are important. Sometimes candidates are confrontational, or just plain strange. New wrinkles and off-the-cuff deviations can draw media attention. Anything out of the ordinary might catch the eye. A candidate might hold up the opponent's campaign literature or cite a scandal story. A debate in Vermont "featured interesting apparel and a heated discussion of a wide variety of topics including; aluminum nanoparticles, the 'Zionist regime,' bathrooms at highway rest areas, and a potential nuclear disaster near the city of Burlington" (Walker and Campbell 2014).

Aggressive tactics can bring media backlash. When a 2008 debate between Minnesotans Norm Coleman and Al Franken took an angry tone, with both candidates hurling accusations at each other, minor-party contender Dean Barkley started to look like a viable alternative (Condon 2008). New Yorker Jimmy McMillan rose to notoriety in multiple elections by regularly working the phrase "the rent is too damn high" into his responses. Jon Huntsman saw his popularity with hardline conservatives slip during the 2012 Republican primaries when he chose to speak in Mandarin on stage. And in 2014, Charlie Crist and Rick Scott gave the media eminently watchable TV when Scott delayed the beginning of a debate while contesting Crist's use of a cooling fan at his lectern.

Candidates should be well prepared, because the media are primed to seize on gaffes. Candidates who deviate from the preset message place themselves at risk. Gerald Ford may have sunk his chances to win the 1976 election when he opined in the course of a debate with Jimmy Carter, "[T]here is no Soviet dominance of Eastern Europe." Michael Dukakis seemed to miss the point of the question, "If [your wife] Kitty Dukakis were raped and murdered, would you favor an irrevocable death penalty for the killer?" when the Massachusetts governor replied, "No, I don't, and I think you know that I've opposed the death penalty during all of my life," and went on to discuss constitutional issues. Sarah Palin's performance in the 2008 vice presidential debate seemed *overly* scripted and insufficiently responsive to either the questions or her opponent—illustrating the downside of a trend toward preparing candidates with briefing books, canned replies, cutting attacks, and clever defensive maneuvers. A meme from that debate: Palin's flirty wink to the viewing audience.

## Editorial Boards

Newspaper editorial boards often meet with candidates before granting an endorsement. These meetings are akin to debates, except that the questioning is typically from a single news outlet to a single candidate. Candidates are typically asked about politics and policy, and the answers are often reported in the board's endorsement. Video of the question-and-answer session might be released to the public. A meeting with the *Milwaukee Journal Sentinel* board accelerated the downward spiral of businessman Herman Cain's presidential campaign when, seemingly unable to sort out a question on foreign policy, Cain admitted that he had "all this stuff twirling around in my head" (*Milwaukee Journal Sentinel* 2011).

As Election Day nears, daily and weekly newspapers declare their preferences in editorial endorsements. Reporters play an advisory role in the endorsement process; they are sometimes asked for their opinions, but the final determination is typically not theirs to make. Campaigns that get the nod might reprint the endorsement for last-minute literature drops. Unfortunately, the editorial decision could wind up going the wrong way.

A strong showing is not always necessary to win. Joni Ernst, who was firmly ahead in her race for the U.S. Senate, skipped the editorial boards in Iowa and thus avoided questioning (Jacobs 2014a). John Kasich in running for reelection as Ohio's governor, appeared before the editorial board of the *Cleveland Plain Dealer* without a tie and barely acknowledged that his opponent, who was invited to the meeting along with the governor, was sitting in the room (Gomez 2014). Ernst lost endorsements while Kasich gained the *Plain Dealer*'s nod; both candidates won their respective contests.

## Opinion Outlets

Candidates for local office are rarely invited to appear on national talk shows, but opportunities might be available on local radio and television and on the editorial page. The prevailing wisdom is that "placing an op-ed is one of the most difficult things to do in public relations. Especially if your client or candidate is not a well-known figure" (Shirley 1997, 23). The reason: Lots of people want to get their opinions in the paper, so editors have a large number of op-eds from which to choose. An alternative route is a humble letter to the editor. A campaign might try to get letters into a broad range of newspapers in hopes that the candidate's arguments will be read far and wide. And in today's diverse media environment, newspapers might be skipped in favor of guest columns in politically oriented blogs run by traditional media outlets or those that are strictly new media.

### Social Media

Bloggers have gained prominence as watchdogs, muckrakers, incen-diaries, and fact checkers. Traditional news outlets allow readers to post instant reactions to unfolding news events, heightening the sense of participation—and sometimes the reality of participation, as in the case of political amateurs like "Obama Girl," who released a catchy, funny, and seductive video supporting her favored candi-date. YouTube and other video-sharing sites allow small campaigns to post clips and forward them to supporters. Poignant segments from campaign events, such as the kickoff, a debate, a press confer-ence, or an endorsement from a respected luminary, might be posted online and spread around the country.

In the 2008 campaign, online social networking emerged as an im-portant component of campaign strategy. Social networks had been around for several years but had rarely been used in campaign poli-tics. Online tools have included chat rooms, messaging, video and photo posting, blogging and video blogging, discussion forums, file sharing, and more. The growth of Facebook soon eclipsed competi-tors, and candidates learn how to use it, and other forms of social media, in a manner that works for their particular campaign and style (Miller 2013b).

Twitter is now a key communications tool—for candidates mak-ing quick announcements, for journalists commenting on issues, for bloggers pushing stories, and for political enthusiasts who had rarely been given a public outlet before the advent of social media. Ted Cruz used social media to good effect in his 2012 election to the U.S. Senate. Cruz announced his candidacy on a conference call with bloggers who leaned toward his brand of politics and kept close touch with them throughout the campaign. A consultant who worked on the race reported that "Ted met with bloggers in per-son and via phone often, and the campaign created a robust blogger action center encouraging bloggers to post supportive widgets, and created a segmented email list to update bloggers from" (Harris 2012). The campaign supplemented "organic"—that is, authentic user—support with promoted tweets.

One downside of using social media to keep in touch with constituents is its encouragement of rapid response without reflection. In 2012, Louisiana congressman John Fleming used his Facebook account to chastise Planned Parenthood's "abortion by wholesale" with a link to a satirical article in the Onion about an "$8 Billion Abortionplex." Fleming deleted the post and the Onion's editor released a statement in response: "We're delighted to hear that Rep. Fleming is a regular reader of America's Finest News Source and doesn't bother himself with The New York Times, Washington Post, the mediums of television and radio, or any other lesser journalism outlets" (Weinger 2012). A columnist in the *Shreveport Times* listed the mistake as one of "a few reasons not to re-elect Fleming" (Stephens 2014).

Another downside of social media is that communications directors may feel they need to keep pace with the tornadic flurry of texts and tweets. An instinct developed prior to political media saturation that all public comments require attention may not work in the Digital Age. And the allure of easy delivery may itself be problematic. A communications consultant warns, "Snark, substance-less witticisms, and gotcha moments on social media have replaced the hard spade work of pitching stories, developing relationships with reporters, and the basics of an efficient press operation" (Harris 2014).

## Conclusion

James Carville has called news media "the Beast"—if the campaign does not feed it, it feeds on the campaign. Problems with the Wendy Davis communications team in Texas, from simple logistics to an apparent suspicion of the news media, led to abundant reporting on gaffes and how those gaffes reflected on Davis's candidacy. Political reporter Dave Mann wrote, "Davis' team often treated the press with suspicion, asking repeatedly what a story would say before granting access to staffers, refusing to confirm basic campaign scheduling details and shielding Davis from in-person interviews with some major outlets." "[T]hese are the kind of errors that only journalists care about," Mann said, but they are "the stuff of endless reporter gripe sessions" (Mann 2014; see also Tilove 2014).

Reporters, editors, and bloggers matter, and they are all under pressure. The 24-hour news environment has erased the old deadlines, with regional and statewide news networks transforming the character of local races. Bloggers create and rehash news in real time. Campaigns have long relied on newspapers, radio, and television to carry the earned-media message, and online news consumption is becoming more and more prevalent. Aggregator sites are among the most popular today by bringing together numerous stories of interest to a reader or listener and permitting them to view them from that one place. And as voters start receiving news in their cars and on the run, with direct feeds to handheld devices, the news environment is undergoing drastic change.

# CHAPTER 10

# Direct Voter Contact

Whereas television and radio broadcast messages to a wide demographic, direct voter contact reaches out to individuals in hopes that the right message aimed at the right person can move a voter the right way. Direct contact might come in the form of a candidate visit, a neighborhood volunteer canvass, a phone call, an e-mail, a piece of campaign literature sent through U.S. Postal Service, an SMS text message from a good friend, or promoted message on Facebook. Ironically, with the rise of technologies that allow for detailed, computerized segmentation of the electorate, voter contact becomes easier to achieve on a mass scale, though perhaps less personal. How many voters believe an urgent request for funds was sent from the president's laptop?

This chapter discusses the purposes of direct contact, field experimentation, social pressure, types of direct contact, get-out-the-vote drives, and issues relating to voter protection, ballot integrity, and recounts.

## Purposes of Direct Contact

Direct contact is frequently used to find and register new voters. While the numbers vary from one district to another, citizens aged 65 to 74 have the highest registration rate—roughly 80 percent—whereas those aged 18 to 24 have the lowest—about 54 percent (U.S. Census Bureau 2012). Voter registration can be an important part of a direct contact effort. Subject to local laws, a campaign volunteer might visit the homes of unregistered but eligible people and try to persuade residents to fill out a voter registration card. Unregistered people tend to have weak partisan ties, so when these voters *are* registered, they may or may not be open to the kind of persuasion that will get them to cast a ballot—but these new voters may well be missing from opposition lists. Perhaps the only campaign material new registrants receive will come from the candidate who signed them up.

A training manual from the Florida Democratic Party lists persuasion as one of the top goals of voter contact: "Repetitively move the campaign's message to key groups, areas, and individuals in an effort to persuade them to support your candidate" (Florida Democratic Party n.d., 1). Every election cycle, voters receive pastel-hued self-introductions from candidates, along with black-and-white attacks on the opposition. According to the Florida Democrats, "Over the last decade, direct mail has become a powerful campaign tool. As television and radio costs have skyrocketed, direct mail has become more cost effective." Importantly, this form of contact "can be used to send specific messages directly to target voters" (ibid., 3).

Toward the end of a campaign, the purpose of direct contact shifts to getting out the vote. The stereotype of this activity involves volunteers firing up buses and vans to drive elderly voters to the polls. While GOTV operatives still use this well-tested approach, efforts to maximize turnout among supporters has become increasingly high-tech. Not only is microtargeting helping campaigns focus on the most valuable voters, but also the outreach to voters now relies on blast e-mails, SMS texting, and social media outreach—none of which existed nor could have been readily conceived in the heyday of mass-media campaigning.

## Field Experimentation

Because direct contact is, by definition, aimed at individual voters, it opens opportunities for experimentation. While strategists continue to spend heavily on survey research and still operate from gut instinct, more and more campaigns are testing methods and hypotheses in the real world (Hesla, Leibowitz, and Peavey 2013). A headline in *Campaigns & Elections* announced the "Evidence Based Evolution" (Trish 2012). Until recently, experimental field studies were rarely employed, but the scholarly literature on voter behavior now includes an array of high-quality field experiments measuring the effects of voter mobilization campaigns.

Scholars are keenly aware of weaknesses in survey research: Human recall is imperfect, respondents sometimes lie, and responses can be ambiguous. More importantly, a wide array of factors might influence a voter, so the potential for interference from confounding variables abounds. The difficulty of distinguishing correlation from causation can be acute. Analysts are commonly frustrated in their attempts to isolate the typical impact of a single factor (or group of factors) from infrequent elections that are influenced by countless variables. By manipulating one or a few factors and comparing test groups against control groups, analysts can narrow questions of effect to a more manageable set of problems.

At the turn of the new millennium, scholars Alan S. Gerber and Donald P. Green were publishing results from randomized field experiments on voter mobilization. Voting records in the United States are publicly available, so interested parties, including researchers, can find out who voted in any given election. They will not learn for whom the vote was cast but will know whether or not it *was* cast. Public records are a boon to field experimentation. If a strategist randomly distributes members of a sample into control and treatment groups, and then administers a treatment (like a postcard urging people to go to the polls on Election Day), differences in turnout between the treated and untreated groups might reveal themselves (Gerber and Green 2012), leading to data-informed tactics.

The literature on voter mobilization revolves around a theoretical question: What prompts people to vote? That is, can a campaign prompt a voter to cast a ballot by offering some information (such as the location of the polling place or the stakes in the election), or is a voter more likely to turn out on Election Day when the voter believes participation is part of a larger social activity?

Green and Gerber argue the existing evidence shows the relative power of highly personalized appeals. "Door-to-door canvassing by friends and neighbors" works far better than "[a]utomatically dialed, prerecorded GOTV phone calls" (2008, 10). According to Green and Gerber, "the decision to vote is strongly shaped by one's social environment" (137). Voting is more than a strictly cognitive activity, so techniques that rely on information seem short-sighted: "One may be able to nudge turnout upward slightly by making voting more convenient, supplying voters with information, and reminding them of an imminent election, but these effects are small in comparison to what happens when voters are placed in a social milieu that urges participation" (ibid.).

Proponents of a more cognitive orientation may counter the social voting theory with the findings of Allison Dale and Aaron Strauss (2009).

In 2006, Dale and Strauss tested whether a simple reminder could increase turnout. If straightforward information could mobilize voters, then the theory of social influence requires adjustment. Working alongside political organizations, the analysts set aside portions of targeted populations as control groups and sent SMS text messages reminding people to vote. The result was a three percentage point increase in turnout among voters who received that message. At the price of about 10 cents per SMS, the cost per vote gained was $3.00. Dale and Strauss conclude that "voter mobilization organizations can boost turnout with a message delivered through an impersonal medium" (2009, 300).

Experimental findings raise questions about external validity— that is, the degree to which the results of a given test will have similar effect in other times and places. Dale and Strauss (2009) took note of a 1925 mail experiment that boosted turnout by nine percentage points. Over the years, as postboxes became crowded with junk, the effect of traditional mail outreach diminished. Now that all kinds of text messages fill smartphones, SMS reminders may not carry the same impact as they did in 2006.

Beyond their findings on particular mobilization tactics, experimental research is changing the way strategists think about voter mobilization and research on voter behavior.

1. *Randomized, controlled field experimentation has popularized cost-sensitive analysis.* A tactic that can increase voter turnout by four percentage points sounds better than a tactic that increases turnout by 2 percent, *unless* the doubly effective method comes at triple the price. Cost-based metrics allow for meaningful comparisons across tactical options, as discussed in chapter 4.
2. *The cost of mobilizing voters is quite high.* Dale and Strauss found a bargain when they computed text messaging at $3 per vote gained. Green and Gerber worked out higher costs for other tactics: door-knocking is inexpensive (about $29 per vote gained) compared to paid phone calls (about $53 to $90 per vote gained) (2008, 139).
3. *Analysts must pay attention to the relationship between effect size and sample size.* Where effects are small, only a very large sample will detect causation at an accepted level of significance. A massive sample can demonstrate a statistically significant effect that is too small to mean much. Significant results are not always meaningful, and vice versa. Hence the virtue of cost-based analysis.

Experimental research cannot displace opinion surveys, but field experimentation continues to progress. Scholars are looking at political phenomena from new angles; strategists are "version-testing" campaign Web sites to increase click-throughs and donations. "The next generation of experiments," Green speculates, "will take advantage of ready access to a wide array of different geographic media markets and maybe even individual level media markets with the ability to increasingly target messages to individuals" (*Campaigns & Elections* 2012).

A smart campaign operative might (randomly) remove some voters from a mailing list in order to have a control group against which to measure data from the treatment group of recipients (perhaps in the run-up to a traditional survey). An operative's "big idea"—and big ideas based on political hunches frequently end badly (Tetlock 2009)—can be tested by scientific methods. GOP strategist Adam B. Schaeffer and Nancy Smith counsel, "We do not know what works until we test it, repeatedly, using experiments," because "[r]andomized-controlled experiments allow us to block out all the other 'noise' and pinpoint precisely how a message or tactic changes voter behavior" (2013). Schaeffer argues that knowledge gained from one cycle can be refined in the next, and wonders if a narrow loss such as Ken Cuccinelli's 2013 defeat by 2.5 percentage points in Virginia might have been preventable with "a full embrace of true experiments and rigorous research" (ibid.).

## Social Pressure

In a landmark experiment, Gerber and Green found that face-to-face voter mobilization efforts were more effective than impersonal modes such as telephone calls (2000). Since publication of that research, scholars have widened their agenda to a long list of questions about the effectiveness of social pressure tactics, explicit and implicit (see Green and Gerber 2008). Much experimental research supports the idea that group solidarity can enhance voter turnout. Costas Panagopoulos finds that unmarried women and minorities are receptive to "positive social pressure"—for example, "invoking positive emotions, such as pride," mobilizes people to vote (2013, 266).

Social pressure has been called "GOTV for the Little Guy" (Malchow 2013). In the 2014 runoff for San Diego mayor, the Republican candidate noticed that a large number of Republicans have missed the general election. The campaign team wrote, "Several weeks out from

Election Day, we launched social pressure mail, phone, text and field programs" (Roe, Dichiara, and Puetz 2014). The mail included hand-written letters and brash "mailers, with the voter's name in bold letters, which read, 'John Doe, public records show you failed to vote in the primary'" (ibid., 40). The campaign reported little blowback to the aggressive tactic, but some analysts suggest that vote-shaming is risky (Bump 2014b).

Social pressure has been defined in terms of voters' need for the approval of others. Green and Gerber argue, "[S]ocial pressure communications typically involve three ingredients: They admonish the receiver to adhere to a social norm, indicate that the receiver's compliance will be monitored, and suggest that the monitored behavior will be publicized" (Green and Gerber 2010).

Controlled field experimentation has allowed political scientists to test many forms of voter outreach by varying, among other things, the mode of contact. Findings presage interest in further experimentation by scholars who asked whether social pressure could activate a sense of civic duty among voters. Personal contact can be expanded beyond face-to-face engagement to include feelings of surveillance. In a classic experiment, strategist Hal Malchow sent mailers to prospective voters in a 2009 New Jersey race that included a voter's turnout histories and some friendly suasion: "We hope to be able to thank you in the future for being the kind of citizen who makes our democracy work" (Issenberg 2010). Turnout was significantly enhanced.

Gerber, Green, and Christopher Larimer have found social pressure can have a deep impact on voter turnout when the pressure is repeated, and the strategic implications are clear: "Although we are not advocates of shaming tactics or policies, their cost-effectiveness makes them an inevitable development in political campaign craft" (2008, 42; but also see Mann 2010).

Digital age social pressure has been transmitted among a voter's online "friend" network. In a large-scale (61 million persons) experiment, Robert M. Bond and colleagues ran a controlled experiment on Facebook users during the 2010 midterm election. News feeds were populated with either an informational message or a social-pressure message, or neither (for a control). The social pressure message included an "I Voted" button and data on others who had also voted (including some pictures). Results from the experiment "suggest the Facebook social message increased turnout directly by about 60,000 voters and indirectly through social contagion by another

280,000 voters, for a total of 340,000 additional votes," or about 0.14% of the voting age population (Bond and Fowler 2012, 297).

## Types of Direct Contact

Direct voter contact (DVC) can be separated into four categories: *candidate, volunteer, mail* (including e-mail and SMS texts), and *social media*. Each form of politicking has its own costs and benefits, and each is likely enhanced by shrewd targeting and wise timing. Candidate contact taps a limited resource: a candidate's own time and energy. Volunteer efforts rely on (and perhaps build up) supporter enthusiasm. A mail drive is less intimate but can be cast more broadly. Finally, social media campaigning, which encourages supporters to reach out to friends, family, and Internet acquaintances, depends heavily on technologies and relationships that did not exist in the recent past.

### *Candidate Contact*

The pinnacle of DVC is a conversation between a candidate and a voter. Voters who meet a candidate might be persuaded by physical appearance or body language. Facial expressions, hand movements, and vocal inflections can mean a great deal. Also, the candidate is taking time to have a conversation, and that suggests the importance of the voter. Personal campaigning humanizes a candidate. In time when many people are obsessed with their social media presence, voters might appreciate the chance to see their candidates as people, not products.

Some candidates use coffee klatches and cocktail parties to meet voters. A supporter invites neighbors to his or her home, and the candidate drops by for a visit. Holding several get-togethers on the same evening allows the candidate to touch base with a large number of voters. Major-party candidates might attend house parties virtually with recorded messages or online appearances. Alternatively, candidates might visit regularly scheduled meetings of civic and business organizations or accept invitations to speak to these groups. Appearing at a factory during a shift change or at a subway stop during rush hour can mean a lot of voter contact over a short period of time— many dozen hands might be shaken in 15 minutes during a morning when little else is going on. Giving voters an opportunity to chat informally helps candidates build strong connections.

A candidate can go overboard with handshakes, however. If a candidate believes the best way to meet voters is to visit the local mall or county fair or to stand on the street corner because "thousands of people will be there," it is worth considering that scattershot approaches are antithetical to new-style campaigning. The campaign organization would not likely know people's residency, partisan predisposition, or registration status. It would be a return to the scattershot approach. Efficient campaigning is not about meeting as many people as possible; untargeted activities can be an inefficient use of time.

Given that time is a scarce resource, targeting would seem the best option. Targeting is particularly important when candidates knock on doors and chat with the people they meet inside.

*The Walk Plan.* Candidate walks start with "walk sheets" containing the names, party affiliations, and perhaps some biographical data on the occupants of each house in a targeted neighborhood. The walk sheet might read:

- 1 Maple Street: Alma Jones (R), Morris Jones (R)
- 3 Maple Street: DeShawn Williams (D), Imani Williams (D), Deja Williams (D)
- Maple Street: Enrique Hernandez (I)
- 9 Maple Street: Betty Hill (D), Camila Jimenez (R)

By listing only the voters who live in odd- or even-numbered houses, the candidate can work one side of the street at a time. Party affiliations allow the candidate to skip disobliging households if the lists have not been filtered to exclude unhelpful voters. Rather than going into a neighborhood with a modest idea of individual voter concerns, microtargeting can help candidates be selective about their approach.

In preparation for the walk, cards can be mailed to each household (or, if the campaign is short on funds, the materials can be hand-delivered by volunteers). These "prewalk cards" might contain a picture of the candidate and a small note, something like:

I'll be stopping by in the next few days to visit. I hope we get a chance to discuss your concerns and what I might do in the state legislature to help.

Prewalk cards can serve several purposes. They get the candidate's name and message out, prime the voter for a visit, and can provide a picture of the candidate so the voter knows who is coming to the door. Prewalk card suggests that the candidate will "listen to the people" even if the resident is not at home.

*The Walk.* Volunteers from the neighborhood can introduce the candidate to all the residents, maybe providing background information along the way ("Mrs. Smith is a retired teacher who loves bird-watching"), or giving a quick rundown of the area ("We used to have a toy factory here"). The volunteer can carry the walk sheet (allowing the candidate to shake hands), keep the candidate on task, provide directions, and serve as the "bad cop" when needed. If a cheerful voter is eager to have the candidate in for coffee and cookies, the volunteer will suggest that they need to be moving along.

After shaking hands at the door and engaging in a brief discussion, the candidate might provide an informational pamphlet in hopes that the voter will read the material once he or she goes back inside. Immediately after the meeting, the volunteer can record summaries of the conversation: the name of the person contacted, the voter's concerns, the voter's hobbies, and so forth.

If the voter is not at home, the candidate might leave a handwritten note on the back of the literature:

Sorry I missed you. I stopped by to say hello and discuss your concerns, and perhaps we can get a chance to talk another time. Please feel free to call.

The notes can be written in advance so that the candidate and the volunteer are able to move steadily along.

Careful attention to details distinguish a targeting walk plan from an untargeted canvass in which the candidate simply knocks on doors. To the voters who were found at home, a follow-up mailing might be sent after the visit. The mailing thanks the voter for his or her time and highlights the candidate's commitment to voter input. Any information or material that the voter requested should probably be sent forthwith. Data gained during these sorts of efforts can be integrated into campaign databases, allowing for additional targeting of advertisements and later contacts.

### Volunteer Outreach

A volunteer canvass mirrors the candidate walk plan except that members of the campaign team, not the candidate, go door-to-door.

Like a candidate's prewalk card, a note might be sent indicating that "a volunteer will be stopping by soon." Door-to-door workers will hopefully be familiar with the campaign's message; training sessions and scripts can help, and the importance of careful recordkeeping as to who was home (and who was not) and the interests of the contacted voters might be stressed. A follow-up note from the candidate might say, "Thanks for chatting with one of my volunteers." In the closing days of the campaign, this sort of canvass can become a door-to-door blitz.

Unlike the canvass, "literature drops" entail simply placing a piece of campaign literature on the porch or in the doorjamb; they are not meant to involve a conversation. A drop can be done by anyone, including volunteers unfamiliar with the candidate—even kids. The idea is to cover an area quickly. Drops might be much less expensive than mailings (no postage required) or less time-consuming than a conversation during a canvass, and they may be helpful in improving early name recognition or during a last-minute push.

Literature on several different topics can be dropped according to probable household interests in hopes that a tailored message would prove more successful in motivating potential voters to cast their ballot than would a generic piece of campaign literature. In the contemporary campaign environment, volunteers might expect their walk lists to come with data-overlay maps that pinpoint where each house can be found along with records of past contacts. Deliberations about proper targeting should probably include the density of voters, so as to avoid rural areas with large lawns that take time to walk and large dogs that prevent the walking.

Telephone banks are another way to reach many voters in short order. They keep volunteers busy, particularly those not able to walk door-to-door, and they are relatively inexpensive. Empirical evidence suggests that telephone contacts made by local volunteers seem to be an efficient means of turning out voters, while computerized "robo calls" appeared to be less effective (Green and Gerber 2008). Additionally, robo calls are subject to a range of legal restrictions (Weisbaum 2014).

A full-service phone operation has three elements: persuasion, identification, and activation. A persuasion pitch targets voters with a brief message. In a voter-identification process, the key would be a few short questions regarding the voters' preferences in the coming election—who they intend to vote for, what their main concerns are, and so on. This information is carefully recorded, and voters are marked as "for," "against," or "undecided." Undecideds might be given another call, mailed information on the candidate, or perhaps visited by a volunteer. Activation calls urge persuaded voters to go to the polls on Election Day. The activation list might start with those labeled "for" during the identification phase, but the list might also include those deemed merely *likely* to support the candidate.

The number of phone contacts that can be made during a given period of time can be predicted with a good deal of accuracy by multiplying the number of volunteers by the number of hours each volunteer will spend on the phone by the number of calls a volunteer can make per hour. Some evenings will have more volunteers than others and some will see fewer hours of service, but a campaign can estimate how long it will take to make a series of telephone contacts before the end of the campaign. Some campaigns hire professional telemarketing firms to carry out this operation.

### Direct Mail, E-Mail, and SMS

Direct mail can be a powerful weapon in new-style campaigning due to its precision and because it operates quietly. GOP strategist Richard Viguerie has said that "direct mail is like a water moccasin—silent but deadly" (quoted in Meredith 2004/2005, 37). If a campaign fears that fish-and-game voters are worried about gun rights, a direct mail campaign might identify these voters and send a pro-gun message to this narrow group.

Direct mail allows the campaign to create a running narrative whereby each piece builds on the prior mailing. Through the course of the campaign, a detailed story can be told. Direct mail can also complement other outreach activities, such as radio and television advertisements. Voters hear the message on their way home from work and then read the same message as they open their mail in the evening. Mailers also allow for the creative use of pictures, graphics, and charts. A piece of direct mail might reproduce an editorial, an endorsement, or a scathing (but helpful) news story. It might offer a picture of the candidate or the opponent, or it might present a telling photograph. Direct mail is not cheap, but it can be highly targeted— much more so than television and radio advertising.

Many campaigns hire direct mail firms to produce, label, and mail their literature, though others call upon volunteers to do all the work. Many volunteers enjoy the camaraderie. Large tables can be set up in one location, and a team of helpers can eat pizza, drink soda, and affix labels to mailers. If a campaign is fortunate enough to have a legion of unpaid assistants, it might consider addressing mailings by hand. Some voters who discard mass-produced literature might still open a hand-addressed envelope. Hand-addressing may be a good way to communicate a specific message to a targeted group of voters. The job is labor-intensive even for short lists, but a student won a seat in the West Virginia House of Delegates at the age of 18—she was too young to vote in the primary—after sending 3,500 handwritten letters. Her father, a state senator, said it was one of the "tricks I wanted to do for a long time" (Hesse 2014).

Simply adding a Web address to a postcard can leverage the mailer's impact. An advocacy campaign for a gambling initiative in Ohio attached an application for an absentee ballot to a large flyer urging citizens to "Vote by Mail. Vote Yes on Issue 3." A 2014 postcard sent by the Kentucky Republican Party used holograms to seemingly morph Democratic Senate candidate Alison Grimes into Barack Obama (Jaffe 2014). All of which is to say that mail can be more than just mail.

Microtargeting is taking a strong role in the direct mail business as well. If voters are ranked by their persuadability or their likelihood of voting, it makes sense to mail them based on those scores. Technology strategist Ravi Singh has said: "I don't necessarily have to print 5,000 or 50,000 pieces. Rather than waiting for a scheduled drop, I can do pieces in response to my strategies" (Blanchfield 2007). While microtargeting is primarily employed by high-level campaigns with financial clout, campaign organizations farther down the ballot are also beginning to use this tactic, forcing new innovations in mail. "The next frontier," believes a team of Democratic consultants, "is embedding computer chips in direct mail pieces. . . . Just wave your mobile phone over the mail piece [and the] computer chip will then match tested messaging to the user's profile and online history, generating a personalized message for the user" (Mack and Henry 2012).

Direct mail takes time to produce and to move through the postal system. Several days can pass while the campaign and mail consultant produce, label, and send a piece of literature. And yet, while other methods are faster, consultant Liz Chadderdon argues that, no matter how much people may utilize or rely upon the Internet, they will always have a physical address they call home (2009).

E-mail is not replacing postal mailers outright but is a growing part of new-style message strategy, raising new challenges. Using a commercial e-mail service can be important because spam filters are sensitive to e-mail that Internet providers deem unwanted, and moving mail through the system without getting blacklisted is increasingly difficult for amateur messaging. A Democratic operation acknowledges the further problem of impersonality, with, perhaps, a touch of irony: "We want to be as personal as possible. It's all part of a tremendous science that is now very important to campaigns" (Weber 2014). A Republican operative adds that "technology has been a real game-changer in voter contact. The more you can personalize and segment different voters, the more you can communicate with them about specific issues" (Weber 2014). As a result, voters end up receiving e-mails that "appear more like pleas from a penniless buddy or an ex-girlfriend" than a formal communication from a candidate seeking one's support or money (ibid.).

SMS text messaging was used to some effect in the 2008 presidential election, especially by the Obama team, which, as noted previously, announced the choice of Joe Biden as vice presidential running mate via text message (though traditional news outlets actually broke the story first [Puzzanghera 2008]). Texts might be intended to rally supporters, solicit funds, or organize campaign events. By virtue of its permission-based nature—federal regulations require permission from a cell phone owner to send such a text message—text messaging serves primarily to build support among those already prepared to vote for a specific candidate, making it less-than-ideal for reaching undecided voters.

### Social Media

Howard Dean's presidential campaign was an early adopter of online grassroots technology—or as it is now known, *social media*. Dean's campaign manager, Joe Trippi, later wrote that the 2004 election

> was the opening salvo in a revolution, the sound of hundreds of thousands of Americans turning off their televisions and embracing the only form of technology that has allowed them to be involved again, to gain control of a process that alienated them decades ago. (2004, xviii–xix)

The reach of the 2008 Obama effort was massive, including some 13 million e-mail addresses, 7,000 distinct messages over a billion separate e-mails, a groundbreaking SMS texting program, 5 million voters signed up on social networking sites such as MySpace and

BlackPlanet, and a half billion dollars collected from the Internet (Vargas 2008). In 2012, Obama's numbers were more impressive. He had an additional 30 million Facebook friends, 22 million Twitter followers, $101 million in additional digital donations, and almost 500,000 total additional donors compared to his first campaign four years earlier. (Cohen 2012).

Strategist Kellen Giuda believes there will soon be a basic shift in strategy "from static information, such as mailers and robo-calls, toward real-time interaction. . . . Steadily, the age of political communication through static mediums is going to fade away as targeted real-time interaction takes its place" (Giuda 2012). Social networking sites such as Facebook and Twitter allow campaigns to reach a new, typically young and tech-savvy, group of voters. Potential supporters can add the candidate as a "friend," post comments on the candidate's profile, and share this information with online associates.

Capitalizing on the power of blogs, campaign Web sites, and social networking sites, Obama's supporters overwhelmed the McCain team in 2008 and Romney's in 2012. A visit to my.barackobama.com during the 2008 campaign allowed supporters to coordinate such events as an "Obama small family farms house meeting" (Caldwell 2008). These gatherings could be organized by supporters who had no formal connection to the campaign. In this way social media communication can occur horizontally, friend to friend, not vertically from the campaign down to the voters. With increasing opportunities to build support around their favorite candidates in the form of blogs, online commentaries, and video postings, campaign professionals are likely to find a double-edged sword. On one side, the opinions of a voter's friends, family, and other associates are a powerful source of political persuasion; on the other side, bloggers and other members of the Internet community are difficult to manage or keep on message.

Since social media is about relationships, "having a running start building those connections is a distinct benefit" (Rutledge 2013). In 2012, Obama had technological expertise and an established network up and running. Obama was able to dominate social media because his team understood how social networks actually work. As was explained after the election, "the real power of social media is not in the number of posts or Tweets but in user engagement measured by content spreadability" (Rutledge 2013).

A central advantage of a motivated social media base is speed. In 1996, Democrat Loretta Sanchez was able to defeat conservative Republican congressman Bob Dornan in California in part because she ran an under-the-radar outreach campaign that did not catch Dornan's attention until the final months of the election; Dornan had difficulty responding because he relied on direct mail fundraising for much of his campaign war chest (Burton and Shea 2003, 89–111). This episode can be compared to the near-defeat of Congresswoman Michele Bachmann of Minnesota in the final weeks of the 2008 cycle. When Bachmann said in an interview, "I am very concerned that [Obama] may have anti-American views" and "The American media [should] take a great look at the views of the people in Congress and find out, are they pro-America or anti-America?" the liberal blogs fired up, video was posted on political Web sites, e-mails raced among Democrats, and Bachmann's opponent raised $450,000 in 24 hours (Aquino 2008). In the new era of social media, campaigns will rarely fly under the radar.

## Get-Out-The-Vote Drives

The value of last-minute campaigning can be seen in the Oneonta, New York, school board election of Rosemary Shea, the late mother of this book's coauthor, Dan Shea. With an hour to go before the polls closed, the campaign team had exhausted its list of favorable voters. Two or three calls had been made to each. Determined to work until the last minute, the candidate scoured the list of those who had not yet voted. With 15 minutes left, she drove across town to visit a household of three would-be Democratic voters, convincing them to get into her car and be driven to the polls so that they could fulfill their "civic duty." With seconds to go, all three cast their ballots. Out of the thousands of votes cast, Shea won the election by exactly three.

GOTV efforts are among the most important activities undertaken during a campaign. While democratic principles call on everyone to vote on Election Day, the goal of a campaign's GOTV drive is to concentrate on voters most likely to support the candidate. Many approaches can be used to figure out the best contacts, including voter identification calls, demographic and survey research, and electoral history. One rule of thumb is to target roughly 10 percent of the votes needed for victory; "If you are running a state legislative race and need 15,000 votes to win, you must have at least 1,500 identified supporters whom you will push to the polls" (Allen 1990, 38). Last-minute pushes are designed to get the candidate's voters to the polls, not simply to kick up turnout across the board.

Donald Green and Alan Gerber (2008) have presented research showing what does and does not work when trying to get out the vote, charting the cost-effectiveness of different techniques. Are automated robo calls worth the time and money? They think not. Does it help to have a celebrity make the voice recording? Perhaps no. Are in-person visits effective? Yes, but are they more cost-effective than telephone-based programs? Sometimes. In the field, techniques that rely on volunteers have proven effective, particularly when the efforts are organized according to a thoughtful method.

The team might begin planning its GOTV drive about a month before Election Day. A plan may require assigning a coordinator, laying out specific tasks, setting deadlines for crucial jobs, naming the people responsible for completing them, and listing the resources needed for implementation. Shortly before the election, a GOTV mail piece might be sent to base voters. This mailer could stress the importance of the election and the difference that every vote can make. It might be a good idea to include an anecdote of an election won by just a few votes. If the campaign is strapped for cash, pamphlets can be hand-delivered.

As technology has advanced, new voting options have emerged. Many voters are casting ballots by mail. Early voting at centralized locations has also become quite popular. Early voters may have comprised nearly 32 percent of all voters in the 2012 election (McDonald 2013). In some states, residents can vote weeks ahead of the election. As of 2014, 33 states allowed some form of no-excuse early voting (NCSL 2014). Advocates say ease of voting is a boon for the democratic process and that absentee-style voting is quick, convenient, and less costly than traditional Election-Day voting, and the public seems willing to move in this direction.

Changes in voting procedures have important implications for campaign operatives. Quite possibly, eager voters might cast their votes early. These votes will already be "in the box," or "banked"; no more persuasion is needed. Mail-in ballots can encourage participation among low-frequency voters—those who are registered but have skipped a few elections or who vote only in presidential contests. Senior citizens might fall into this category. Whenever a new pool of voters is added to the electorate, uncertainty is created. Will electoral targeting prove accurate? Will new voters break for candidates of one party or the other?

Early voting procedures also shift strategic timing. Campaign workers must heed deadlines for the submission of mail-in or absentee and early voting ballots, making sure that would-be voters has this information as needed. In jurisdictions that provide such information, absentee lists might be secured from boards of elections. Volunteers can review these registries and "chase" the absentees with campaign mail until the absentee ballot shows as received by the board of elections. Campaigns might find an "Election Day" stretched to three or four weeks. Instead of building up to a single moment in time, a campaign might have to spread its most intense efforts—media buys, news events, and campaign mailings—over a month-long period, with attention paid to the first few days after the voting window opens.

On the eve of the election, intensity increases. The entire GOTV target group could be contacted by phone. The message on the phone might be quite similar to the message in a mailer already sent. Early on Election Day, e-mail and text messages might be shipped to likely supporters who still need to go out and vote. Some jurisdictions allow "poll watching." On the morning of the election, volunteers go to each polling place, find a comfortable place to sit, and record the names of each person who votes. The resulting lists are communicated to headquarters, where the names of those who have voted are scratched off a master list. By keeping track of which voters have already gone to the polls, the campaign knows who still needs a reminder.

Many people vote early in the morning or after work. Some people need assistance getting to the polls; child care and rides to the polling stations might be offered. This process continues throughout the evening, relying on updated lists from the poll watchers in order to keep track of recent voters. Prospective supporters are called until the polls close. A rally might be held in a targeted neighborhood. Massive literature drops might help, along with yard sign blitzes, literature distribution near polling places, and record retention at campaign headquarters before the soon-to-be-former staff make for the door with souvenirs. And the books will need to be closed out before finance reports are due.

## Voter Protection, Ballot Integrity, and Recounts

Recount procedures gripped public attention during the six weeks following the 2000 presidential contest. Many people were surprised by the complexity of recounts and the fragility of election results. Every time ballots were counted, vote totals changed. In 2002, the

Help America Vote Act tried to correct many of the problems encountered in 2000. Most agree, however, the potential for irregularities and miscounts continues. In a well-prepared campaign, a voter protection plan might begin by assembling the laws on access to the voting booth and recount procedures.

With an increasing number of states requiring specific forms of identification—and with many voters uninformed about ID requirements or opportunities to cast "provisional ballots" in case of a problem—campaign organizations may want to consider either positioning advocates at the polling place or bringing voters to the ballot booth en masse. In Ohio, some African American churches drive "Souls-to-the-Polls" on the Sunday before Election Day. Web sites advertise pick-up locations for rides to early-voting sites and phone numbers to call for information. In 2014, a state representative in Cincinnati was slated to "provide rides to the polls as well host a prayer vigil at 2 P.M." (ocsea.org 2014).

The 2014 Souls-to-the-Polls almost did not happen. In recent years, tightened rules on voter registration and voting have raised heated controversy about access to the ballot booth. On one side of the argument, stricter ID requirements are said to ensure equal protection by preventing ineligible voters from casting ballots. Opponents of ID requirements argue that in-person voter fraud is exceedingly rare and that preventing whatever illegitimate votes may be cast comes at a cost of denying rights to qualified voters (especially lower-income, older, and minority voters) who lack appropriate identification and would have to take expensive measures amounting to a "poll tax" to get such ID. Ohio officials tried to standardize polling times for early voting. When it was announced that standardization meant elimination of voting on the Sunday before Election Day, voting rights advocates sued the state and won the battle with hours to spare.

With balloting subject to political and legal wrangling, an attorney with a working knowledge of state election law might be retained. Legal questions should be clarified well before Election Day—in terms of initiating a recount (if the campaign loses) and opposing a recount (if the campaign wins), and campaigns might consider placing trained volunteers at the polls to watch for irregularities. Among those who would sit on a recount team, legal and political responsibilities should probably be made clear, contact information shared, and the necessary addresses and telephone numbers of election offices, election commissioners, and appropriate judicial authorities readied. Recounts are generally initiated on Election Night or the following morning so there is little time to waste.

Some jurisdictions have automatic recounts for close elections, but whether the process is automatic or must be requested it will likely be a time-consuming and labor-intensive affair. Outright election fraud is far less frequent than accidental mishaps. The focus is often on mistakes in tabulation. In 2000, the problem in Florida was a combination of poor ballot design, voter error, faulty voting procedures, and improper instructions. In the razor-thin outcome of the 2008 U.S. Senate race in Minnesota, the question of victory boiled down to the validity of a few hundred ballots—and the issue took several months and a series of court challenges to settle. Attention must be paid to the legal implications of the recount and the attendant communications issues, for, in politics, the court of public opinion is also important.

Operatives on all sides should understand that election results are hard to overturn even when the evidence seems clear. During the 2000 recount season, an attorney shared the story of an election his client had lost by 30 votes. One precinct, which went 55 to 125 for the opposition, showed clear indications of machine malfunction, although the exact problem could not be located in the device itself. With a seeming undervote of a hundred ballots,

> we canvassed the precinct and got about 150 affidavits from people who said they had voted for the Democrat. I checked them against the precinct sign-in list and every one of them had been there. At the hearing, I proffered the affidavits to show that my client had been the victim of a machine malfunction. The judge said he trusted the machine. My client decided not to take an appeal. (Still 2000)

Some candidates believe it more dignified to bow out gracefully than to fight for a contested victory.

## Conclusion

An enthusiastic volunteer effort suggests that the community supports the candidate, and this image might bring still more volunteers and increased support. A visible outpouring of help by members of the community gets the bandwagon rolling. This same enthusiasm might bring media attention and campaign funds. Candidates flanked by volunteers send a positive message. Potential contributors take notice, as do editors and reporters. An air of grassroots popularity can be a self-fulfilling prophecy. If the campaign is low on funds and receives a last-minute endorsement, a volunteer operation can spread the word. With careful planning, it can bring the right message to the right voters without the waste that accompanies broadcast media targeting large demographic groups.

The effort should probably start with the candidate. It is difficult to ask volunteers to lend a hand if the candidate is unwilling to do so. The candidate's friends might want to "do strategy," not implementation, but these friends might be reminded of the need to knock on doors. Some local parties are as robust as they have been at any time in the past 40 or 50 years, and a growing number of politically active organizations are in the field. Many Democrats are assisted by labor unions and many Republicans get a boost from business organizations. Yet another source of volunteers is the pool of student organizations at a local college or university. The rise of youth-oriented political groups in the 2004 and 2008 elections was impressive. At the other end of the spectrum are senior citizens. Older Americans are politically active and often have a good deal of spare time for making phone calls.

As with all other facets of electioneering, political judgment is vital. In some places door-to-door volunteers are common on Sunday; in others, this would be taboo; in still others Saturday would be off limits. On any day, campaigns should be wary of calling too early in the morning or too late at night. Yard signs are acceptable in some places but not in others. Professionals must understand the social, religious, and political norms of any area in which they undertake grassroots campaigning. And they must treat volunteers properly, which might require a candidate to attend volunteer functions and express gratitude. Pizza, bagels, soda, and coffee go a long way, and on Election Night everyone can enjoy an extravagant blowout.

A political race should be fun, or at least a learning experience. Even as microtargeting and media advertising have surpassed many traditional campaign activities, politics remains a very human endeavor. Campaigning can be one of the most rewarding missions that a person can accept. The rush of Election Night can be thrilling. Candidates, consultants, and campaign staff want to win, but professionals should not forget that it is only an election. There will be others. Win or lose, life will go on.

# PART IV

# THE FUTURE OF ELECTIONEERING

# CHAPTER 11

# New Players and New Campaigns

Electioneering is not static and money will always be looking for political power. New kinds of campaigns have attracted politicians, citizens, and donors. The archetype of these campaigns is the emergence of "outside money."

Donors who want to contribute to a campaign—whether $10 or $1 million—will find numerous outlets for that desire. The hydraulic theory of money and politics suggests money is like water: It can be diverted, but the flow is hard to stop (Malbin et al. 2002). The history of campaign finance (discussed in chapter 7) shows the evolution of financial resources flowing through candidates' official organizations. But donors who "max out" or who want to take a different approach to influencing public policy through the electoral process can bypass candidates and operate on their own. Moreover, the domain of "campaigns" is not confined to those that center on candidates. Policy is made through voter initiatives, referenda, and the courts, with spending on these kinds of campaigns reaching new levels. Borrowing from a famous line in the movie *Jurassic Park*—"Life finds a way"—observers of the new players and new campaigns can easily believe, "*Money* finds a way."

The hydraulic theory was illustrated by a running joke on the "Colbert Report." Stephen Colbert created his own so-called super PAC, "Making a Better Tomorrow, Tomorrow" with the help of former Federal Election Commission (FEC) chair Trevor Potter. Filing papers with the FEC and incessantly seeking, and finding, loopholes that allowed amazing flexibility in the use of financial resources led to a 2012 Peabody Award for the series' informative content. Colbert explained that the "whole thing came about by accident" in a rare out-of-character interview on public radio:

> We were just trying to do a parody ad of a Tim Pawlenty ad, and I couldn't figure out how to end it. And then I said, "Well how does his ad end?" And his ad ended with just a simple card on the screen that said "LibertyPAC.com"—whatever his political action committee was. And I said, "OK, just put a Colbert PAC.com at the end." (Fresh Air 2012)

Colbert gained official sanction from the FEC and raised a considerable amount of cash, and along the way he could "illustrate how easy it is to give money to somebody else and really have control over what happens" (ibid.). Colbert argued the emerging way of politics is about the "new flush of cash into our political system that is in large part untraceable or traceable only after the fact when it's too late" (ibid.).

This chapter discusses the increasing impact of outside groups, judicial elections, and noncandidate campaigns on the practice of American electoral campaigns.

## Outside Groups

For some candidates, the money game has become one of the most frustrating aspects of campaigning. How does one become competitive without first getting assistance? But how does one get assistance without first becoming competitive?

Cold-blooded legislative campaign committees have a long tradition of targeting efforts at the most competitive races (see Shea 1999). If a candidate's chances are good, help might be forthcoming, but a long-shot candidate will get little support. As a would-be congressional candidate described his first encounter with the Democratic Congressional Campaign Committee (DCCC), "All they did . . . was show me a list of [PACs] and then tell me that the PACs wouldn't talk to me until I was the designated candidate. They promised me nothing. I could count on no help from them at all" (Fowler and McClure 1989, 37). The plight of Democratic senator Mary Landrieu in Louisiana in 2014 demonstrates the power of these organizations. The Democratic Senatorial Campaign Committee (DSCC) canceled over $1.5 million in broadcast buys between November 5 and her run-off election in December after the party lost the Senate (Hohmann and Haberman 2014).

From the early part of the 20th century, corporations and unions were explicitly banned by federal election law from donating to candidates. As a result, candidates had to work directly with voters and campaign committees to seek funding. Campaign committees, such as the National Republican Campaign Committee (for Republican members of Congress) or the Democratic Legislative Campaign Committee (for Democratic state legislatures), serve as leading-edge consultancy operations. Governors have followed suit. In 2004, the Missouri Democratic Party took in $3 million from the Democratic Governors Association (DGA) and the Republican state committee received some $1.8 million from its own governors' association. In all, the DGA raised $24 million in 2004, and the Republican Governors Association (RGA) raised some $34 million (Bogardus 2005). In 2012 the RGA raised a whopping $130 million (RGA 2014).

As discussed in chapter 7, political parties used a soft money "loophole," as critics called it, to use money for "party building" that looked to many observers like ads endorsing candidates—except that the ads did not directly call for the victory or defeat of any particular candidate. Lacking "direct advocacy," such ads seemed for have become a way to promote a candidate without really doing so.

The 2002 Bipartisan Campaign Reform Act was intended to eliminate the effect of soft money by adding a variety of burdensome restrictions. Industry professionals did not seem to fear that money would be drained from campaigns. Presumably, some of the money that would have gone to the parties went instead to groups organized under Section 527 of the Internal Revenue Code. Groups such as Swift Boat Veterans for Truth and MoveOn.org said they were providing education to the public without any express advocacy and without coordinating with any campaign and were therefore exempt from federal taxation. (The FEC determined that some violations had occurred and levied fines.) Section 527 is the framework that governs many of the outside groups that operate in the political sphere but since the Supreme Court loosened restrictions on "direct advocacy" a "527" is typically used in narrow reference to groups that do not engage in that activity. (The RGA and DGA operate as 527 groups.)

The legal regime changed in 2010 with two federal court cases: *Citizens United v. Federal Election Commission* and *SpeechNow.org v Federal Election Commission*. The first, *Citizens United*, found that corporations, because they are legal persons with rights and because campaign spending had previously been held to be a form of political speech, could not be prevented from engaging in express advocacy.

(It was immediately assumed that this ruling would extend to labor unions.) Shortly thereafter the U.S. District Court for the District of Columbia ruled in *SpeechNow.org* that 527s could not be prevented from collecting unlimited funds from individuals, insofar as doing so would encroach on the free speech of prospective donors. As a result, donors could give without their names having to appear on every ad they paid to produce. A scholar writing on Slate.com believed, "The theory was that, per Citizens United, if independent spending cannot corrupt, then contributions to fund independent spending cannot corrupt either" (Hasen 2012).

The announcement raised expectations, and fears, that a great deal more money would be making its way into the American campaign process. New super PACs were designated as independent expenditure-only committees so they could raise and spend unlimited sums for or against political candidates. As of December 2014, over 1,000 such groups had been recognized and combined they have spent over $340 million in the 2014 midterm election cycle (VandenDolder 2014).

Restrictions on campaign contributions were further loosened by the Supreme Court in *McCutcheon v. Federal Election Commission*. Previously, individual donations to federal candidates were limited in the amount of money that could be given to any single candidate and to the total amount that can be donated to separate candidates. *McCutcheon* struck down the aggregate cap on how much an individual may donate to candidates, PACs, and parties in an election cycle. One observer "predicted that it would empower a new class of elite donors and lead to the creation of massive joint fundraising committees—teams of candidates, party committees and other groups that could pursue big donors together and split the proceeds of a single giant check" (Choma 2014).

While the ruling was lauded in some circles for permitting donors to give directly to candidates and parties (thus addressing some of the questions about "dark money" in American campaigns), others believed those who wished to have the greatest influence would continue to do so under the shroud of secrecy. Justice Breyer's dissent in *McCutcheon* drew parallels to concerns still existing since Watergate: "Where enough money calls the tune, the general public will not be heard" (Haberman 2014). According to a critic of the rulings: If it were dealing with gun control rather than campaign finance, the result would be something equivalent to the Court saying: "Everyone who can afford it can now have their own nuclear arsenal. Good luck" (Hill 2014).

Outside groups appear to be having a significant impact on the political landscape. A central storyline of the 2014 midterm elections was the money involved in electioneering. The key story of financing the midterms "was not which side had more resources, but that such a large chunk of the cost was paid for by a small group of ultra-wealthy donors using outside groups to bury voters with an avalanche of spending" (Choma 2014). Even more telling has been the impact on electoral outreach. Despite more money being spent overall, the average winning campaign has actually declined in terms of money spent by candidates. Political groups independent of candidates spent more than $814 million to influence congressional elections in 2014, a record for the midterms and nearly twice the spending in 2010, Federal Election Commission records show (Willis 2014).

In the 2012 cycle, outside independent groups in aggregate spent just shy of $200 million on House races and over $250 million on the Senate (Campaign Finance Institute 2012b). These days, a congressional candidate may be pleasantly surprised, or maybe outraged, by television advertisements emanating from party committees, 527 groups, super PACs, and 501(c)(4) organizations.

Senator John McCain remarked in early 2012, "I guarantee there will be a scandal, there is too much money washing around politics, and it's making the campaigns irrelevant" (Jaffe 2012). Concerns about disclosure, corruption, coordination, distortion, and inequality all surround these alleged "WMDs of campaign finance" (Heineman 2012). Super PACs are complicating candidates' efforts to control their messages (Gold 2014a). This dynamic was highlighted during the 2012 Republican primary season when Newt Gingrich publicly called on a super PAC that was supporting his own bid for the presidency to stop running an attack ad that questioned Mitt Romney's record on job creation (Huisenga 2014).

Super PACs introduce new questions about electioneering, including the aforementioned problems with unlimited donations, the ability for big donors to secretly donate (like former Bain Capital manager Ed Conrad with Romney's Restore Our Future [Blumenthal 2011b]), the potential failure of regulators (as seen with the FEC's struggles to determine what it meant by coordination early in the process of recognizing super PACs [Wang 2011]), and the potential for coordination between campaigns and these allegedly independent groups (especially considering the activities of Karl Rove's American Crossroads [Blumenthal 2011a]). And politicians are aware of the advantages these organizations offer. Per an e-mail from a staffer for Wisconsin Governor Scott Walker sent to supporters: "As the

Governor discussed . . . he wants all the issue advocacy efforts run thru one group to ensure correct messaging. . . . We had some past problems with multiple groups doing work on 'behalf' of Gov. Walker and it caused some issues . . . the Governor is encouraging all to invest in the Wisconsin Club for Growth" (Richmond and Johnson 2014).

No longer must campaign organizations do all the work. As opposition researcher Jeff Berkowitz explains: "When you had a direct connection between a campaign and the research being done, there is only so far you could go. Now, with these Super PACs, anyone who believes deeper investigation needs to be done doesn't have to wait for the campaign or the party committee to agree on them. They can just fund it themselves and move forward" (Reid 2011). Many of these entities have gone negative. In the 2012 presidential elections, "Republican super PACs [spent] three times as much opposing Obama as they have backing Romney, $46 million to $14 million . . . The most telling stat—both in terms of how negative super PACs are and how much Democrats are being outspent—is that Republican super PACs spent more trying to sink Mitt Romney during the Republican primaries than the president's Democratic allies have spent in favor of him during the entire campaign, $4.7 million to $3.2 million" (Graham 2012).

The Tea Party movement has benefited greatly from outside spending in recent election cycles (Miller 2014). Many candidates who would not have received money from the parties due to ideology or likelihood of success in general elections have been able to garner support from outside groups. Although Tea Party candidates were out-raised almost 5–1 in 2014 Senate races, the amounts they did receive forced primary opponents to take their campaigns more seriously than they may have in previous years (Blake 2014). In all, the six largest Tea Party super PACs have spent nearly $40 million supporting candidates (Gold 2014b). In the 2012 Republican presidential primary, billionaire casino owner Sheldon Adelson allowed Newt Gingrich to limp through the season by writing checks to Winning Our Future—the official pro-Gingrich super PAC (Confessore and Lipton 2012). Likewise, a Louisiana energy executive allowed Rick Santorum to prolong his campaign with almost $3 million in cash infusions to the Red, White, and Blue fund, helping his efforts (Murphy 2012). Without these types of donors and organizations, the Republican primary would likely have ended sooner, allowing Romney to more efficiently move toward a general election strategy.

For candidates and campaigns, super PACs will continue to be double-edged swords in coming election cycles. When the Supreme Court opened elections to greater outside spending, American campaigns were fundamentally changed. Super PACs seem to be making electoral contests more negative (Sonmez 2012). And candidates and campaigns have no ability to control the messaging. Candidates and campaign staff are not permitted to coordinate efforts with a super PAC. Thus, some campaigns find themselves at the mercy of messages they neither create nor prefer. As elections pass, both super PACs and candidates may determine what is allowed (even as regulators continually attempt to do the same). But, without question, the potential influence outsiders have on elections is a new facet of American campaigns and one that will likely remain.

## Judicial Elections

Thirty-eight states hold elections for judicial posts, including partisan and nonpartisan contests, and up-or-down retention elections. Historically, these campaigns were neither seen nor heard; they were quiet affairs focused on character and experience. Voter drop-off for judicial races was large, given that these campaigns were less partisan (and in some states nonpartisan), usually noncontroversial, and often at the very bottom of a long ballot so voters needed to be highly aware and very resilient if they were to cast an informed vote for judicial candidates. With rare exceptions springing from a scandal or a high-profile decision—sometimes involving the recall of sitting judges—most races were low-cost, low-profile, and low-interest political events.

The situation is changing. A 2012 report written by Justice at Stake, the Brennan Center for Justice, and the National Institute on Money in State Politics highlights what some operatives have witnessed for a decade. The report argues that many judicial races seem "alarmingly indistinguishable from ordinary political campaigns—featuring everything from Super PACs and mudslinging attack ads to millions of dollars of candidate fundraising and independent spending" (Bannon et al. 2012, 1). A number of these campaigns link judicial candidates with the accused criminals who have come before their courts. It seems that "[c]ampaigning for judgeships in America, once described as decent, docile, and dirt-cheap, even if drab and dull, are today nosier, nastier, and costlier" (Gibson 2012, 105).

A vivid illustration of this change was captured in a 2005 documentary, *The Last Campaign,* which follows the 2004 reelection campaign of West Virginia Supreme Court Justice Warren McGraw. McGraw had been a well-known figure in West Virginia politics for three decades—a member of a prominent Democratic family, brother of the attorney general. Most pundits expected an easy reelection and the candidate himself seemed indifferent to fundraising, paid consultants, television advertisements, and all forms of new-style electioneering. McGraw's campaign mostly comprised parades, candidate forums, and small tokens such as combs and emery boards to voters. And yet, during his time on the bench, McGraw had handed down a number of decisions very unpopular with state business leaders and coal company executives, including Don Blankenship of Massey Energy. These leaders, along with the U.S. Chamber of Commerce and national conservative organizations, set their sights on defeating McGraw (and several other state judges), with Blankenship reportedly putting $2.5 million into the effort to defeat McGraw.

Other such contests have followed. "Louis Butler [a Wisconsin Supreme Court Justice] worked to put criminals on the street," the narrator warns, "like Reuben Lee Mitchell, who raped an 11-year-old girl with learning disabilities. . . . Can Wisconsin families feel safe with Louis Butler?" (Kroll 2014, 1). Butler's opponent, Michael Gableman, had amassed a hefty war chest from business leaders, who were keenly aware of Butler's role in striking down a $350,000 limit on pain-and-suffering damages in malpractice suits, and a second case where individuals harmed by lead paint exposure could sue multiple companies at the same time. All told, $1.2 million was spent by the candidates in this race, a staggering sum in Wisconsin. But it was the outside money that caught widespread attention: $3.6 million was spent by outside groups, almost 90 percent of all money was spent on television ads related to the race. Butler was defeated—the first Wisconsin Supreme Court justice to lose his seat in 40 years (Kroll 2014). North Carolina Supreme Court judge Robin Hudson used to describe her races as "sleepy" (Gass 2014). Then television ads sponsored by the conservative super PAC Justice for All NC accused Hudson of letting criminals off the hook. Hudson watched as huge sums of money poured in from across the nation.

About a quarter of the states that elect judges or magistrates ban candidates from making personal solicitations. The idea behind the bans is to help ensure impartiality, but the plaintiffs argue that this restriction is a violation of the First Amendment's free speech protections, and is inconsistent with a host of recent court decisions. It is perhaps not surprising in the wake of *Citizens United* that outside spending on judicial elections has increased sevenfold since 2000. An estimated $56.4 million was contributed to high court races in the 2012 election cycle, with roughly one-half of this amount coming from outside groups and parties, much of it spent on television. The most expensive high court elections that year occurred in Michigan, Wisconsin, Florida, and North Carolina (Bannon et al. 2012). Michigan had the most expensive Supreme Court race in the country in 2012, with outside groups spending $13.85 million on issue ads (Gass 2014). Many experts suggest the state judicial spending may be much higher than is currently understood, given that state financial disclosure laws vary and are often weaker than those at the national level (Kroll 2014).

In April 2015, the U.S. Supreme Court ruled that Florida's ban on personal solicitations was constitutional. The main arguments of the parties surrounded questions of free speech, impartiality of the legal system, integrity of courts, and the right of due process guaranteed to individuals who come before the court. Judges pose difficulties for campaign finance given the positions they are running for and how they differ from other political positions. Former judges and justices came down on both sides of the argument, suggesting a division within the views of those on the bench about these changes in the campaign climate. Ultimately, the Court found that the state's interest in the integrity of the judicial system allows for different regulations in these races.

The transformation of judicial races suggests a number of implications for campaign operatives. As these races become more competitive and expensive, experts may be in greater demand, though specialized skills may be required. But in many ways judicial campaigns are unique. There is less applicable prior voting data to structure strategy. Little is known about voter propensities when it comes to picking judicial candidates. Will they focus on qualifications and character, or will voters rely on retrospective evaluations? How will partisanship shape vote choice in judicial contests, particularly when a candidate's affiliation is not listed on the ballot—as is the case in over a dozen states? Does it make a difference if the voters are aware of candidates' party affiliations in an officially non-partisan race? When several races occur in the same year, will voters make ticket-based evaluations? Fundraising will present challenges, particularly if the ban on personal solicitations remains.

## Noncandidate Campaigns

Not all campaigns have candidates. Some consultants specialize in helping individuals with a shared interest to pursue successful ballot measures, from environmental issues to school levy renewals. This new area of campaign growth and expansion requires a different set of considerations than a candidate-based effort. Some would argue that noncandidate campaigns could (and possibly should) be easier to manage. Without a candidate, there are no opportunities for an off-the-cuff comment to be made or decades of stories, writings, and ideas to worry about emerging through an opponent's opposition research. Unlike campaigns with candidates, noncandidate campaigns lack a personal touch. Potential voters tend to know where they stand on an issue (whether they are fully informed or not) and consequently may reach a voting decision without seeking out information from a campaign. As a result, noncandidate campaigns present new considerations for seasoned managers.

Noncandidate campaigns fall into a few different categories. From local tax levies to statewide initiatives, the bonding characteristic of each is the allowance of citizens to directly determine public policy. Initiatives allow citizens to attempt to initiate policy while referenda permit them to either agree or disagree with passed legislation and recalls serve as a vote of confidence on a sitting official. Many people believe these elections are the very definition of direct democracy. There were 2,421 statewide initiatives between 1904 (citizen-initiated) and 2012 (Initiative and Referendum Institute 2013). Adding in referenda, there have been 200 statewide ballot issues per year among the 27 states that allow for referenda and initiatives. In 2014, roughly 100 initiatives alone accounted for over $1 billion in campaign spending (Rehm 2014).

Abortion, death penalty, stem-cell research, marijuana legalization, same-sex marriage, and euthanasia have all appeared on the ballot in different states in recent electoral cycles. Such policies touch on morality and generate strong responses. As a result, voters may not need new information, just mobilization. In 2011, Ohio voters launched an effort to reverse a bill passed by the state legislature that curtailed collective bargaining rights for state workers. In order to gain the signatures necessary to get the referendum put on the ballot, supporters held drive thru petition signings at county courthouses, parks and labor halls (Willard and Fazekas 2012).

And the issues may have the effect of mobilizing voters in ways the help candidates. Even in the midterm elections of 2014, which were successful for Republicans nationally, ballot measures were viewed as progressive policy issues that might help progressive candidates. Reid Wilson of the *Washington Post* explains:

> I'd point to initiatives like minimum wage measures in Arkansas and Alaska and a medical marijuana initiative in Florida. . . . All three of those are designed to bring specific voters . . . low-income voters, if they're going to vote to raise their own minimum wage, they're likely to vote for the Democratic candidates for U.S. Senate. (Rehm 2014)

The Brookings Institute released a report titled "Harry Reid Should Love Marijuana: How Legalization Could Help Keep the Senate Blue" (Hudak 2014). It did not. Yet despite not mirroring national success for progressive candidates, these ballot initiatives allowed pundits to suggest that perhaps the cycle was not a complete loss for the Democratic side.

Ballot measures and noncandidate campaigns have seen heavy spending, as in the competing campaigns of the Koch brothers (wealthy industrialists with a track record of giving to conservative and libertarian policy and advocacy groups) and Tom Streyer (a wealthy environmental advocate). In 2014, Streyer spent approximately $50 million of his own money, supporting candidates who have strong environmental records and ballot measures that favored the environment (Rutenberg 2014). The Koch brothers—through their PAC, Americans for Prosperity (AFP)—even devoted funding to defeat efforts to fund expansion of the Columbus Zoo, a well-loved institution in central Ohio. AFP referred to the levy as a money grab in literature drops to potential voters. In response, the zoo hired a public relations firm and featured famed zoologist Jack Hanna in support of the initiative, but the levy ultimately gained only about 30 percent of the vote. The Ohio AFP director offered a clear explanation for the Koch interest in an Ohio zoo: "There is no issue we won't get involved in if you're going to raise taxes" (McCarter 2014).

Campaign organizations that have traditionally planned on a two-way debate about the issues may now face well-financed interests from outside the district. Former New York City mayor Michael Bloomberg has been using outside money in an effort to influence local politics. David Clarke, a black Democrat aligned with the National Rifle Association, was seeking reelection in Milwaukee when he received word that Bloomberg was spending over $200,000 in an effort to have him defeated. Before narrowly winning his primary, Clarke exclaimed, "Wow, this is big-time now" (Burns 2014b). And citizens end up being forced to have to decipher the true intentions of such outside efforts: "It's a difficult environment for voters to know everything about a particular ballot measure anyway, in a normal election. You have to actually do some digging or find that article on the Internet or newspaper that has that in-depth information, and that's actually a pretty demanding task for low- and medium-information voters" (Whyte 2014).

## Conclusion

New players enter the political arena every election cycle; untapped donors emerge; local business owners seek seats on county commissions and school boards; and nationally recognized figures seek congressional office. The players and rules have undergone dramatic change. Aside from opening doors to more outside money than ever before, a significant uptick in the number of judicial and issue-based campaigns have altered how electioneering operates in the American context. But an influx of money does not guarantee electoral success. Expertise is needed to determine how best to spend increased donations.

Outsiders may sometimes they hurt the candidates they want to support. In 1998, Lily Eskelsen (now the president of the National Education Association) was hurt by the decision of Americans for Limited Terms to run hundreds of thousands of dollars' worth of ads against her opponents. The ads focused on term limits, not the issues that Eskelson wanted to pursue (Goodliffe 2000, 171). And outsiders are not always successful. An effort supported by The Koch brothers—significant financial supporters of libertarian and conservative think tanks and campaigns, specifically the Tea Party supporting American for Prosperity—were defeated while bankrolling school board candidates in Douglas County School District in Colorado (Simon 2013).

Candidates benefiting from outside spending may be a means to an end for donors with larger (or smaller) agendas. Individual candidates might not matter nearly as much as the ideologies they espouse. Candidates may come and go, and loyalty may extend only so far as what an elected official has done lately. Outsiders may lack local knowledge, or their spending might attract retaliation. And the parties are not ready to stand aside. With the coming of the 2014 midterms, as some party regulars worried that Tea Party candidates, who might benefit from outside money, could harm efforts to take the Senate, the Republican Party "issued a stern warning to outside groups that the establishment is ready and willing to strike back in critical [states]" (Kucinich 2013).

Campaign managers, staffers, and candidates have learned to adapt to changes in order to be efficient and effective. Yet when new players and new rules emerge, it creates a more jarring ebb and flow in the standard campaign operating procedure. In the case of super PACs, judicial elections, and the new-found fascination and interest in noncandidate campaigns, America has been exposed to elements of campaigning never experienced before.

# CHAPTER 12

# The Evolving Style

Political strategists often speak in martial language because

politics and war follow the same principles: armies face off in
battle, each with different plans, different strengths and weaknesses, limited resources, generals with different styles, all sharing
the same goal of crushing the enemy. (Sweitzer 1996, 46)

For a political strategist, campaigns are civilized warfare, a form of
single combat (see Burton and Shea 2003; Pitney 2000). But politics is also a form of commercial marketing (see Lees-Marshment
2012; Lees-Marshment, Conley, and Cosgrove 2014). The language
of voter contact speaks of "gross rating points," "spot production,"
"list management," and "demographic research." Campaigns need a
"business plan to raise venture capital" (Pelosi 2010, 141).

Adlai Stevenson, who railed against those who "merchandise candidates for high office like breakfast cereal," would be dismayed at
the present state of affairs. For more than half a century, political
campaigns have absorbed innovative technologies with amazing
speed. Databases, desktop video editing software, and app-driven
smartphones have become standard. Advanced technologies such
as SMS text-casting are used in high-profile campaigns and some
down-ballot races. As with all other areas of life, the tools employed
by an organization transform the structure of the organization itself,
and the tools of political campaigns are the tools of entrepreneurial
commerce.

This final chapter highlights technologies that reinforce the new-
style business of electioneering, limiting factors on the industries

expansion, and implications for connections between candidates and voters.

## Politics, Technology, and Business

When the political parties dominated campaign politics, the relationship between bosses and voters was a one-to-one affair, with ground-level leaders listening directly to voter concerns and shaping their pitches accordingly (perhaps with the added incentive of a Thanksgiving turkey or a government job). With the rise of candidate-centered campaigns, the relationship involved mass outreach, a one-to-many relationship; no longer did the parties customize their approaches to individual voters, but instead the candidates reached out to a mass audience. The technology available to contemporary campaigns allows for the tailoring of messages to individual voters in a business revolution that is bringing profound changes to the relationship between voters and candidates. In the process, campaign consultants are trying to reestablish one-to-one relationships, this time on a mass scale.

The "mass customization" of politics can be seen in the increasing power of database management and the astounding proliferation of communications technology. The developments go hand-in-hand. Media can be purchased with prepackaged audiences. Database management software produces specialized lists of voters, and these voters can be targeted by new modes of communication.

While many businesses have moved to the Cloud-based operations, campaign managers might rely on simple spreadsheets (Shaw 2014, 33–35). Low-tech procedures make sense for small races because the start-up costs of professional databasing can be high. As the expense of data management declines, down-ballot campaigns are likely to go digital.

Professionalism is transforming campaigns. The difference is not just the media of message dissemination but also the strategy that new-style electioneering sustains. Early mass media took a shotgun approach. The candidate's media strategy—to the extent it had a well-planned line of attack—broadcast the message widely. The goal was to reach as many people as possible. This meant getting the message out through newspapers, rallies, and district-wide door-to-door canvassing. Each of these tactics was able to contact a great many people, though they were not always reaching the most persuadable voters. Little could be done to link the right message with the right person. In the Digital Age, scrupulous efforts are made to discover voter preferences through survey research, and a carefully rifled message, it is hoped, will be directed to each persuadable voter group and to each individual voter.

In the Golden Age of Parties, campaigns were constituent parts of a centralized chain of command. By the early days of new-style campaigns, the decomposition of party structures meant a trend toward multiple hierarchies, with each candidate running his or her own operation. As the transformation toward candidate-centered campaigns was unfolding, candidates began to rely on outside consultancies. The resurgence of political parties reflects this trend. The parties are no longer just a pecking order of elected officials and staff. They are clearinghouses for money, expertise, and political information. One result is a new party structure in which campaigns are more adaptable to change in the political environment because they can tap the expertise of outside consultants.

Another result is that electioneering has evolved into a business-oriented profession. It has a professional organization, standards of conduct, an industry magazine, and a collection of norms and practices that set consultants apart from the old party bosses and their own candidates. Professional consultants can have more in common with their colleagues on the other side of the partisan aisle than with outspoken ideologues within their chosen party. But most important, the profession has been locked in place by the increasing technological complexity of new-style electioneering. This was true as far back as 1980, when Sidney Blumenthal wrote, "The arrival of new techniques based on computers—direct mail, voter identification methods, sophisticated polling—reinforces the role of consultants." The reason for the shift to professionals, according to Blumenthal, was simple: "In order to have access to the new technology, a candidate needs a consultant. He can't run a viable, much less a respectable, campaign without one" (1980, 3).

As a business, consulting operates on profit motives, and profit motives are often averse to old-style racial, ethnic, and gender barriers (Burton and Miracle 2014). An increasing number of women as well as members of minority groups are getting involved in the industry (Panagopoulos, Dulio, and Brewer 2011; Williams 2014; *Campaigns & Elections* 2011). Progress is not uniform. An "audit" of consultant hiring "found that half of all funds raised by the [Democratic] Party over the past two cycles were used to hire consultants to engage multiracial voters; however, of the firms who received a total of $515 million in disbursements, only 1.7% ($8.7 million) went to firms that were minority-owned or had a minority principal" (Chen 2014).

Merging politics and technology requires substantial funding. Telemarketing costs money, and so does sophisticated Web design. Voter lists cost money, too. New-style campaigns can cost a *lot* of money, because they rely on specialized expertise. In the late 1990s, before "data geeks" became newsworthy, an article in *Campaigns and Elections* titled "Can Political Candidates Afford to Allow Their Data to Be Managed by Anyone but a Professional?" suggested that professionals "can take the burden of mission critical database management and related targeted communications off of the plate of the campaign manager" (Grefe 1997/1998, 18). The logic is compelling. Electoral competition requires technical proficiency; technical proficiency is capital-intensive, and because campaign organizations cannot afford to absorb the initial costs by themselves, campaign managers, who may well be employed as consultants in their own right, must rely on a range of outside consultancies.

User-friendly software can help almost any techno-savvy supporter build a Web site. The difficulty is that Web sites built by amateurs can look amateurish. Surfers are accustomed to a visually attractive Web experience, and they will be disappointed by a poorly designed site. Web sites need to be optimized for search engines. Unless the designer is thoroughly familiar with varieties of server platforms and distinctions among Web browsers and browser versions, the candidate's site might not display properly or it might lack a "call to action." Top-notch sites require first-rate talent if for no other reason than to promote data security. To be (reasonably) hacker-proof—a particular concern for political Web sites, which are prime targets for mischief—the technology team must know more about server technology than nearly all other Internet users. If the campaign deploys e-commerce applications for campaign contributions, the need for paid professionals increases. The relative value of volunteer Web designers is diminished, and it becomes more and more doubtful that an in-house campaign staffer will be capable of designing a stable, secure, and up-to-date Web site.

The capital costs of research, development, and experience would be hard to shoulder within any single candidate operation. Loyalists might be incapable of developing an integrated television, radio, Internet, call center, and mail outreach program. Polling and electoral

targeting are becoming more sophisticated. The abundance of information available at the turn of the 21st century has made opposition research an advanced skill. The competitive nature of electoral
politics ensures that each new technology escalates the need for campaigns to be faster, stronger, and more capable of doing battle with
techno-savvy opponents. In the 21st century, it would seem that only
the uninformed or poorly resourced would try to run a major campaign without drawing on experienced consultants using advanced
technology.

In the late 1800s, the capital costs of campaign management were
borne by the major parties, as knowledge was stored within Tammany-
style organizations. If, in the Digital Age, traditional parties were
still intact, there might be little need for consultants. But in the
1960s and 1970s, with the rise of individualized campaign operations, party structures loosened and consultants picked up the slack.
(Consultants, for their part, are loyal to party organizations in that
they represent certain political ideals and require a ready stock of clients.) Few consultants are interested in joining party hierarchies and
they might treat their selection of candidates as a business decision.
James Carville's minimalist criteria from his days as an active consultant for American campaigns seems representative of the culture:
"I will work for a Democrat who I can get along with who is neither
a bigot nor a crook" (Matalin and Carville 1995, 55). Scholar David
Dulio found that "over half . . . of all the consultants in [his] study
reported that they once worked for a candidate who they were later
sorry to see serve in office" (2004, 79). Consultants can also become
annoyed by tactical meddling from candidates and their families
(Williams 2014).

The decline of parties led to a fragmented political marketplace
and the rise of independent consultancies. Some of the resurgence of
political parties can be attributed to the recognition that party organizations harness the power of professional expertise by distributing
money and referrals to candidates in targeted races. But while parties
respond to the new consultant-centered environment, the fact that
they are contracting with outside political consultants demonstrates
a concession to the new reality: Independent campaign operatives
have taken over the management of political campaigns.

Campaign consultants provide specialized expertise. Imported
from the private sector, television advertising and research-driven
market segmentation were deployed in the 1952 Dwight Eisenhower
campaign, which drew on the services of television advertising

pioneer Rosser Reeves, whose best-known slogan was "M&M's—Melts in your mouth, not in your hands." In 1968, Richard Nixon relied on a specially selected media team that included *Mike Douglas Show* executive producer Roger Ailes. In 1996, Bill Clinton used Bob Squier of Squier Knapp Ochs, a Washington-based media firm that handled a wide variety of clients. As if to demonstrate that the component parts of media consultancy are truly interchangeable, Ailes, who had also worked for Ronald Reagan and George H.W. Bush, would later return to television as president of the Fox News Channel, and Squier, whose knowledge of damage control was virtually unrivaled, helped America Online respond to bad publicity when customers complained about interruptions in service.

George Stephanopoulos, when he first met James Carville, reflected on the changes that had taken place since John F. Kennedy's time: "There were still amateurs who loved the game in 1991, but campaigns were now run by professionals" (1999, 45). More recently, campaign organizations include data scientists, who can come into conflict with old hands who can "sense" what is happening on the ground with a canny blend of observation and instinct. General campaign management has become the business of integrating a variety of professional services.

From the early 1990s into the 21st century, the campaign marketplace required increasing specialization. According to one observer, general consultants like Carville, who supervised political campaigns from top to bottom, had become "dinosaurs of the consulting world" (Glasser 2000a). The profits that can be had by skillful entrepreneurs and the increasing complexity of political campaigns make for a campaign context in which specialization is sometimes prized over broad-spectrum talent. A large campaign might hire a strategist who charges a monthly fee, a professional fundraiser who keeps a percentage, a pollster who charges per completed survey, an opposition researcher who runs up billable hours, a media consultant who bases costs on a mix of production fees and commissions, an ad placement consultant who takes an additional cut of the media buys, a telemarketer who invoices the campaign for a retainer plus a cost per call, and a direct mail consultant whose fees vary according to the type of mail requested, the lists used, and the size of the mailings sent. The strategist, in turn, might purchase consumer data from an outside vendor and voter lists from yet another vendor, and the media consultant might work with a new-media specialist who subcontracts visual production, site hosting, and e-commerce services to another set of experts.

## Mitigating Forces

Despite the centrifugal forces that break up campaigns and distribute their parts to a wide range of outside contractors, campaign decentralization is limited by constraints inherent in political operations. In most small, municipal-level campaigns, the benefits of consultancy are not realized. Examples abound. Ed Baum, the Republican for city council discussed in chapter 4, gained his seat with a self-run campaign that cost a few thousand dollars. Baum's team was made up of friends and acquaintances, and his strategy was developed by reading a few good books. He built name recognition with yard signs and ran ads in the local paper. After his victory Baum sat down and figured out what went right and what could be improved. The need for a highly paid political consultant in this sort of race seems remote, and a skeptical candidate might wonder if money spent on consultants is worth the expenditure, since the advice offered by professionals is difficult to measure and often turns out wrong (see Martin and Peskowitz 2014.; Nyhan 2014; Terris 2014a).

Aside from economic calculations, a number of other factors mitigate against the power of consultants in campaigns and elections. First, the public is not infinitely malleable—some candidates do not persuade voters. In media-driven California politics, Michael Huffington's losing campaign for Senate in 1994 and Al Checchi's disastrous bid for the gubernatorial nomination in 1998 suffered from backlash against candidates who seemed to be buying the election. Huffington was seen as an "empty suit" whose $30 million campaign was orchestrated by his then wife, Arianna. Checchi's advertisements and campaign materials, coordinated by top consultants Mark Penn and Bob Shrum, reflected the corporate professionalism that could be expected from a $40 million campaign run by an airline executive but were never able to connect the candidate with the voters. As media consultant Alex Castellanos has said, "You know, sometimes the problem is not the label on the can, it's the dog food. And sometimes there's just dog food dogs don't like" (1998). In campaign politics, media can make a difference, but rarely can they make *all* the difference.

Second, loyalty still counts. Although candidates look to outside consultancies, they continue to rely on inside advisers. Wise candidates form kitchen cabinets of trusted friends and colleagues. Both major-party presidential candidates in 2000 commanded loyalty: Al Gore had long depended on his former chiefs of staff—Peter Knight, Roy Neel, Jack Quinn, and Ron Klain—all of whom worked high up in the vice president's campaign; George W. Bush's inner circle was filled with staffers who had demonstrated loyalty for years in the Texas governor's office. Barack Obama would later find his strongest supporters within his sphere of Chicago loyalists and many of Romney's advisers spoke with a New England accent. Candidates turn to intimates for confidential advice, alternative interpretations of polling data, and a listening ear for the musings and frustrations of the candidates in the middle of a tough campaign. Consultants—who must treat politics as a business, who are probably working for several clients at once, and who may fade from view days after the election—are not always privy to internal decision making.

Third, the same technological advances that complicate campaigns can also simplify the campaign process. With more than half a million electoral offices in the United States, there is a rich market for campaign goods and services. No one size fits all, but the commonalities that allow for modularized content also create a market for the modularized tools of the trade. Campaign handbooks provide generalized advice (Burton and Miracle 2014). A new-style candidate at ease with computer technology can, over the course of a long weekend, download voter lists, combine this information with precinct data, and display the results on a computer-generated map. Digital technology can reduce the costs of shooting video, and ill-funded candidates can post their ads on YouTube.

Fourth, good management demands limitations on the number of consultants involved in a campaign. With each stratum of consultants comes a new risk of media leaks, cost-control problems, and administrative headaches. Simple communication can become problematic. Managing a large number of profit-driven consultants who need to work together can be daunting for the ablest of political candidates. That was one of the problems on the Checchi campaign, it has been said, where battles reportedly broke out among consultants who became overly aggressive in seeking fees (Glasser 2000b). Even when the consultants are all cooperating with one another, the distributed nature of campaign consulting can lead to a counterproductive "silo effect," whereby a campaign organization's well-paid tacticians are spread across the country and must coordinate their efforts through the narrow bandwidth of a weekly conference call.

Fifth, efficiency has limits. If, in a general election, there are not enough persuadable voters to make up the difference in support between the candidates, then even perfect efficiency will not close the gap (see O'Connor and Chinni 2014).

Finally, an electorate that demands authenticity will perhaps see something untoward in the hiring of people whom James A. Thurber and Candice J. Nelson have called "campaign warriors" (2000). Mercenaries are little more respected in politics than in battle, and the very fact that an opponent's campaign has hired an out-of-state consultant can be used to impugn the opposition. Consultants who use the same tricks of the trade over and over again might have a homogenizing effect on American politics. Voters seek authenticity in their candidates. When long-time Boston mayor Tom Menino died, politicos lamented he was of a dying breed of personal politicians, recalling a 2008 survey showing 57 percent of voters had actually met the mayor (see Patton 2012). Visible indications that a campaign is mass-customized threatens to chip away at a candidate's image of authenticity. For many, the rise of political consultants and voter targeting signifies a move away from the politics of personal connection and toward an era of hyper-mediated politics.

## Political Connections

Did the citizens of earlier times enjoy a closer connection to public officials than those of the Digital Age? In some ways, they did; in other ways, they did not. At no time was there truly a Golden Age of American politics. Never has money failed to provide access to politicians, nor was there a moment when campaigns did not attempt to change the public mind for political reasons. The Civil War was a violent extension of partisan and sectional politics. Later, Mark Hanna, William McKinley's strategist, took in $250,000 from John D. Rockefeller's Standard Oil, the fortunes of which were endangered by populist presidential candidate William Jennings Bryan. What passes for mean-spirited politics in the Digital Age pales in comparison to the partisan witch hunts of Joseph McCarthy.

There is, however, a sense in which all these comparisons are irrelevant. First, each tends toward the extreme. The Civil War, Rockefeller, and McCarthy are outliers in the American experience. Second, the forms of voter contact provided by campaign organizations have changed so radically that comparisons between old- and new-style campaigns are inherently problematic.

One of the most common bases of comparison is the infamous political operation of George Washington Plunkitt. Plunkitt was reported to boast personal knowledge of everyone whom he represented: "I know every man, woman, and child in the Fifteenth District, except them that's been born this summer—and I know some of them, too" (Riordon 1995, 25). While there may be self-aggrandizement in his claim, certainly the urban political machines, which merged social and political affairs, fostered a more personalized connection between voters and elected officials.

A closer read of *Plunkitt of Tammany Hall* shows an attenuated relationship between candidates and constituents. Plunkitt got his start when he built a political following of voters who would cast their ballots the way he requested. The voters in his base of support were "marketable goods" (Riordon 1995, 8). The budding politician used his newfound assets to link up with the party leaders at district headquarters, which, in turn, was beholden to city and state organizations, on up to the national party level. In the day of the party machines, hierarchies were stratified through multilayered echelons. The idea that one of Plunkitt's loyal supporters might have a substantive conversation with a governor or president is all but unthinkable. In some ways, the old party structure was highly personalized. Plunkitt had an immediate relationship with his initial supporters, as indeed his first loyalists were a cousin and his friends. Then again, low-level supporters had little contact with leaders high up the political chain of command. Party hierarchies mediated relationships between leaders and voters by inserting thick layers in between.

New-style campaigns have fundamentally changed old-style relationships, bringing novel forms of voter alienation. As campaign scholar Christopher Arterton argued years before microtargeting became the coin of the realm:

> Modern politics have eviscerated [the old party] networks, replacing them with polling and mass communications. In the process, the individual voter has become a cipher, a statistical construct rather than a living, breathing person. Targeting involves creating an electoral majority by sending out messages to voters on the basis of the probability of support, depending on certain demographic characteristics or known "facts" about the individuals in a given group. Given the large number of citizens involved, campaigners cannot treat (or even conceptualize) these voters as individuals. In fact, to some degree, the

individuals themselves are unimportant. As long as the total number of supporters can be pushed over the 50 percent mark, one voter is more or less substitutable by another. (2000, 22)

Depersonalization was a hallmark of American politics in the period following the decline of traditional parties.

The fall of old party hierarchies resulted partly from the forging of new relationships between voters and candidates. When Ronald Reagan campaigned in the 1980 primaries, he "went over the heads" of the party leadership by speaking directly to Republican voters. The appeal was made on the airwaves—it was in no sense a personal, one-to-one relationship—but Reagan's politics were arguably a great deal more personalized than the "smoke-filled rooms" of Plunkitt's day. Nixon could run his own campaigns because television allowed him to bypass the established party leadership. George McGovern received the Democratic nomination in 1972 in large part because he had mastered the art of direct mail. Jimmy Carter made effective use of television to present himself as an outsider at the precise moment when the political marketplace demanded such a president. In 1992, Bill Clinton used town hall meetings to great effect, dispensing with the questions of skeptical reporters. In 2000 and 2004, George W. Bush "connected" with the voters better than his adversaries. And in 2008, Hillary Clinton, once the front-running choice of established Democratic Party stalwarts, was selected to become secretary of state by president-elect Barak Obama, who seemed to master the electronic media. With the rise of the Tea Party movement, numerous candidates joyfully ran against the GOP's party "Establishment" (Miller 2013a).

As campaign operatives review chatter on the Web, watching opponents trying to define the electoral competition, "campaigns must fight an online tug-of-war between good press and bad. They have to create enough positive stuff to outweigh the negative" (Berg 2008). A more horizontal media environment, in which candidates now compete with lay politicos who publicly talk to one another at the speed of the Web, means that campaigns need to keep up with Facebook and Twitter and Tumblr and Reddit, watch what activists are saying online, figure out if a "virtual town hall" is worth the effort, deal with the integration of a new variety of message outlets, and manage a new ecology of Web content that has the barest resemblance to the old, two-party, two-candidate, two-message competitive world of mass-media politics.

Younger voters are turning to alternative sources for their political information. For many years, *The Daily Show* attracted wide audiences of people who used Jon Stewart as their main source of news. *Saturday Night Live,* which brought Sarah Palin look-alike Tina Fey back on board for the 2008 campaign, is a mainstay of political news, where candidates mingle with the performers who make fun of them. Blogging has grown enough to receive national attention from political strategists at all levels. Campaign volunteers initiate and maintain blogs that trumpet their candidates, and candidate Web sites sometimes encourage voters to establish their own outlets for commentary. The holy grail of earned media is the news event that "goes viral" on the Internet. With the rise of amateur involvement increasing the complexity of contemporary electioneering, the help of campaign professionals may be more crucial than it ever has been.

Blumenthal noted that "consultants . . . embody many of the virtues espoused by the turn-of-the-century Progressives. They are usually dispassionate critics of politics, wary of control by party bosses" (1980, 7). The institutionally corrosive power of technology in the hands of outside consultants has sealed the fate of traditional party hierarchies. Precision targeting and sophisticated marketing techniques hold out one-to-one customer relationships as their ideal (see Chatlos and Barger 2014). New-style campaigns do not necessarily foster the warm, enduring relationships found in sentimental depictions of American politics, that have public officials knowing each voter personally, but neither do they create the remote interactions of mass-media advertising. Arterton believed Internet technology could help "establish a new, more personalized connection between candidate and voter," perhaps helping to "restore some balance and mutual respect to the relationship" (2000, 22).

Less serious observers tend to romanticize new-style politics with talk of the rich new connections that might accompany an interactive Web environment. Those who read political blogs, and comments on blogs, and comments on those comments will sense a coarsening of political speech and perhaps conclude that narrow-casted media give activists the ammunition they need to intensify an ideological arms race. Democratization of communication technology seems to have a Balkanizing influence.

A review of contemporary elections suggests that technology has neither brought candidates and voters closer together nor pushed them farther apart. The nature of the relationship has been altered so profoundly that comparisons between old- and new-style politics are difficult to render. When a candidate's voter contact strategy targets individual voters with exactly the right message, does it make politics more or less personalized? When party leaders enlist independent consultants to win state senate races, have the parties reconsolidated their power or ceded it to outsiders? The critical transformation that is taking place in American elections has filtered down from presidential campaigns to mayoral races, and bickering among supporters on all sides. As students of politics try to appreciate the accompanying changes in governance, they must unravel the new style.

Central to understanding contemporary political campaigns is a recognition that professional electioneering is a novel enterprise. It is no longer a high art—if it ever was such—in which the intuitive faculties of candidates would impress the electorate with spontaneous oratory and principled debate. Nor is it a pure science in which the voter is held up for detached observation by pollsters and then manipulated by media consultants. Instead, in the competitive environment created by America's two-party system, campaign operatives must constantly refine their expertise, merging technology and creativity in the search for electoral success. Consultant-centered campaigns are less beholden to the old party structures than their predecessors were, as candidates have released themselves to set up their own campaign operations and have come to rely on professionals who know the strategies and tactics of campaign management. New-style electioneering is both an art and a science—the product of ingenuity as well as research, experience, and analysis. Consultant-based electioneering is best understood as a new campaign craft.

# References

AAPOR Standards Committee. 2008. *Guidelines and considerations for survey researchers when planning and conducting RDD and other telephone surveys in the U.S. with respondents reached via cell phone numbers.* Deerfield, IL: American Association for Public Opinion Research.

AAPOR Standards Committee. 2010. *New considerations for survey researchers when planning and conducting RDD and other telephone surveys in the U.S. with respondents reached via cell phone numbers.* Deerfield, IL: American Association for Public Opinion Research. Available at http://www.aapor.org/AAPORKentico/Education-Resources/Reports/Cell-Phone-Task-Force-Report.aspx. Retrieved January 4, 2015.

Abramowitz, A. 2010. *The disappearing center.* New Haven, CT: Yale University Press.

Acohido, B. 2008. Sponsored-link ads play campaign role. *USA Today*, September 5.

Agranoff, R. 1972. *The new style in election campaigns.* Boston: Holbrook.

Allen, C. 1990. GOTV. *Campaigns and Elections*, October.

Allen, C. 1996. *Taking back politics: An insider's guide to winning.* Toronto: Jalapeno Press.

Allen, M., and K.P. Vogel. 2014. Inside the Koch data mine: Meet the guys building the right's new machine. *Politico*, December 8. Available at http://www.politico.com/story/2014/12/koch-brothers-rnc-113359.html. Retrieved January 4, 2015.

American Association for Public Opinion Research. 2007. AAPOR statements on "push" polls. June. Deerfield, IL: American Association for Public Opinion Research.

American Association of Political Consultants. 1996. AAPC Board of Directors declaration regarding "push polling." Washington, DC: AAPC.

American Association of Political Consultants. 2009. AAPC Board of Directors declaration regarding the use of disclaimers on new media communications. August 26. Washington, DC: AAPC.

American Association of Political Consultants. 2012. Code of ethics. Available at http://www.aapc.org/about-us/code-of-ethics/.

American Press Institute. 2014. The personal news cycle: How Americans choose to get their news. March 16. Available at http://www.american pressinstitute.org/publications/reports/survey-research/personal-news-cycle/single-page/. Retrieved January 4, 2015.

Andersen, K., M.B. Stepno, A. Braiterman, D. Brigida, M. Davis, C. Golden, T. Krackeler, S.U. McLaughlin, K. Swank, and C. Weeden. 2012. Best practices for fundraising success. Blackbaud. Available at https://www.blackbaud.com/files/resources/7–12.desktop.book.web.pdf. Retrieved January 4, 2015.

Aquino, J. 2008. Bachmann's comments spur opponent's fundraising spurt. *Minneapolis Star Tribune*, October 19.

Arbour, B. 2014. *Candidate-centered campaigns: Political messages, winning personalities, and personal appeals.* New York: Palgrave Macmillan.

Arceneaux, K., M. Johnson, and C. Murphy. 2012. Polarized political communication, oppositional media hostility, and selective exposure. *Journal of Politics* 74:174–186.

Arnold, J. n.d. Planning your campaign budget. *Winning Campaigns*. Available at http://www.winningcampaigns.org/Winning-Campaigns-Arch ive-Articles/Planning-Your-Campaign-Budget.html. Retrieved January 4, 2015.

Arnold, M. 1999. TV spot production: A political campaign primer. *Campaigns and Elections*, September, 62.

Arterton, C. 2000. New relationships. *Campaigns and Elections*, April, 22.

Atlas, M. 1989. Gambling with elections: The problems of geodemographics. In *Campaigns and elections: A reader in modern American Politics*, ed. L.J. Sabato, 126–135. Glenview, IL: Scott, Foresman.

Backstrom, C.H., and G. Hursh-Cesar. 1981. *Survey research.* New York: Macmillan.

Baker, P. 1996. Contrasting GOP strategies mark Senate primary in Va. *Washington Post*, May 26.

Baker, R., J.M. Brick, N.A. Bates, M. Battaglia, M.P. Couper, J.A. Dever, K.J. Gile, and R. Tourangeau. 2013. Report of the AAPOR task force on non-probability sampling, June. Available at https://www.aapor .org/AAPORKentico/AAPOR_Main/media/MainSiteFiles/NPS_TF_ Report_Final_7_revised_FNL_6_22_13.pdf. Retrieved January 4, 2015.

Balaban, J.J. 2014. The coming revolution in cable television. *Campaigns and Elections*, February 17. Available at http://www.campaignsandelec tions.com/magazine/1713/the-coming-revolution-in-cable-television. Retrieved January 4, 2015.

Baldwin, T. 2006. Republicans bank on precision bombardment in war for votes. *Times Online*, October 19. Available at http://www.timesonline .co.uk/tol/news/world/us_and_americas/article605662.ece. Retrieved February 23, 2010.

Balz, B. 2008. Aides say team interviewed Palin late in the process. *Washington Post*, September 3. Available at http://www.washingtonpost.com/ wp-dyn/content/article/2008/09/02/AR2008090203462.html.

Banks, A. 2008. Dirty tricks, South Carolina, and John McCain. *Nation Online*, January 14. Available at http://www.thenation.com/article/dirty-tricks-south-carolina-and-john-mccain. Retrieved February 28, 2010.

Bannon, A., E. Velasco, L. Casey, and L. Reagan. 2012. The new politics of judicial elections, 2011–12. The Brennan Center for Justice. Available at http://newpoliticsreport.org. Retrieved January 4, 2015.

Barnard, L., and D. Kreiss. 2013. A research agenda for online advertising: Surveying campaign practices, 2000–2012. *International Journal of Communication* 7:2046–66.

Barr, A. 2009. South Carolina Gov. Mark Sanford admits affair. *Politico*. Available at http://www.politico.com/news/stories/0609/24146.html. Retrieved April 10, 2010.

Bartels, L. 2014. Colorado's "war on women" and the U.S. Senate race: The sequel. *Denver Post*, September 24. Available at http://www.denverpost .com/election2014/ci_26598933/colorados-war-women-and-u-s-senate-race. Retrieved January 4, 2015.

Bartels, L.M. 2014. Remembering to forget: A note on the duration of campaign advertising effects. *Political Communication* 31:532–44.

Bayer, M.J., and J. Rodota. 1989. Computerized opposition research. In *Campaigns and elections: A reader in modern American Politics*, ed. L.J. Sabato, 19–25. Glenview, IL: Scott, Foresman.

Beaudry, A., and B. Schaeffer. 1986. *Winning local and state elections*. New York: Free Press.

Beiler, D. 1990. Precision politics. *Campaigns and Elections*, February/ March.

Beiler, D. 2000. The body politic registers a protest. In *Campaigns and elections: Contemporary case studies*, eds. M.A. Bailey, R.A. Faucheux, P.S. Herrnson, and C. Wilcox, 71–82. Washington, DC: CQ Press.

Berelson, B.R., P.F. Lazarsfeld, and W.N. McPhee. 1954. *Voting*. Chicago: University of Chicago Press.

Berg, J. 2008. Scrub your online image. *Campaigns and Elections*, July, 52.

Biersack, B. 2012. The big spender always wins? The Center for Responsive Politics, January 11. Available at http://www.opensecrets.org/ news/2012/01/big-spender-always-wins/. Retrieved January 4, 2015.

Bierschbach, B. 2014. How social media is changing political campaigns in Minnesota. *Minnesota Post*, September 8. Available at http://www .minnpost.com/politics-policy/2014/09/how-social-media-changing-political-campaigns-minnesota. Retrieved January 4, 2015.

Bike, W.S. 1998. *Winning local elections: A comprehensive guide to electoral success.* Juneau, AK: Denali.

Bishop, B. 2008. *The big sort: Why the clustering of like-minded America is tearing us apart.* New York: Houghton Mifflin.

Blake, A. 2014. The tea party has a big fundraising problem. *Washington Post*, May 13. Available at http://www.washingtonpost.com/blogs/the-fix/wp/2014/05/13/the-tea-partys-big-fundraising-problem/. Retrieved January 4, 2015.

Blanchfield, T.A. 2006. Make a Deal, Get a Donation. *Campaigns and Elections*, September.

Blanchfield, T.A. 2007. Watch your mailboxes: Direct mail gurus develop new ways to be seen. *Campaigns and Elections*, May 19.

Blumberg, S.J., and J.V. Luke. 2014. Wireless substitution: Early release of estimates from the National Health Interview Survey, July–December 2013. Available at http://www.cdc.gov/nchs/data/nhis/earlyrelease/wireless201407.pdf. Retrieved December 4, 2015.

Blumenthal, P. 2011a. Karl Roves' "fully coordinated" super PAC ads drive the FEC to deadlock. *Huffington Post*, December 1. Available at http://www.huffingtonpost.com/2011/12/01/karl-roves-stephen-colbert-fully-coordinated-super-pac-ads_n_1123999.html. Retrieved January 4, 2015.

Blumenthal, P. 2011b. Pro-Romney super PAC mystery donor comes forward. *Huffington Post*, October 6. Available at http://www.huffingtonpost.com/2011/08/06/romney-super-pac-mystery-donor-bain_n_920151.html. Retrieved January 4, 2015.

Blumenthal, S. 1980. *The permanent campaign: Inside the world of elite political operatives.* Boston: Beacon Press.

Boatright, R.G. 2013. *Getting primaried: The changing politics of congressional primary challenges.* Ann Arbor, MI: University of Michigan Press.

Boatright, R.G. 2014. *Congressional primary elections.* New York: Routledge.

Bocskor, N. 2013. How a fundraising plan comes together. *Campaigns and Elections*, May 12. Available at http://www.campaignsandelections.com/magazine/1755/how-a-fundraising-plan-comes-together. Retrieved January 4, 2015.

Bogardus, K. 2005. Old parties learn new tricks. Center for Public Integrity. Available at http://projects.publicintegrity.org/partylines/report.aspx?aid=691.

Bond, R., and J.H. Fowler. 2012. Facebook experiment in social influence and political mobilization. *Journalist's Resource*, September 19. Available at http://journalistsresource.org/studies/politics/digital-democracy/facebook-61-million-person-experiment-social-influence-political-mobilization#. Retrieved January 4, 2015.

Boorstin, D.J. 1964. *The image: A guide to pseudo-events in America.* New York: Harper & Row.

Borman, K. 2014. Fundraising questions candidates should be asked before they run. *Campaigns and Elections*, July/August.

Bovee, J. 1998. How to do opposition research on the Internet. *Campaigns and Elections*, September.

Bowers, J.R., and S. Daniels, eds. 2011. *Inside political campaigns: Chronicles and lessons from the trenches*. Boulder, CO: Lynne-Rienner.

Bradshaw, J. 1995. Who will vote for you and why: Designing strategy and theme. In Thurber and Nelson 1995, 30–46.

Bresnahan, J., and M. Raju. 2014. David Perdue: "I spent most of my career" outsourcing. *Politico*, October 3. Available at http://www.politico.com/story/2014/10/david-perdue-georgia-senate-race-2014–111589.html#ixzz3Nurw9U3Y. Retrieved January 4, 2015.

Brockman, D.E., and D.P. Green. 2014. Do online advertisements increase political candidates' name recognition or favorability? Evidence from randomized field experiments. *Political Behavior* 36:263–89.

Broder, D.S. 1972. *The party's over: The failure of politics in America*. New York: Harper & Row.

Brown, R. 2008. "Godless" link prompts lawsuit. *New York Times*, October 31.

Bryson, M.C. 1976. The *Literary Digest* poll: Making of a statistical myth. *American Statistician* 30 (November):184–85.

Bumiller, E. 2008. Palin disclosures raise questions on vetting. *New York Times*, September 1.

Bump, P. 2013. Does more campaign money actually buy more votes: An investigation. *Wire: News from the Atlantic*, November 11. Available at http://www.thewire.com/politics/2013/11/does-more-campaign-money-actually-buy-more-votes-investigation/71473/. Retrieved January 4, 2015.

Bump, P. 2014a. 40 painful seconds of Alison Lundergan Grimes refusing to say whether she voted for President Obama. *Washington Post*, October 9. Available at http://www.washingtonpost.com/blogs/the-fix/wp/2014/10/09/40-painful-seconds-of-alison-lundergan-grimes-refusing-to-say-whether-she-voted-for-president-obama/. Retrieved January 4, 2015.

Bump, P. 2014b. Do those "we know whether you voted" warnings actually work? An expert weighs in. *Washington Post*, October 31. Available at http://www.washingtonpost.com/blogs/the-fix/wp/2014/10/31/do-those-we-know-whether-you-voted-warnings-actually-work-an-expert-weighs-in/. Retrieved January 5, 2015.

Burden, B.C., and D.C. Kimball. 2004. *Why Americans split their tickets: Campaigns, competition, and divided government*. Ann Arbor, MI: University of Michigan Press.

Burns, A. 2014a. Thad Cochran's fight: Up close and all too personal. *Politico*, May 28. Available at http://www.politico.com/story/2014/05/

thad-cochrans-fight-up-close-and-all-too-personal-107197.html#
ixzz3NuW2xDMt. Retrieved January 4, 2015.

Burns, A. 2014b. Buying Main Street: Billionaires swamp local races.
*Politico*, August 15. Available at http://www.politico.com/story/
2014/08/michael-bloomberg-koch-brothers-tom-steyer-110055
.html. Retrieved January 4, 2015.

Burton, M.J. 2010. A defense of machine learning procedures in quantitative political analysis: Modeling and validation. Paper accompanying
poster session presented at the annual meeting of the Midwest Political Science Association, April.

Burton, M.J. 2014. The Republican primary season: Strategic positioning
in the GOP field. In *Campaigning for President 2012: Strategy and
tactics*, ed. Dennis W. Johnson, 43–56. New York: Routledge.

Burton, M.J., and T. Miracle. 2014. The emergence of voter targeting: Learning to send the right message to the right voter. In Lees-Marshment,
Congley, and Cosgrove 2014, 26–43.

Burton, M.J., and D. Shea. 2003. *Campaign mode: Strategic vision in congressional elections*. Lanham, MD: Rowman & Littlefield.

Cabel Roe, J., D. Dichiara, and S. Puetz. 2014. Electing a GOP mayor in
a Dem stronghold. *Campaigns and Elections*, April 21. Available at
http://www.campaignsandelections.com/magazine/1707/electing-a-
gop-mayor-in-a-dem-stronghold. Retrieved January 4, 2015.

Cafferty, Jack. 2012. Why do people give money to candidates who have no
chance of winning? *CNN*, January 5. Available at http://caffertyfile.blogs
.cnn.com/2012/01/05/why-do-people-give-money-to-candidates-
who-have-no-chance-of-winning/. Retrieved January 4, 2015.

Caldwell, A. 2008. Obama small family farms house meeting. Organizing
for America. Available at http://my.barackobama.com/page/event/
detail/4gwgx.

*Campaigns and Elections*. 2006a. Ten questions for Gary Maloney: Inside
opposition research. September, 23.

*Campaigns and Elections*. 2006b. Ten questions for Michael Gehrke: Inside
opposition research. September, 22.

*Campaigns and Elections*. 2011. Political pages. April, 36–37.

*Campaigns and Elections*. 2012. The evolution of experimentation. July/
August, 22–26.

Campaign Finance Institute. 2012a. House campaign expenditures: Incumbents and challengers, major party general election candidates by
election outcome, 1974–2012 (full cycle, mean net dollars). Available
at http://www.cfinst.org/pdf/vital/VitalStats_t3.pdf. Retrieved January 4, 2015.

Campaign Finance Institute. 2012b. Non-Party Independent Expenditures in
House and Senate Elections, 1978–2012 (in dollars). Available at http://
www.cfinst.org/pdf/vital/VitalStats_t14.pdf. Retrieved January 4,
2015.

Campaign Finance Institute. 2012c. Senate campaign expenditures: In-cumbents and challengers, major party general election candidates by election outcome, 1980–2012. Available at http://www.cfinst.org/pdf/vital/VitalStats_t6.pdf. Retrieved January 4, 2015.

Campaign Finance Institute. 2012d. Campaign funding sources: House and senate major party general election candidates, 1984–2012. Available at http://www.cfinst.org/pdf/vital/VitalStats_t8.pdf. Retrieved January 4, 2015.

Campbell, A. 1960. Surge and decline: A study of electoral change. *Public Opinion Quarterly* 24:397–418.

Campbell, A., P. E. Converse, W. E Miller, and D. E. Stokes. 1960. *The American voter*. Chicago: University of Chicago Press.

Campbell, J. E. 2003. The stagnation of congressional elections. In *Life after reform: When the Bipartisan Campaign Reform Act meets politics*, ed. M. Malbin, 141–57. Lanham, MD: Rowman & Littlefield.

Campbell, J. E. 2008. *The American campaign: U.S. presidential campaigns and the national vote*. College Station: Texas A&M University Press.

Cassidy, J. 2014. Why didn't anyone see the G.O.P. tidal wave coming? *New Yorker*, November 7. Available at http://www.newyorker.com/news/john-cassidy/cassidys-count-didnt-anyone-see-gop-wave-coming. Retrieved January 5, 2014.

Castellanos, A. 1998. Interview on *The: 30 second candidate*. PBS. Available at http://www.pbs.org/30secondcandidate.

The Center for Responsive Politics. 2014a. The money behind the elections. Available at https://www.opensecrets.org/bigpicture/. Retrieved January 4, 2015.

The Center for Responsive Politics. 2014b. Reelection rates over the years. https://www.opensecrets.org/bigpicture/reelect.php. Retrieved January 4, 2015.

Chadderdon, L. 2009. Going strong; these direct mail gurus say their medium is far from dead. *Politics*, May, 22.

Chatlos, S., and J. Barger. 2014. Tech transformation and the human touch. *Campaigns and Elections*, January/February, 8–10.

Chemi, E. 2014. Food politics: The United States of bacon and kale. *Businessweek*, August 15. Available at http://www.businessweek.com/articles/2014–08–15/kale-for-democrats-bacon-for-republicans-an-american-food-map. Retrieved January 4, 2015.

Chen, A. 2014. PowerPAC + releases first-of-its kind audit on diversity in Democratic spending. *PowerPAC +*, June 26. Available at http://www.powerpacplus.org/powerpac_releases_first_of_its_kind_audit_on_diversity_in_democratic_spending. Retrieved January 4, 2015.

Choma, R. 2013. The 2012 election: Our price tag (finally) for the whole ball of wax. The Center for Responsive Politics, March 13. Available at http://www.opensecrets.org/news/2013/03/the-2012-election-our-price-tag-fin/. Retrieved January 21, 2015.

Choma, R. 2014. Money won Tuesday, but rules of the game changed. The Center for Responsive Politics, November 5. Available at http://www.opensecrets.org/news/2014/11/money-won-on-tuesday-but-rules-of-the-game-changed/. Retrieved January 4, 2015.

Christensen, K.S. 2009. Building a database for fundraising. *Politics*. April, 54–55.

Cohen, R. 2012. "Wow!" on social media metrics from the Obama campaign. *NonProfit Quarterly*, December 4. Available at https://nonprofitquarterly.org/management/21443-wow-on-social-media-metrics-from-the-obama-campaign.html. Retrieved January 4, 2015.

Cohn, N. 2014a. Demise of the southern Democrat is now nearly complete. *New York Times*, December 4. Available at http://www.nytimes.com/2014/12/05/upshot/demise-of-the-southern-democrat-is-now-nearly-compete.html?_r=0&abt=0002&abg=0. Retrieved January 4, 2015.

Cohn, N. 2014b. Southern whites' loyalty to G.O.P. nearing that of blacks to Democrats. *New York Times*, April 23. Available at http://www.nytimes.com/2014/04/24/upshot/southern-whites-loyalty-to-gop-nearing-that-of-blacks-to-democrats.html?abt=0002&abg=1. Retrieved January 4, 2015.

Cole, J., M. Suman, P. Schramm, L. Zhou, and A. Salvador. 2013. Surveying the digital future. Available at http://www.digitalcenter.org/wp-content/uploads/2013/06/2013-Report.pdf. Retrieved January 4, 2015.

Condon, P. 2008. Senate candidates clash in last debate. Associated Press, November 3.

Confessore, N., and E. Lipton. 2012. A big check, and Gingrich gets a big lift. *New York Times*, January 9. Available at http://www.nytimes.com/2012/01/10/us/politics/sheldon-adelson-a-billionaire-gives-gingrich-a-big-lift.html?pagewanted=all. Retrieved January 4, 2015.

Connell, M. 1999/2000. A guide to finding a smart Internet strategy for 2000. *Campaigns and Elections*, December/January, 58.

Connelly, M., J. Huang, and J. Merrill. 2014. Exit polls. *New York Times*, November 4. Available at http://www.nytimes.com/interactive/2014/11/04/us/politics/2014-exit-polls.html?utm_source=top_nav&utm_medium=web&utm_campaign=election-2014&_r=2. Retrieved January 4, 2015.

connor17. 2008. Response to: McCain unveils his surprise veep pick at a conservative southwest Ohio stronghold. *Cleveland Plain Dealer*, August 29. Available at http://blog.cleveland.com/openers/2008/08/dayton_arizona_sen_john.html. Retrieved January 4, 2015.

Corn, D. 2012. Romney tells millionaire donors what he really thinks of Obama voters. *Mother Jones*, September 17. Available at http://www.motherjones.com/politics/2012/09/secret-video-romney-private-fundraiser. Retrieved January 4, 2015.

Cornfield, M. 2006. Late money. *Campaigns and Elections*, July, 46.

Cotter, C.P., J.L. Gibson, J.F. Bibby, and R.J. Huckshorn. 1984. *Party organizations in American politics*. Pittsburgh: University of Pittsburgh Press.

Cover, A.D. 1985. Surge and decline in congressional elections. *Western Political Quarterly* 38:606–19.

Craig, S.C., and D.B. Hill. 2010. *The electoral challenges: Theory meets practice*, 2nd ed. Washington, DC: CQ Press.

Crowder-Meyer, M. 2009. The party's still going: Local party strength and activity in 2008. In *The state of the parties*, 6th ed., eds. J. Green and D. Coffey, 115–34. Lanham, MD: Rowman & Littlefield.

Dale, A., and A. Strauss. 2009. Don't forget to vote: Text message reminders as a mobilization tool. *American Journal of Political Science* 53: 787–804.

Daley, S. n.d. Write an optimized political press release. *Online Candidate*. Available at http://www.onlinecandidate.com/articles/write-an-optimized-political-press-release. Retrieved January 4, 2015.

D'Aprile, S. 2008. What leadership PACs really reveal. *Campaigns and Elections*, May, 14.

D'Aprile, S. 2010. The staggering price of money. *Campaigns and Elections*, May, 28–33.

Deaver, M.K., and M. Herskowitz. 1987. *Behind the scenes*. New York: William Morrow.

DeSilver, D. 2013. Only 1 in 7 House districts were competitive in 2012. Pew Research Center, November 5. http://www.pewresearch.org/fact-tank/2013/11/05/only-1-in-7-house-districts-were-competitive-in-2012/. Retrieved January 4, 2015.

Devine, T. 2008. How to leak like a pro. *Campaigns and Elections*, August, 62.

Diamond, E., and S. Bates. 1992. *The spot: The rise of political advertising on television*. Cambridge, MA: MIT Press.

Dimock, M., C. Doherty, J. Kiley, and R. Oates. 2014. Political polarization in the American public: How increasing ideological uniformity and partisan antipathy affect politics, compromise and everyday life. Pew Research Center, June 12. Available at http://www.people-press.org/files/2014/06/6–12–2014-Political-Polarization-Release.pdf. Retrieved January 4, 2015.

Dinkin, R.J. 1989. *Campaigning in America: The history of election practices*. New York: Greenwood Press.

Dionne, E.J. 1987. Gary Hart, the elusive front-runner. *New York Times*, September 18. Available at http://www.nytimes.com/2014/09/21/magazine/gary-hart-the-elusive-front-runner.html?_r=0. Retrieved January 4, 2015.

Ditonto, T.M., A.J. Hamilton, and D.P. Redlawsk. 2014. Gender stereotypes, information search, and voting behavior in political campaigns. *Political Behavior* 36:335–58.

Dittmar, K. 2015. *Navigating gendered terrain: Stereotypes and strategy in political campaigns*. Philadelphia, PA: Temple University Press.

Dixon, M. 2014. Crist hits Scott for self-financing, defends campaign stop in courthouse. *Political Fix Florida*, November 1. Available at http://www.politicalfixflorida.com/2014/11/01/crist-hits-scott-for-self-financing-defends-campaign-stop-in-courthouse/. Retrieved January 4, 2015.

Dobbs, M. 2008. Hillary's Balkan adventures, part II. *Fact Checker* Available at http://blog.washingtonpost.com/fact-checker/2008/03/hillarys_balkan_adventures_par.html.

Doherty, C., S. Keeter, and R. Weisel. 2014. The party of nonvoters: Younger, more racially diverse, more financially strapped. Pew Research Center, October 31. Available at http://www.people-press.org/files/2014/10/10–31–14-Party-of-Nonvoters-release.pdf. Retrieved January 4, 2015.

Dolan, K. 2014. *When does gender matter?: Women candidates and gender stereotypes in American elections*. New York: Oxford University Press.

Downs, A. 1957. *An economic theory of democracy*. New York: Harper & Row.

Draper, R. 2008. The making (and remaking and remaking) of McCain. *New York Times*, October 26.

Drinkard, J., and J. Lawrence. 2004. Online, off and running: Web a new campaign front. *USA Today*, October 26. Available at http://usatoday30.usatoday.com/news/politicselections/2003–07–14-online-cover-usat_x.htm.

Druckman, J.N., M.J. Kifer, and M. Parkin. 2007. The technological development of congressional candidate Web sites: How and why candidates use Web innovations. *Social Science Computer Review* 25:425–42.

Dulio, D.A. 2004. *For better or worse? How political consultants are changing elections in the United States*. Albany, NY: State University of New York Press.

Dutwin, D., and M.H. Lopez. 2014. Considerations of survey error in surveys of Hispanics. *Public Opinion Quarterly*, published online prior to print, July 22.

Edelman, A., and J. Straw. 2014. New York Rep. Michael Grimm threatens reporter after being asked about fundraising allegations. *New York Daily News*, January 29. Available at http://www.nydailynews.com/news/politics/new-york-rep-michael-grimm-threatens-reporter-asked-fundraising-allegations-article-1.1594857. Retrieved January 4, 2015.

Einstein, K.E., and D.M. Glick. 2014. Do I think BLS data are BS? The consequences of conspiracy theories. *Political Behavior*, published online prior to press, September 4.

Elazar, D.J. 1993. *The American mosaic: The impact of space, time, and culture on American politics*. Boulder, CO: Westview Press.

Ellin, A. 2012. GOP jobs report manipulation claims dismissed. *ABC News*, October 5. Available at http://abcnews.go.com/blogs/business/2012/10/does-the-white-house-manipulate-jobs-numbers/. Retrieved January 4, 2015.

Elon Poll. 2014. Hagan leads Tillis with wide gender gap among likely voters. September 15. Available at http://www.elon.edu/e-net/Article/100374. Retrieved January 4, 2015.

Everett, B. 2014. Harry Reid apologizes to Asians over "Wong" comment. *Politico*, August 22. Available at http://www.politico.com/story/2014/08/harry-reid-asian-apology-110260.html. Retrieved January 4, 2015.

Ferguson, A. 1996. Live free or cry: The truth about New Hampshire. *Weekly Standard*, January, 42–47.

Fields, A., and R. Kominski. 2012. America: A nation on the move. *Random Samplings*. Available at http://blogs.census.gov/2012/12/10/america-a-nation-on-the-move/. Retrieved January 4, 2015.

Fineman, H., and P. Blumenthal. 2012. Political consultants rake it in, $466 million and counting in 2012 cycle. *Huffington Post*, June 5. Available at http://www.huffingtonpost.com/2012/06/05/political-consultants-2012-campaign-big-money_n_1570157.html?utm_hp_ref=profits-of-politics. Retrieved January 4, 2015.

Fiorina, M.P. 1981. *Retrospective voting in American national elections*. New Haven, CT: Yale University Press.

Fiorina, M.P., S.J. Abrams, and J.C. Pope. 2006. *Culture war? The myth of a polarized America*. 2nd ed. New York: Pearson Education.

Fletcher, F., and M. L. Young. 2012. Political communication in a changing media environment. In *The SAGE Handbook of Political Communication*, eds. H.A. Semetko and M. Scammell, 36–48. Thousand Oaks, CA: SAGE.

Florida Democratic Party. n.d. *Voter contact strategies and targeting*. Tallahassee, FL: Florida Democratic Party. Available at http://www.fladems.com/sync/documents/Training_Manual_Voter_Contact.pdf. Retrieved February 25, 2010.

Fowler, L.L., and R.D. McClure. 1989. *Political ambition: Who decides to run for Congress*. New Haven, CT: Yale University Press.

Fresh Air. 2012. Colber "re-becoming" the nation we always were. National Public Radio, October 4. Available at http://www.npr.org/2012/10/04/162304439/colbert-re-becoming-the-nation-we-always-were. Retrieved January 4, 2015.

Friedenberg, R.V. 1997. *Communication consultants in political campaigns: Ballot box warriors*. Westport, CT: Praeger.

Friedman, L.M. 1993. *Crime and punishment in American history*. New York: Basic Books.

Fuller, J. 2014. The newest ad in the Florida governor's race will make you thankful the election is almost over. *Washington Post*, October 27. Available at http://www.washingtonpost.com/blogs/the-fix/wp/2014/10/27/the-newest-ad-in-the-florida-governors-race-will-make-you-thankful-the-election-is-almost-over/. Retrieved January 4, 2015.

Gaddie, R.K. 2004. *Born to run: Origins of the political career*. Lanham, MD: Rowman & Littlefield.

Gass, H. 2014. Justice for sale?More money flowing to judicial elections. *Christian Science Monitor*, November 2.

Gelman, A. 2014a. How Bayesian analysis cracked the red-state, blue-state problem. *Statistical Science* 29:26–35.

Gelman, A. 2014b. Republicans aren't really a blue-collar party. *Washington Post*, April 25. Available at http://www.washingtonpost.com/blogs/monkey-cage/wp/2014/04/25/republicans-arent-really-a-blue-collar-party/. Retrieved January 4, 2015.

Gelman, A., L. Kenworthy, and Y. Su. 2010. Income inequality and partisan voting in the United States. *Social Science Quarterly* 91:1203–19.

Gelman, A., D. Park, B. Shor, J. Bafumi, and J. Cortino. 2008. *Red state, blue state, rich state, poor state: Why Americans vote the way they do*. Princeton, NJ: Princeton University Press.

Gelman, A., and D. Rothschild. 2014. Modern polling needs innovation, not traditionalism. *Washington Post*, August 4. Available at http://www.washingtonpost.com/blogs/monkey-cage/wp/2014/08/04/modern-polling-requires-both-sampling-and-adjustment. Retrieved on January 4, 2015.

Gerber, A.S., and D.P. Green. 2000. The effects of canvassing, telephone calls, and direct mail on voter turnout: A field experiment. *American Political Science Review* 94:653–63.

Gerber, A.S., and D.P. Green. 2012. *Field experiments: Design, analysis, and interpretation*. New York: W.W. Norton.

Gertner, J. 2004. The very, very personal is the political. *New York Times*, February 15.

Gibson, J.L. 2012. *Electing judges: The surprising effects of campaigns on judicial legitimacy*. Chicago: University of Chicago Press.

Gibson, J.L., C.P. Cotter, J.F. Bibby, and R.J. Huckshorn. 1983. Assessing party organizational strength. *American Journal of Political Science* 27:193–222.

Giuda, K. 2012. Microtargeting in real time. *Campaigns and Elections*, March 15. Available at http://www.campaignsandelections.com/campaign-insider/671/microtargeting-in-real-time. Retrieved January 4, 2015.

Glad, P.W. 1964. *McKinley, Bryan, and the people*. Philadelphia: Lippincott.

Glasser, S.B. 2000a. Hired guns fuel fundraising race. *Washington Post*, April 30.

Glasser, S.B. 2000b. Winning a stake in a losing race. *Washington Post*, May 1.

Gold, M. 2014. Big spending by parties, independent groups drowns airwaves in negative attacks. *Washington Post*, October 22. Available at http://www.washingtonpost.com/politics/big-spending-by-parties-independent-groups-drowns-airwaves-in-negative-attacks/2014/10/21/b4447f66–593c-11e4-b812–38518ae74c67_story.html. Retrieved January 4, 2015.

Gold, M. 2014b. Tea Party PACs reap money for midterms, but spend little on candidates. *Washington Post*, April 26. Available at http://www.washingtonpost.com/politics/tea-party-pacs-reap-money-for-midterms-but-spend-little-on-candidates/2014/04/26/0e52919a-cbd6–11e3-a75e-463587891b57_story.html. Retrieved January 4, 2015.

Goldfarb, Z.A. 2007. With opposition research, tone is revealing. *Washington Post*, June 16.

Gomez, H.J. 2014. Gov. John Kasich ignores Ed FitzGerald in their only meeting of election season: 5 observations. *Cleveland Plain Dealer*, October 25. Available at http://www.cleveland.com/open/index.ssf/2014/10/gov_john_kasich_ignores_ed_fit.html. Retrieved January 4, 2015.

Goodliffe, J. 2000. The 1998 Utah Second Congressional District race. In *Outside money: Soft money and issue advocacy in the 1998 congressional elections*, ed. D.B. Magleby, 171–85. Lanham, MD: Rowman & Littlefield.

Graf, J. 2008. New media: The cutting edge of campaign communications. In *Campaigns on the cutting edge*, ed. R.J. Semiatin, 48–68. Washington, DC: CQ Press.

Graham, D.A. 2012. The incredible negative spending of super PACs—in 1 chart. *Atlantic*, October 15. Available at http://www.theatlantic.com/politics/archive/2012/10/the-incredible-negative-spending-of-super-pacs-in-1-chart/263643/. Retrieved January 4, 2015.

Green, D.P., and A.S. Gerber. 2006. Can registration-based sampling improve the accuracy of midterm election forecasts? *Public Opinion Quarterly* 70:197–223.

Green, D.P., and A.S. Gerber. 2008. *Get out the vote: How to increase voter turnout*. 2nd ed. Washington, DC: Brookings Institution Press.

Green, D.P., and A.S. Gerber. 2010. Introduction to social pressure and voting: New experimental evidence. *Political Behavior* 32:331–36.

Green, D.P., A.S. Gerber, and C.W. Larimer. 2008. Social pressure and voter turnout: Evidence from a large-scale field experiment. *American Political Science Review* 102:33–48.

Green, D. P., M. C. McGrath, and P. A. Arnow. 2013. Field experiments and the study of voter turnout. *Journal of Elections, Public Opinion and Parties* 23:27–48.

Grefe, E.A. 1997/1998. Can political candidates afford to allow their data to be managed by anyone but a professional? *Campaigns and Elections*, December/January.

Grey, L. 2007. *How to win a local election.* 3rd ed. Lanham, MD: M. Evans.

Gross, D.A., and P. Miller. 2000. The 1998 Kentucky Senate and Sixth District races. In *Outside money: Soft money and issue advocacy in the 1998 congressional elections*, ed. D.B. Magleby, 187–210. Lanham, MD: Rowman & Littlefield.

Gulati, G.J., and C.B. Williams. 2007. Closing the gap, raising the bar: Candidate Web site communication in the 2006 campaigns for Congress. *Social Science Computer Review* 25:443–65.

Guzzetta, S.J. 2006. *The campaign manual: A definitive study of the modern political campaign process.* 7th ed. Alexandria, VA: Political Publications.

Guzzetta, S.J. 2010. *The campaign manual: A definitive study of the modern political campaign process.* 8th ed. Ronkonkoma, NY: Linus Publications.

Haberman, C. 2014. The cost of campaigns. *New York Times*, October 19. Available at http://www.nytimes.com/2014/10/20/us/the-cost-of-campaigns.html?_r=1. Retrieved January 4, 2015.

Halperin, M., and J.F. Harris. 2006. *The way to win: Taking the White House in 2008.* New York: Random House.

Hamilton, A. 2011. Opposition research 101: From Andrew Jackson to Herman Cain. *WNYC*, November 4. Available at http://www.wnyc.org/story/168559-getting-goods-opposition-research-and-politics/. Retrieved January 4, 2015.

Hancock, L. 2014. Two days on the bus: Frugal Hardy scraps together campaign in daunting senate bid. *Casper Star-Tribune*, October 25. Available at http://trib.com/news/state-and-regional/govt-and-politics/two-days-on-the-bus-frugal-hardy-scraps-together-campaign/article_1e904fd4-da5d-57f5-bc2b-fd52c1658a9d.html. Retrieved January 4, 2015.

Harris, M. 2014. Is Twitter ruining young press operatives? *Campaigns and Elections*, August 11. Available at http://www.campaignsandelections.com/magazine/1687/is-twitter-ruining-young-press-operatives. Retrieved January 4, 2015.

Harris, V. 2012. A social media-fueled upset. *Campaigns and Elections*, September/October, 30–3.

Hartford Courant, 2014. Greenberg denounces DCCC research book in web ad, August 28. Available at http://articles.courant.com/2014-08-28/politics/hc-mark-greenberg-esty-dccc-0829-20140828_1_shady-landlord-esty-campaign-super-pacs. Retrieved January 4, 2015.

Hartman, J.K. 2012. Columbus Dispatch unveils sub-tabloid format. *Editor & Publisher*, September 10. Available at http://www.editorandpublisher.com/Columns/Article/Columbus-Dispatch-Unveils-Sub-Tabloid-Format. Retrieved January 4, 2015.

Hasen, R.L. 2012. The numbers don't lie. *Slate*, March 9. Available at http:// www.slate.com/articles/news_and_politics/politics/2012/03/the_su preme_court_s_citizens_united_decision_has_led_to_an_explosion_ of_campaign_spending_.html. Retrieved January 4, 2015.

Hawley, G. 2013. *Voting and migration patterns in the U.S.* New York: Routledge.

Heffter, E. 2008. Darcy Burner's claims of a Harvard econ degree an exaggeration. *Seattle Times*, October 23. Available at http://seattletimes .nwsource.com/html/localnews/2008298919_webburner23m.html.

Heileman, J. and M. Halperin. 2010. Game change: Obama and the Clintons, McCain and Palin, and the race of a lifetime. New York: Harper.

Heineman, Jr., B.W. 2012. Super PACs: The WMDs of campaign finance. *Atlantic*, January 6. Available at http://www.theatlantic.com/politics/ar chive/2012/01/super-pacs-the-wmds-of-campaign-finance/250961/. Retrieved January 4, 2015.

Helliker, K. 2007. Political ads stage a comeback in newspapers. *Wall Street Journal Online*, July 26. Available at http://www.wsj.com/articles/ SB118541344062578440. Retrieved February 28, 2010.

Henderson, N. 2014. Mark Udall has been dubbed "Mark Uterus" on the campaign trail. That's a problem. *Washington Post*, October 13. Available at http://www.washingtonpost.com/blogs/the-fix/wp/2014/10/ 13/mark-udall-has-been-dubbed-mark-uterus-on-the-campaign-trail- thats-a-problem/. Retrieved January 4, 2015.

Herrnson, P.S. 2012. *Congressional elections: Campaigning at home and in Washington.* 6th ed. Washington, DC: CQ Press.

Hershey, M.R. 1984. *Running for office: The political education of campaigners.* Chatham, NJ: Chatham House.

Hesla, M., A. Leibowitz, and E. Peavey. 2013. The state of the political industry. *Campaigns and Elections*, May/June.

Hesse, M. 2014. West Virginia's Saira Blair is learning to balance college life, state politics. *Washington Post*, December 6. Available at http:// www.washingtonpost.com/lifestyle/style/west-virginias-saira-blair- is-learning-to-balance-college-life-state-politics/2014/12/06/6475df0 8–7407–11e4-a5b2-e1217af6b33d_story.html. Retrieved January 4, 2015.

Hewitt, J. 1999. Sending effective press releases. *Campaigns and Elections*, April.

Hicks, J. 2008. Fossella is said to be ending re-election bid. *New York Times*, May 20, 1.

Hill, S. 2014. McCutcehon's silver lining: How it could undermine super PACs. *Atlantic*, April 3. Available at http://www.theatlantic.com/ politics/archive/2014/04/-em-mccutcheon-em-s-silver-lining-how-it- could-undermine-super-pacs/360070/. Retrieved January 4, 2015.

Hill, W.W. 2013. Should more polls be interpreted as too close to call? *PS: Political Science & Politics* 46:329–32.

Hillygus, D.S., and T.G. Shields. 2008. *The persuadable voter: Wedge issues in presidential campaigns.* Princeton, NJ: Princeton University Press.

Hines, C. 1992. The Reagan–Bush era: Reagan's simple message hit the spot. *Houston Chronicle*, August 16.

Hockaday, T., and M. Edlund. 1999. Banner advertising as a voter outreach tool. *Campaigns and Elections*, May.

Hohmann, J. 2014a. The Michelle Nunn memos: 10 key passages. *Politico*, July 28. Available at http://www.politico.com/story/2014/07/michelle-nunn-memos-10-key-passages-109463.html#ixzz3NFYtyh94. Retrieved January 4, 2015.

Hohmann, J. 2014b. Why Mark Begich's "Willie Horton" ad matters. *Politico*, September 3. Available at http://www.politico.com/story/2014/09/mark-begich-ad-110559.html. Retrieved January 4, 2015.

Hohmann, J., and M. Haberman. 2014. Democrats bail on Mary Landrieu. *Politico*, November 6. Available at http://www.politico.com/story/2014/11/democrats-ads-mary-landrieu-112647.html. Retrieved January 4, 2015.

Holbrook, T. 1996. *Do campaigns matter?* Thousand Oaks, CA: SAGE.

Hruby, P. 2012. Learning to love oppo researchers, whistle-blowers of democracy. *Washington Times*, July 17. Available at http://www.washingtontimes.com/news/2012/jul/17/diligent-but-maligned-opposition-researchers-searc/#ixzz3Lzydf4YM. Retrieved January 4, 2015.

Hudak, J. 2014. Harry Reid should love marijuana: How legalization should keep the Senate blue. *Brookings*, August 20. Available at http://www.brookings.edu/blogs/fixgov/posts/2014/08/20-harry-reid-marijuana-keep-the-senate-blue-hudak. Retrieved January 4, 2015.

Huisenga, S. 2012. Gingrich to super PAC: Fix negative ad or take it down. *National Journal*, January 13. Available at http://www.nationaljournal.com/2012-presidential-campaign/gingrich-to-super-pac-fix-negative-ad-or-take-it-down-20120113. Retrieved January 4, 2015.

Hurt, C. 2004. Kerry bags geese but plays down gory details. *Washington Times*, October 22.

Hutchens, J. 1996. Buying cable time: How to get your money's worth. *Campaigns and Elections*, June.

Ingram, M. 2012. Is Twitter good or bad for political journalism? *Businessweek*, August 28. Available at http://www.businessweek.com/articles/2012–08–28/is-twitter-good-or-bad-for-political-journalism. Retrieved January 4, 2015.

Initiative and Referendum Institute. 2013. Initiative use. January. Available at http://www.iandrinstitute.org/IRI%20Initiative%20Use%20(2013–1).pdf. Retrieved January 4, 2015.

Issa, N., and L. Jacobson. 2014. Congress has 11% approval ratings but 96% incumbent reelection rate, meme says. *PolitiFact*, November 11.

Available at http://www.politifact.com/truth-o-meter/statements/2014/nov/11/facebook-posts/congress-has-11-approval-ratings-96-incumbent-re-e/. Retrieved January 4, 2015.

Issenberg, S. 2008. Obama trumpets message of unity in Europe: "The walls . . . cannot stand." *Boston Globe*, July 25.

Issenberg, S. 2010. Nudge the vote. *New York Times*, October 29. Available at http://www.nytimes.com/2010/10/31/magazine/31politics-t.html?pagewanted=all&gwh=F9E31887BF538D4039DAE32FF6A AFB59&gwt=pay. Retrieved January 4, 2015.

Issenberg, S. 2012a. How President Obama's campaign used big data to rally individual voters. *MIT Technology Review*, December 19. Available at http://www.technologyreview.com/featuredstory/509026/how-obamas-team-used-big-data-to-rally-voters/. Retrieved January 3, 2015.

Issenberg, S. 2012b. *The victory lab: The secret science of winning campaigns*. New York: Crown.

Jacobs, J. 2014a. Ernst cancels meeting with Register's editorial board. *Des Moines Register*, October 23. Available at http://www.desmoines-register.com/story/news/elections/2014/10/23/ernst-declines-meeting-with-register-editorial-board/17782955/. Retrieved January 4, 2015.

Jacobs, J. 2014b. Self-funding campaigns can backfire on candidates. *USA Today*, April 23. Available at http://www.usatoday.com/story/news/2014/04/23/self-funding-campaigns-can-backfire-on-candidates/8080485/. Retrieved January 4, 2015.

Jacobs, L.R. 2005. Communicating from the White House: Presidential narrowcasting and the national interest. In *The executive branch*, eds. J.D. Aberbach and M.A. Peterson, 174–217. New York: Oxford University Press.

Jacobson, G.C. 1989. Strategic politicians and the dynamics of U.S. House elections, 1946–86. *The American Political Science Review* 83:773–93.

Jacobson, G.C. 2013. *The politics of congressional elections*. 8th ed. New York: Pearson Longman.

Jacobson, G.C. 2015. How do campaigns matter? *Annual Review of Political Science*: 18.

Jaffe, A. 2012. McCain warns on campaign money: "There will be a scandal." *National Journal*, January 29. Available at http://www.nationaljournal.com/2012-presidential-campaign/mccain-warns-on-campaign-money-there-will-be-a-scandal—20120129. Retrieved January 4, 2015.

Jaffe, A. 2014. GOP mailer turns Grimes into Obama. *Hill*, October 30. Available at http://thehill.com/blogs/ballot-box/senate-races/222314-gop-mailer-turns-grimes-into-obama. Retrieved January 4, 2015.

Jalonick, M.C. 2000. Greatest hits II: Democratic House candidate sites. *Campaigns and Elections*, July.

Jamieson, K.H. 1996. *Packaging the presidency.* 3rd ed. New York: Oxford University Press.

Jamieson, K.H., and J.N. Cappella. 2008. *Echo chamber: Rush Limbaugh and the conservative media establishment.* New York: Oxford University Press.

Johnson, D.W. 2007. *No place for amateurs: How political consultants are reshaping American democracy.* 2nd ed. New York: Routledge.

Johnson, D.W. 2011. *Campaigning in the twenty-first century: A whole new ballgame?* New York: Routledge.

Johnson, D.W. 2015. *Political consultants and American elections: Hired to fight, hired to win.* New York: Routledge.

Johnson, D.W. Forthcoming, 2016. *Democracy for hire: A history of American political consulting.* New York: Oxford University Press.

Johnson-Cartee, K.S., and G.A. Copeland. 1991. *Negative political advertising: Coming of age.* Hillsdale, NJ: Lawrence Erlbaum Associates.

Jones, J.M. 2014a. U.S. whites more solidly Republican in recent years. *Gallup*, March 24. Available at http://www.gallup.com/poll/168059/whites-solidly-republican-recent-years.aspx. Retrieved January 4, 2015.

Jones, P.E. 2014b. Revisiting stereotypes of non-white politicians' ideological and partisan orientations. *American Politics Research* 42:283–310.

Jones, S. 1964. *The presidential election of 1896.* Madison: University of Wisconsin Press.

Kanfer, R. 1991. Direct to the bank. *Campaigns and Elections*, July.

Kang, C., and M. Gold. 2014. With political ads expected to hit a record, news stations can hardly keep up. *Washington Post*, October 31. Available at http://www.washingtonpost.com/business/technology/with-political-ads-expected-to-hit-a-record-news-stations-can-hardly-keep-up/2014/10/31/84a9e4b4–5ebc–11e4–9f3a-7e28799e0549_story.html. Retrieved January 4, 2015.

Kaplan, R.L. 2000. Getting the most out of your professional fundraiser. *Campaigns and Elections*, February.

Kapochunas, R. 2009. Facebook: Opposition research dream come true. *CQ Politics*, June 26.

Katz, B.A., and C. Katz. 2009. Online politics is also local. *Campaign Guide*. Available at http://www.completecampaigns.com/article.asp?articleid=1. Retrieved February 25, 2010.

Kay, Tim. 2014. The case for keeping cable in your media mix. *NCC Media*. Available at http://nccmedia.com/2014/02/01/ncc-medias-tim-kay-the-case-for-keeping-cable-in-your-media-mix/. Retrieved January 4, 2015.

Kayden, X., and E. Mahe Jr., eds. 1985. *The party goes on.* New York: Basic Books.

Keeter, S., C. Kennedy, A. Clark, T. Tompson, and M. Mokrzycki. 2007. What's missing from national landline RDD surveys? The impact of the growing cell-only population. *Public Opinion Quarterly* 7:772–92.

Keeter, S., L. Christian, K. Purcell, and A. Smith. 2010. Assessing the cell phone challenge to survey research in 2010. Pew Research Center, May 20. Available at http://www.pewresearch.org/files/old-assets/ pdf/1601-cell-phone.pdf. Retrieved January 4, 2015.

Key, V.O. 1966. *The responsible electorate.* New York: Vintage Books.

King, G. 1997. *A solution to the ecological inference problem: Reconstructing individual behavior from aggregate data.* Princeton, NJ: Princeton University Press.

Kingsley, D. 2010. Google can't save your bacon. *Campaigns and Elections*, April.

Kirk, C. 2014. The ugliest elections, charted. *Slate*, November 4. Available at http://www.slate.com/articles/news_and_politics/politics/2014/11/_ 2014_midterm_election_s_most_negative_races_most_political_at tack_ads_by.html. Retrieved January 4, 2015.

Klemanski, J.S., and D.A. Dulio. 2006. *The mechanics of state legislative campaigns.* Belmont, CA: Thomson Higher Education.

Klemanski, J.S., D.A. Dulio, and M. Switalski. 2015. *Campaigns from the ground up: State house elections in a national context.* Boulder, CO: Paradigm.

Knobloch-Westerwick, S., B.K. Johnson, and A. Westerwick. 2014. Confirmation bias in online searches: Impacts of selective exposure before an Election on political attitude strength and shifts. *Journal of Computer-Mediated Communication* Early View.

Kohut, A., C. Doherty, M. Dimock, and S. Keeter. 2012. Trends in American values: 1987–2012: Partisan polarization surges in Bush, Obama years. Pew Research Center, June 4. Available at http://www.people-press.org/files/legacy-pdf/06-04-12%20Values%20Release.pdf. Retrieved January 4, 2015.

Kolodny, R., and D.A. Dulio. 2003. Political party adaptation in US congressional campaigns: Why political parties use coordinated expenditures to hire political consultants. *Party Politics* 9:729–46.

Kornblut, A.E. 2004. Strategist focuses on president's devotees. *Boston Globe*, August 30.

Krauthammer, C. 2008. The audacity of selling hope. *Washington Post*, February 15.

Kroll, A. 2014. Is your judge for sale? *Mother Jones*, December.

Kucinich, J. 2013. The (GOP) empire promises to strike back. *Washington Post*, November 5. Available at http://www.washingtonpost.com/ blogs/post-politics/wp/2013/11/05/the-empire-promises-to-strike-back-some-more/. Retrieved January 4, 2015.

Kurtz, H. 1992a. Clinton, Bush ads go separate ways: While Democrat targets specific states, Republican uses nationwide approach. *Washington Post*, September 23.

Kurtz, H. 1992b. The story that just won't check out. *Washington Post,* February 19.

LaPotin, K. 2011. Lesson in self research. *Campaigns and Elections,* November 9. Available at http://www.campaignsandelections.com/campaign-insider/773/a-lesson-in-self-research. Retrieved January 4, 2015.

Lazarsfeld, P.F., B. Berelson, and H. Gaudet. 1944. *The people's choice: How the voter makes up his mind in a presidential campaign.* New York: Duell, Sloan, & Pearce.

Lees-Marshment, J., ed. 2012. *Routledge handbook of political marketing.* New York: Routledge.

Lees-Marshment, J., B. Conley, and K. Cosgrove. 2014. *Political marketing in the United States.* New York: Routledge.

Leinweber, D.J. 2007. Stupid data miner tricks: Outfitting the S&P 500. *Journal of Investing* 16:15–22.

Leiserowitz, A.A., E.W. Maibach, C. Roser-Renouf, N. Smith, and E. Dawson. 2013. Climategate, public opinion, and the loss of trust. *American Behavioral Scientist* 57:818–37.

Lerman, A.E., and M.L. Sadin. 2014. Stereotyping or projection? How white and black voters estimate black candidates' ideology. *Political Psychology,* Early View.

Levendusky, M.S. 2013. Why do partisan media polarize viewers? *American Journal of Political Science* 57:611–23.

Lewis, B. 2013. Why candidates hate fundraising. *Campaigns and Elections,* October 1. Available at http://www.campaignsandelections.com/magazine/1738/why-candidates-hate-fundraising. Retrieved January 4, 2015.

Lewis-Beck, M.S., W.G. Jacoby, H. Norpoth, and H.F. Weisberg. 2008. *The American voter revisited.* Ann Arbor: University of Michigan Press.

Lightman, D. 2009. GOP "trackers" stalk Dems in hunt for "macaca" moment. *McClatchy Washington Bureau,* March 16.

*Literary Digest.* 1936a. Landon, 1,293,669; Roosevelt 972,897. October 31, 5–6.

*Literary Digest.* 1936b. What went wrong with the polls? November 14, 7–8.

Lodge, M., and C.S. Taber. 2013. *The rationalizing voter.* New York: Cambridge University Press.

Lopez, M.H., J.M. Krogstad, E. Patten, and A. Gonzalez-Barrera. 2014. Latino voters and the 2014 midterm election. Pew Research Center, October 16. Available at http://www.pewhispanic.org/2014/10/16/latino-voters-and-the-2014-midterm-elections. Retrieve March 14, 2015.

Lopez, M.H., and A. Gonzalez-Barrera. 2012. Latino voters support Obama by 3–1 ratio, but are less certain than others about voting. Pew Research Center, October 11. Available athttp://www.pewhispanic.org/

files/2012/10/2012_NSL_latino_vote_report_FINAL_10–18–12.pdf. Retrieved January 4, 2015.

Lorber, J. 2012. Obama's campaign quick to capitalize on text-to-donate option. *CQ Roll Call*, October 24. Available at http://cdn.rollcall.com/news/Obama-Campaign-Quick-to-Capitalize-on-Text-to-Donate-Option-218432–1.html?popular=true&cdn_load=true&zkPrintable=1&nopagination=1#sthash.xRZKqNWc.dpuf. Retrieved January 4, 2015.

Luntz, F.I. 1988. *Candidates, consultants, and campaigns: The style and substance of American electioneering*. Oxford, UK: Blackwood.

MacEachern, D. 2014. Guilt by association campaign against Judge Herrod. *Arizona Central*, October 20. Available at http://www.azcentral.com/story/dougmaceachern/2014/10/20/herrod-judge-maricopa-campaign/17618211/. Retrieved January 4, 2015.

Mack, K., and S. Henry. 2012. The future of direct mail is digital. *Campaigns and Elections*, September 17. Available at http://www.campaignsandelections.com/magazine/1796/the-future-of-direct-mail-is-digital. Retrieved January 4, 2015.

Maisel, S. 1990. The incumbency advantage. In *Money, elections, and democracy: Reforming congressional campaign finance*, eds. M.L. Nugent and J.R. Johannes, 119–41. Boulder, CO: Westview Press.

Malbin, M.J. 2006. *The election after reform: Money, Politics and the Bipartisan Campaign Reform Act*. Lanham, MD: Rowman & Littlefield.

Malbin, M.J. 2013. Small donors: Incentives, economies of scale, and effects. *Campaign Finance Institute*. Available at http://www.cfinst.org/pdf/papers/06_Malbin_Small-Donors.pdf. Retrieved January 4, 2015.

Malbin, M.J., C. Wilcox, M. Rozell, and R. Skinner. 2002. New interest group strategies—a preview of post McCain-Feingold politics? *Campaign Finance Institute*, April 19. Available at http://cfinst.org/transcripts/pdf/CFI_RevTranscript_41902.pdf. Retrieved January 4, 2015.

Malchow, H. 2008. *Political targeting*. 2nd ed. Washington, DC: Predicted Lists.

Malchow, H. 2013. Social pressure: A GOTV tactic for the little guy. *Campaigns and Elections*, September/October, 35–36.

Mann, C. 2010. Is there backlash to social pressure? A large-scale field experiment on voter mobilization. *Political Behavior* 32:387–407.

Mann, D. 2014. Wendy Davis' media fail. *Texas Observer*, January 31. Available at http://www.texasobserver.org/wendy-davis-keystone-cops-routine-press/. Retrieved January 4, 2015.

Maor, J. 2001. Writing campaign speeches that connect. *Campaigns and Elections*, August.

Marinucci, C. 2006. Campaign 2006: Gubernatorial race. *San Francisco Chronicle*, June 9.

Marquardt, A. 2008. *Obama says Palin's family off limits*. September 2. Available at http://www.cnn.com/2008/POLITICS/09/01/obama.palin/index.html.

Martin, G., and Z. Peskowitz. 2014. How to judge your consultant. *Campaigns and Elections*, December 4. Available at http://www.cam paignsandelections.com/campaign-insider/2371/how-to-judge-your-consultant. Retrieved January 4, 2015.

Martin, J., and A. Parnes. 2008. McCain: Obama not an Arab, crowd boos. *Politico*, October 10. Available at http://www.politico.com/news/stories/1008/14479.html#ixzz3M05WPiBf Muslim. Retrieved January 4, 2015.

Mason, J. 2012. Anatomy of a White House win: How Obama outmaneuvered Romney. *Reuters*, November 7. Available at http://www.reuters.com/article/2012/11/07/usa-campaign-obama-strategy-idUS L1E8M7E1R20121107. Retrieved January 4, 2015.

Matalin, M., and J. Carville. 1995. *All's fair: Love, war, and running for president.* New York: Touchstone.

McCarter, J. 2014. Why do the Koch brothers hate the Columbus zoo? *Daily Kos*, May 6. Available at http://www.dailykos.com/story/2014/05/06/1297343/-Why-do-the-Koch-brothers-hate-the-Colum bus-zoo#. Retrieved January 4, 2015.

McCarthy, Justin. 2014. Most Americans still see crime up over last year. *Gallup*, November 21. Available at http://www.gallup.com/poll/179546/americans-crime-last-year.aspx?. Retrieved January 4, 2015.

McConnaughy, C.M., I.K. White, D.L. Leal, and J.P. Casellas. 2010. *A Latino on the ballot: Explaining coethnic voting among Latinos and the response of white Americans.* Journal of Politics 72:1199–211.

McDonald, M. 2013. A modest early voting rise in 2012. *Huffington Post*, June 12. Available at http://www.huffingtonpost.com/michael-p-mc donald/a-modest-early-voting-ris_b_3430379.html. Retrieved January 4, 2015.

McGhee, E. 2014. What if election polls are biased against winners? *Washington Post*, December 8. Available at http://www.washingtonpost.com/blogs/monkey-cage/wp/2014/12/08/what-if-election-polls-are-biased-against-winners/. Retrieved January 4, 2015.

McGinniss, J. 1969. *The selling of the president, 1968.* New York: Trident.

McLuhan, M. 1964. *Understanding media: The extensions of man.* New York: McGraw-Hill.

McQuade, D. 2014. Tom Corbett's campaign photoshopped him next to a black woman. *Philadelphia Magazine*, October 17. Available at http://www.phillymag.com/news/2014/10/17/tom-corbett-campaign-photoshop/. Retrieved January 4, 2015.

Medvic, S.K. 2001. *Political consultants in U.S. congressional elections.* Columbus, OH: Ohio State University Press.

Mendolera, K. 152 newspapers shut down in 2011. 2012. *Ragan's PR Daily*, January 12. Available at http://www.prdaily.com/Main/Articles/152_newspapers_shut_down_in_2011_10536.aspx. Retrieved January 4, 2015.

Meredith, M. 2014. Exploiting friends-and-neighbors to estimate coattail effects. *American Political Science Review* 107:742–65.

Meredith, T. 2000. Fundraising events: The dollars are in the details. *Campaigns and Elections*, February, 61.

Meredith, T. 2004/2005. Open the envelope: Getting people to look at the direct mail they receive. *Campaigns and Elections*, December/January, 76.

Miller, W. E., and J. M. Shanks. 1996. *The new American voter*. Cambridge, MA: Harvard University Press.

Miller, W. J., ed. 2013a. *The 2012 nomination and the future of the Republican Party: The internal battle*. Lanham, MD: Lexington.

Miller, W. J. 2013b. We can't all be Obama: The use of new media in modern political campaigns. *Journal of Political Marketing* 2012: 326–47.

Miller, W. J. 2014. Branding the Tea Party: Political marketing and an American social movement. In Lees-Marshment, Conley, and Cosgrove 2014, 112–129.

Milne, J. 2004. *State senate campaigns turn to consultants*. NHPR News, September 20.

*Milwaukee Journal Sentinel*. 2011. Herman Cain on Libya. November 14. Available at http://www.jsonline.com/multimedia/video/?bcpid=139 60334001&bctid=1275195602001. Retrieved January 4, 2015.

Mitchell, A., and R. Weisel. 2014. Political polarization & media habits: From Fox News to Facebook, how liberals, and conservatives keep up with politics. Pew Research Center, October 21. Available at http://www.journalism.org/files/2014/10/Political-Polarization-and-Media-Habits-FINAL-REPORT-11–10–14.pdf. Retrieved January 4, 2015.

Mitofsky, W., J. Bloom, J. Lenski, S. Dingman, and J. Agiesta. 2005. A dual frame RDD/registration-based sample design: Lessons from Oregon's 2004 National Election Pool Survey. *American Statistical Association*, 3929–36.

Morain, D., and T. Hamburger. 2008. Longtime patron may be a problem for Obama. *Los Angeles Times*, January 23.

"Morning Joe." 2014. And now strip clubs are at play in Florida race. MSNBC, October 28. Available at http://www.msnbc.com/morning-joe/watch/and-now-strip-clubs-are-at-play-in-florida-race-34875 7059871. Retrieved January 4, 2015.

Morris, D. 1999. *Behind the Oval Office: Getting reelected against all the odds*. Los Angeles: Renaissance Books.

Morris, D. 2007a. Direct mail? Get a horse! *Campaigns and Elections*, May, 54.

Morris, D. 2007b. Fund-raisers are really fund-reapers. *Campaigns and Elections*, April.

Morris, D. 2008. Money is losing its mojo. *Campaigns and Elections*, February, 50.

Morris, D., and M.E. Gamache. 1994. *Gold-plated politics: The 1992 congressional races*. Washington, DC: CQ Press.

Motyl, M., R. Iyer, S. Oishi, S. Trawalter, and B.A. Nosek. 2014. How ideological migration geographically segregates groups. *Journal of Experimental Social Psychology* 51:1–14.

Murphy, T. 2012. Rick Santorum's mystery donor. *Mother Jones*, February 28. Available at http://www.motherjones.com/politics/2012/02/william-dore-rick-santorum-mystery-donor. Retrieved January 4, 2015.

Nagourney, A. 2004. Bush campaign manager views the electoral divide. *New York Times*, November 19.

Napolitan, J. 1972. *The election game and how to win it*. Garden City, NY: Doubleday.

Napolitan, J. 1986. Some thoughts on the importance of strategy in a political campaign. In *The National Republican Congressional Committee campaign starter manual*, ed. J. Napolitan. Washington, DC: Republican Congressional Campaign Committee.

National Public Radio. n.d. Fairness. Available at http://ethics.npr.org/category/b-fairness/#1-fairness-in-storytelling. Retrieved January 4, 2015.

National Public Radio. n.d. Anonymous sources. Available at http://ethics.npr.org/category/g-transparency/#3-anonymous-sources. Retrieved January 4, 2015.

NCSL. 2014. Absentee and early voting. October 21. Available at http://www.ncsl.org/research/elections-and-campaigns/absentee-and-early-voting.aspx. Retrieved January 4, 2015.

Nelson, C., D.A. Dulio, and S. Medvic, eds. 2002. *Shades of gray: Perspectives on campaign ethics*. Washington, DC: Brookings Institution Press.

Newport, F. 2014. Religion remains a strong marker of political identity in U.S. *Gallup*, July 28. Available at http://www.gallup.com/poll/174134/religion-remains-strong-marker-political-identity.aspx. Retrieved January 4, 2015.

*New York Times*. 2009. For the mayor of New York City. Editorial, October 24.

Nie, N.H., S. Verba, and J.R. Petrocik. 1979. *The changing American voter*. Cambridge, MA: Harvard University Press.

Nielsen, 2014. What's empowering the new digital consumer? Available at http://www.nielsen.com/us/en/insights/news/2014/whats-empowering-the-new-digital-consumer.html. Retrieved January 4, 2015.

Nimmo, D. 1970. *The political persuaders*. Englewood Cliffs, NJ: Prentice Hall.

Nyhan, B. 2012. Enabling the jobs report conspiracy theory. *Columbia Journalism Review*, October 8. Available at http://www.cjr.org/united_states_project/enabling_the_jobs_report_conspiracy_theory.php. Retrieved January 4, 2015.

Nyhan, B. 2013. When coverage gets ahead of the facts. *Columbia Journalism Review*, September 4. Available at http://www.cjr.org/ united_states_project/jack_welch_jobs_conspiracy_claim_more_ persuasive_in_media_scandal_climate.php. Retrieved January 4, 2015.

Nyhan, B. 2014. You lose, we win: Consultants profit even when candidate underperform. *New York Times*, September 2. Available at http:// www.nytimes.com/2014/09/03/upshot/you-lose-we-win-consultants-profit-even-when-candidates-underperform.html?smid=tw-share&_ r=0&abt=0002&abg=1. Retrieved January 4, 2015.

ocsea.org. 2014. Souls to the Polls: Get a ride to the polls across Ohio. October 31. Available at http://votes.ocsea.org/news/2014/10/31/souls-to-the-polls-get-a-ride-to-the-polls-across-ohio. Retrieved January 4, 2015.

O'Muircheartaigh, C. 2008. Sampling. In *The Sage handbook of public opinion research*, eds. W. Donsbach and M.W. Traugott, 194–308. Los Angeles: Sage.

O'Neill, T., and G. Hymel. 1994. *All politics is local and other rules of the game*. Holbrook, MA: Bob Adams.

O'Neill, T., and W. Novak. 1987. *Man of the House: The life and political memoirs of Speaker Tip O'Neill*. New York: Random House.

Ouzounian, R. 1997. Satellites, feeds and computers. *Campaigns and Elections*, August.

Palin, S. 2008a. Exclusive: Palin on foreign policy. CBS-TV transcripts, September 25. Available at http://www.cbsnews.com/stories/2008/09/25/ eveningnews/main4479062.shtml Retrieved February 25, 2010.

Palin, S. 2008b. Palin opens up on controversial issues. CBS-TV transcripts, September 30. Available at http://www.cbsnews.com/stor ies/2008/09/30/eveningnews/main4490618.shtml. Retrieved February 25, 2010.

Panagopoulos, C., ed. 2009. *Politicking online: The transformation of election campaign communications*. New Brunswick, NJ: Rutgers University Press.

Panagopoulos, C. 2012. Campaign context and preference dynamics in U.S. presidential elections. *Journal of Elections, Public Opinion, and Parties*. 22:123–37.

Panagopoulos, C. 2013. Positive social pressure and prosocial motivation: Evidence from a large scale field experiment on voter mobilization. *Political Psychology* 34:265–75.

Panagopoulos, C., and P.W. Wielhouwer. 2008. The ground war, 2000–2004: Strategic targeting in grassroots campaigns. *Presidential Studies Quarterly* 38:347–62.

Panagopoulos, C., D. Dulio, and S.E. Brewer. 2011. Lady luck? Women political consultants in U.S. congressional campaigns. *Journal of Political Marketing* 10:251–74.

Patterson, K.D., and D.M. Shea. 2003. Local political context and negative campaigns: A test of negative effects across state party systems. *Journal of Political Marketing* 3:1–20.

Patton, Z. 2012. The boss of Boston: Mayor Thomas Menino. *Governing.* January. Available at http://www.governing/com/topics/politics/gov-boss-of-boston-mayor-thomas-menino.html. Retrieved January 4, 2015.

Pearson, R. 2014. New Rauner attack ad relies on made-up headlines. *Chicago Tribune,* July 24. Available at http://www.chicagotribune .com/news/nationworld/politics/chi-new-rauner-attack-ad-relies-on-madeup-headlines-20140723-story.html. Retrieved January 4, 2015.

Pelosi, C. 2010. *Campaign boot camp 2.0: Basic training for candidates, staffers, volunteers, and nonprofits.* San Francisco: Berrett-Koehler Publishers.

Pérez-Peña, R. 2009. 4 Michigan markets will lose daily newspapers, as ailing industry tries to cope. *New York Times,* March 24.

Perress, M. 2010. Correcting for survey nonresponse using variable response propensity. *Journal of the American Statistical Association* 105:1418–30.

Pescatore, B., and A. Zusman. 2007. Digging in the dirt: The last cycle's top oppo finds. *Campaigns and Elections,* July.

Petrocik, J. 1996. Issue ownership in presidential elections, with a 1980 case study. *American Journal of Political Science* 40:825–50.

*Pew Research Center.* 2012. The gender gap: Three decades old, as wide as ever. March 29. Available at http://www.people-press.org/2012/03/29/the-gender-gap-three-decades-old-as-wide-as-ever/?src=prc-num ber#gap-in-party-id. Retrieved January 4, 2015.

Phillip, A. 2009. *Senators fly high on taxpayers' dime.* June 11. Available at http://www.politico.com/news/stories/0609/23615.html.

Pine, J.B. 1993. *Mass customization: The new frontier in business competition.* Boston: Harvard Business School Press.

Pineda, A. 2007. Playing to win: Campaign polls and the Latino vote. *Campaigns and Elections,* January.

Pitney, J.J., Jr. 2000. *The art of political warfare.* Norman, OK: University of Oklahoma Press.

Political Pages Directory, 2014. Available at https://www.politicalpagesdi rectory.com/.

Pollard, A.B., III. 2008. President-elect Obama: He was the one we were waiting for. *US News and World Report,* November 5.

Pomper, G.M. 1974. *Elections in America.* New York: Dodd, Mead.

Popkin, S.L. 1991. *The reasoning voter: Communication and persuasion in presidential campaigns.* Chicago: University of Chicago Press.

Porter, E. 2012. Unleashing the campaign contributions of corporations. *New York Times,* August 28. Available at http://www.nytimes.com/

2012/08/29/business/analysts-expect-a-flood-of-corporate-cam paign-contributions.html?pagewanted=all&_r=0. Retrieved January 4, 2015.

Public Policy Polling. 2013. Fox News' credibility declines. February 6. Available at http://www.publicpolicypolling.com/pdf/2011/PPP_Re lease_National_206.pdf. Received January 4, 2015.

Puzzanghera, J. 2008. Obama's VP text message reached 2.9 million people, Nielsen reports. *Los Angeles Times*, August 16.

Radelat, A. 2014. CT House incumbents winning political money race. *Hartford Courant*, July 29. Available at http://www.courant.com/poli tics/hc-ctm-money-race-20140729-story.html. Retrieved January 4, 2015.

Rehm, D. 2014. Growing use of state ballot initiative for political change. *The Diane Rehm Show*, August 27. Available at http://thedianerehm show.org/shows/2014–08–27/growing-use-state-ballot-initiatives-political-change. Retrieved January 4, 2015.

Reid, T. 2011. The golden age of opposition research. *Reuters*, November 14. Available at http://www.reuters.com/article/2011/11/14/us-campaign-opporesearch-newspro-idUSTRE7AD10620111114. Retrieved January 4, 2015.

RGA. 2014. Memo: RGA's 2014 election results. Available at http://www .rga.org/homepage/memo-rgas-2014-election-results/. Retrieved January 4, 2015.

Richmond, T., and M.I. Johnson. 2014. Documents allege Scott Walker pressured groups to donate to campaign. Associated Press, August 22. Available at http://www.huffingtonpost.com/2014/08/22/documents-scott-walker-campaign_n_5702016.html. Retrieved January 4, 2015.

Riordon, W.L., ed. 1995. *Plunkitt of Tammany Hall: A series of very plain talks by ex-senator George Washington Plunkitt.* New York: Signet.

Robbin, J. 1989. Geodemographics: The new magic. In *Campaigns and elections: A reader in modern American Politics,* ed. L.J. Sabato, 106–25. Glenview, IL: Scott, Foresman.

Romano, L. 2004. Kerry hunting trip sets sights on swing voters. *Washington Post*, October 21.

Romney, M. 2005. Why I vetoed contraception bill. *Boston Globe*, July 26.

Roscoe, D.D., and S. Jenkins. 2014. Changes in local party structure and activity, 1980–2008. In *The state of the parties: The changing role of contemporary American politics,* 7th ed., eds. J.C. Green, D.J. Coffey, and D.B. Cohen, 287–302. Lanham, MD: Rowman & Littlefield.

Rutledge, P. 2013. How Obama won the social media battle in the 2012 presidential campaign. The Media Psychology Blog, January 25. Available at http://mprcenter.org/blog/2013/01/how-obama-won-the-social-media-battle-in-the-2012-presidential-campaign/. Retrieved January 4, 2015.

Rutenberg, J. 2014. How billionaire oligarchs are becoming their own political parties. *New York Times*, October 17. Available at http://www.nytimes.com/2014/10/19/magazine/how-billionaire-oligarchs-are-becoming-their-own-political-parties.html. Retrieved January 4, 2015.

Rutenberg, J., and J.W. Peters. 2012. Obama outspending Romney on TV ads. *New York Times*, October 2. Available at http://www.nytimes.com/2012/10/03/us/politics/obama-outspending-romney-on-tv-ads.html?_r=0. Retrieved January 4, 2015.

Sabato, L.J. 1981. *The rise of political consultants: New way of winning elections.* New York: Basic Books.

Sabato, L.J. 1989. How direct mail works. In *Campaigns and elections: A reader in modern American* Politics, ed. L.J. Sabato, 88–99. Glenview, IL: Scott, Foresman.

Sabato, L.J. 1991. *Feeding frenzy: How attack journalism has transformed American journalism.* New York: Free Press.

Sabato, L., M. Stencel, and S.R. Lichter. 2000. *Peepshow: Media and politics in an age of scandal.* Lanham, MD: Rowman & Littlefield.

Safire, W. 2004. Flip flop. *New York Times*, March.

Safire, W. 2008. *Safire's political dictionary.* New York: Oxford University Press.

Salmore, B.G., and S.A. Salmore. 1989. *Candidates, parties, and campaigns.* Washington, DC: CQ Press.

Scaheffer, A., and N. Smith, 2003. Vaccines vs. leeches. *Campaigns and Elections*, December 8. Available at http://www.campaignsandelections.com/magazine/1729/vaccines-vs-leeches.

Schuman, H., and S. Presser. 1981. *Questions and answers in attitude surveys.* San Diego: Academic Press.

Selnow, G.W. 1994. *High-tech campaigns.* Westport, CT: Praeger.

Shaiko, R.G. 2008. Political parties—On the path to revitalization. In *Campaigns on the cutting edge*, ed. R.J. Semiatin, 105–22. Washington, DC: CQ Press.

Shapiro, W. 2012. How to handle oppo research? *Columbia Journalism Review*, July 20. Available at http://www.cjr.org/united_states_project/how_to_handle_oppo_research.php?page=all. Retrieved January 4, 2015.

Shaw, C. 2010. *The campaign manager: Running and winning local elections.* 4th ed. Boulder, Co: Westview Press.

Shaw, C. 2014. *The campaign manager: Running and winning local elections.* 5th ed. Boulder, Co: Westview Press.

Shaw, D.R. 2006. *The race to 270: The Electoral College and the campaign strategies of 2000 and 2004.* Chicago: University of Chicago Press.

Shea, D.M. 1996. Issue voting, candidate quality, and the ousting of a ten-year incumbent. *American Review of Politics* 17:395–420.

Shea, D.M. 1999. The passing of realignment and the advent of the "base-less" party system. *American Politics Quarterly* 27:33–57.

Shea, D.M. 2014. Separated we stand? The impact of ideological sorting on local party dynamics. In *The state of the parties: The changing role of contemporary American politics*, 7th ed., eds. J.C. Green, D.J. Coffey, and D.B. Cohen, 303–22. Lanham, MD: Rowman & Littlefield.

Shea, D.M., and S.C. Brooks. 1995. How to topple an incumbent. *Campaigns and Elections*, June.

Shea, D.M., and S. Medvic. 2009. All politics is local . . . except when it isn't. In *Cases in congressional campaigns: Incumbents playing defense*, eds. R.E. Adkins and D. Dulio, 173–88. New York: Routledge.

Shea, D.M., and B. Reece. 2008. *2008 election preview.* Upper Saddle River, NJ: Pearson.

Shea, D.M., J.C. Strachan, and M.R. Wolf. 2012. Local party viability, goals and objectives in the information age. In *The parties respond: Changes in American parties and campaigns*, 5th ed., eds. M. Brewer and L.S. Maisel, 103–32. Boulder, Co: Westview Press.

Shepard, S. 2012. Sorry, wrong number. *National Journal*, July 19. Available at http://www.nationaljournal.com/magazine/who-responds-to-telephone-polls-anymore-20120719. Retrieved January 4, 2015.

Sherman, J. 2014. Cantor loses. *Politico*, June 11. Available at http://www.politico.com/story/2014/06/eric-cantor-primary-election-results-virginia-107683.html. Retrieved January 4, 2015.

Shirley, C. 1997. Interviewed in "Spin." *Campaigns and Elections*, April.

Sides, J., and L. Vavreck. 2013. *The gamble: Choice and chance in the 2012 presidential election.* Princeton, NJ: Princeton University Press.

Sifton, E. 1998. The serenity prayer. *Yale Review* 86:16–65.

Silver, N. 2012. FiveThirtyEight's 2012 forecast. *FiveThirtyEight*. Available at http://fivethirtyeight.blogs.nytimes.com/fivethirtyeights-2012-forecast/. Retrieved January 4, 2015.

Silver, N. 2014. The polls were skewed toward Democrats. *FiveThirtyEight Politics*, November 5. Available at http://fivethirtyeight.com/features/the-polls-were-skewed-toward-democrats/. Retrieved January 4, 2015.

Simon, H.A. 1983. *Reason in human affairs.* Palo Alto, CA: Stanford University Press.

Simon, J. 2014. Free overseas trip? Yeah, your congressperson has probably taken one. *Washington Post*, May 29. Available at http://www.washingtonpost.com/blogs/the-fix/wp/2014/05/29/free-overseas-trip-yeah-your-congressperson-has-probably-taken-one/. Retrieved January 4, 2015.

Simon, P. 1995. Capitol Hill Nine: Retiring senators discuss why they chose to leave public office. Interview on CBS-TV, *60 Minutes*, December 17.

Simon, P. 1999. *P.S.: The autobiography of Paul Simon.* Chicago: Bonus Books.

Simon, R. 2008. Hillary should be running scared. *Politico.com*, January. Available at http://www.politico.com/news/stories/0108/7739.html. Retrieved February 25, 2010.

Simon, S. 2013. Koch group, unions battle over Colorado schools race. *Politico*, November 2. Available at http://www.politico.com/story/2013/11/koch-group-unions-battle-over-colorado-schools-race-99252.html. Retrieved January 4, 2015.

Simonich, M. 2004. Ex-hostage takes heat from GOP foe: Ohio campaign one of the nation's nastiest. *Pittsburgh Post-Gazette*, October 30.

Sive, R. 2013. *Every day is election day: A woman's guide to winning any office, from the PTA to the White House.* Chicago: Chicago Review Press.

Sockowitz, I. 2008. How to avoid catastrophe in your advance work. *Campaigns and Elections*, April.

Sonmez, F. 2012. Negative ads: Is it the campaigns, or the super PACs? *The Washington Post*, March 22. Available at http://www.washingtonpost.com/blogs/post-politics/post/negative-ads-is-it-the-campaigns-or-the-super-pacs-thursdays-trail-mix/2012/03/22/gIQAOf8VTS_blog.html.

Sorauf, F.J. 1988. *Money in American elections.* Boston: Scott, Foresman.

Spicer, E. 2012. Getting the most out of endorsements. *Campaigns and Elections*, July/August.

Stephanopoulos, G. 1999. *All too human: A political education.* Boston: Little, Brown.

Stephens, M. 2014. A few reasons not to re-elect Fleming. *Shreveport Times*, September 3. Available at http://www.shreveporttimes.com/story/opinion/guest-columnists/2014/09/04/reasons-re-election-fleming/15041161/. Retrieved January 4, 2015.

Stern, M. 2010. Supremes' gift to TV stations: Big bucks. *Media Life Magazine*, January 25. Available at http://www.medialifemagazine.com/supremes-gift-to-tv-stations-big-bucks/. Retrieved January 4, 2015.

Still, E. 2000. Litserv posting to Law-Courts List-serv, December 9.

Stokes, D.E. 1966. Spatial models of party competition. In *Elections and the political order*, eds. A. Campbell, P.E. Converse, W.E. Miller, and D.E. Stokes, 161–78. New York: John Wiley & Sons.

Stolberg, S.G. 2014. Black vote seen as last hope for Democrats to hold senate. *New York Times*, October 18. Available at http://www.nytimes.com/2014/10/19/us/in-black-vote-democrats-see-lifeline-for-midterms.html?_r=0. Retrieved January 4, 2015.

Stoll, H. 2013. Presidential coattails: A closer look. *Party Politics*, June 7, published online before print.

Stonecash, J.M. 2008. *Political polling: Strategic information in campaigns.* 2nd ed. Lanham, MD: Rowman & Littlefield.

Stonecash, J.M. 2014. A perfect storm: Presidential-House elections, policy, and congressional polarization. In *The state of the parties:*

*The changing role of contemporary American politics*, 7th ed., eds. J.C. Green, D.J. Coffey, and D.B. Cohen, 73–86. Lanham, MD: Rowman & Littlefield.

Strasma, K. n.d. Micro targeting: New Wave political campaigning. *Winning Campaigns*. Available at http://www.winningcampaigns.org/ Winning-Campaigns-Archive-Articles/Micro-Targeting-New-Wave-Political-Campaigning.html.

Sullivan, M. 2012. He said, she said, and the truth. *New York Times*, September 15. Available at http://www.nytimes.com/2012/09/16/public-editor/16pubed.html. Retrieved January 4, 2015.

Sweitzer, D. 1996. Kill or be killed: Military strategies can help win campaigns. *Campaigns and Elections*, September.

Sweitzer, D., and D. Heller. 1996. Radio tips: 10 ways to give your campaign ads more punch. *Campaigns and Elections*, May.

Sydnor, C.S. 1952. *Gentlemen freeholders: Political practices in Washington's Virginia*. Chapel Hill: University of North Carolina Press.

Taleb, N.N. 2010. *The black swan: The impact of the highly improbable*, 2nd ed. New York: Random House.

"Talk of the Nation." 2012. The job: Dig up dirt on politicians. *National Public Radio*, May 14. Available at http://www.wbur.org/npr/152683320/ the-job-dig-up-dirt-on-politicians?ft=3&f=152683320. Retrieved January 4, 2015.

Tau, B. 2013. Obama campaign final fundraising total: $1.1 billion. *Politico*, January 19. Available at http://www.politico.com/story/2013/01/ obama-campaign-final-fundraising-total-1-billion-86445.html. Retrieved January 4, 2015.

Terris, B. 2014a. A question for Washington pollsters: How wrong must you be to never work again? *Washington Post*, August 20. http:// www.washingtonpost.com/lifestyle/style/how-wrong-do-you-have-to-be-in-washington-to-never-work-again/2014/08/20/8f2adc 18–2717–11e4–86ca-6f03cbd15c1a_story.html. Retrieved January 4, 2015.

Terris, B. 2014b. Tracking the trackers: What it's like to have the most mind-numbing job in a campaign. *Washington Post*, October 14. Available at http://www.washingtonpost.com/lifestyle/style/tracking-the-trackers-what-its-like-to-have-the-most-mind-numbing-job-in-a-campaign/2014/10/14/a2ed9d46–50a0–11e4–8c24–487e92bc99 7b_story.html. Retrieved January 4, 2015.

Tetlock, P.E. 2009. *Expert political judgment*. Princeton, NJ: Princeton University Press.

Thomas, O. 2009. Gavin Newsom raising money on Twitter. NBC Bay Area News, June 24. Available at http://www.nbcbayarea.com/news/local-beat/Gavin-Newsom-Raising-Money-on-Twitter.html.

Thurber, J.A., and C.J. Nelson, eds. 1995. *Campaigns and elections American style*. Boulder, CO: Westview Press.

Thurber, J.A., and C.J. Nelson. 2000. *Campaign warriors: Political consultants in elections*. Washington, DC: Brookings Institution Press.

Thurber, J.A., and C.J. Nelson. 2004. *Campaigns and elections American style*. 2nd ed. Boulder, CO: Westview Press.

Thurber, J.A., and C.J. Nelson. 2010. *Campaigns and elections American style*. 3rd ed. Boulder, CO: Westview Press.

Thurber, J.A., and C.J. Nelson. 2013. *Campaigns and elections American style*. 4th ed. Boulder, CO: Westview Press.

Tilove, J. 2014. On Wendy Davis' bio: How I didn't get that story. *Austin Statesmen*, January 21. Available at http://www.statesman.com/weblogs/first-reading/2014/jan/21/wendy-davis-bio-how-i-didnt-get-story/. Retrieved January 4, 2015.

Trent, J.S., R.V. Friedenberg, and R.E. Denton. 2011. *Political campaign communication: Principles and practices*. 7th ed. Lanham, MD: Rowman & Littlefield.

Trippi, J. 2004. *The revolution will not be televised: Democracy, the Internet, and the overthrow of everything*. New York: Regan Books.

Trish, B. 2012. The evidence-based revolution. *Campaigns and Elections*, July/August, 28–31.

Tron, B. 1995/1996. Staging media events: What we learned from the "Contract with America." *Campaigns and Elections*, December/January.

Troy, G. 1996. *See how they ran: The changing role of the presidential candidate, Revised and expanded edition*. New York: Free Press.

Tseng, M.M., J. Jiao. 2001. Mass customization. In *Handbook of industrial engineering: Technology and operations management*, ed. G. Salvendy, 684–708. West Lafayette, IN: John Wiley & Sons.

Tufte, E.R. 1975. Determinants of the outcomes of midterm congressional elections. *American Political Science Review* 69:812–26.

Tuttle, S. 1996. Arizona primary of secondary concern. *Arizona Republic*, February 4.

TVB. n.d. National ADS, wired-cable & over-the-air penetration trends. Available at http://www.tvb.org/research/media_comparisons/4729/72512. Retrieved January 4, 2015.

U.S. Census Bureau. 2012. Voting and registration in the election of November 2012—Detailed tables. Available at http://www.census.gov/hhes/www/socdemo/voting/publications/p20/2012/tables.html. Retrieved January 4, 2015.

VandenDolder, T. 2014. What's next for campaign finance reform? *DCInno*, November 13. Available at http://dcinno.streetwise.co/2014/11/13/whats-next-for-campaign-finance-reform/. Retrieved January 4, 2015.

Vargas, J.A. 2008. Obama raised half a billion online. *Washington Post*, November 20. Available at http://voices.washingtonpost.com/44/2008/11/20/obama_raised_half_a_billion_on.html.

Varoga, C. 2008. Online money for local races. *Campaigns and Elections*, October, 44.

Vogel, K.P., and B. Tau. 2014. Gotcha! How oppo took over the midterms. *Politico*, September 19. Available at http://www.politico.com/story/2014/09/2014-election-stories-111114.html#ixzz3MUaeaicv. Retrieved January 4, 2015.

Walker, H., and C. Campbell. 2014. Vermont's gubernatorial debate was very, very special. *Business Insider*, October 14. Available at http://www.businessinsider.com/vermont-gubernatorial-debate-highlights-2014-10. Retrieved January 4, 2015.

Wang, M. 2011. FEC deadlocks (again) on guidance for big-money super PACs. *ProPublica*, December 2. Available at http://www.propublica.org/article/deadlocks-again-on-guidance-for-big-money-super-pacs. Retrieved January 4, 2015.

Wang, W., D. Rothschild, S. Goel, and A. Gelman. 2014. Forecasting elections with non-representative polls. *International Journal of Forecasting*. Available online prior to print.

*The War Room*. 1993. Dir. C. Hegedus and D.A. Pennebaker. Universal City, CA: Universal Studios. DVD.

*Washington Post*. 2012. 2012 presidential campaign finance explorer. December 7. Available at http://www.washingtonpost.com/wp-srv/special/politics/campaign-finance/. Retrieved January 4, 2015.

*Watertown Daily Times*. 2009. Few answers. October 23. Available at http://www.watertowndailytimes.com/article/20091023/opinion01/310239957/-1/opinion.

Wayne, L. 2008. Democrats take page from their rivals' playbook. *New York Times*, October 31.

Weaver, M.R. 1996. Paid media. In *Campaign craft: The strategies, tactics, and art of political campaign management*, ed. D.M. Shea, 201–18. Westport, CT: Praeger.

Weaver, V.M. 2012. The electoral consequences of skin color: The "hidden" side of race in politics. *Political Behavior* 34:159–92.

Weber, J. 2014. Campaigns craft attention grabbing, personalized emails to woo voters, raise cash. *Fox News*, November 2. Available at http://www.foxnews.com/politics/2014/11/02/campaigns-craft-attention-grabbing-personalized-emails-to-woo-voters-raise-cash/. Retrieved January 4, 2015.

Weigel, D. 2006. The political bull's-eye: Persuading the right people with microtargeting. *Campaigns and Elections*, February, 20.

Weigel, D. 2011. You're all nuts! *Slate*, April 25. Available at http://www.slate.com/articles/news_and_politics/politics/2011/04/youre_all_nuts.html. Retrieved January 4, 2015.

Weinger, M. 2012. John Fleming links to Onion story on Facebook. *Politico*, February 6. Available at http://www.politico.com/news/stories/0212/72507.html#ixzz3NG7DN26e. Retrieved January 4, 2015.

Weisbaum, H. 2014. How to block those unwanted political robocalls. *Today Money*, September 3. Available at http://www.today.com/

money/how-block-those-unwanted-political-robocalls-1D80122958. Retrieved January 4, 2015.

Weisberg, H.F. 2005. *The total survey error approach: A guide to the new science of survey research.* Chicago: University of Chicago Press.

Weisberg, H.F., J.A. Krosnick, and B.A. Bowen. 1996. *An introduction to survey research and data analysis.* 2nd ed. Thousand Oaks, CA: Sage.

White, J.K., and D.M. Shea. 2004. *New party politics: From Jefferson and Hamilton to the Information Age.* 2nd ed. Belmont, CA: Wadsworth.

White, T.H. 1961. *The making of the president, 1960.* New York: Atheneum.

Whyte, L.E. 2014. Corporations, advocacy groups spend big on ballot measures. The Center for Public Integrity, October 26. Available at http://www.publicintegrity.org/2014/10/23/15998/corporations-advocacy-groups-spend-big-ballot-measures. Retrieved January 4, 2015.

Willard, D., and M. Fazekas. 2012. Turning the tide in Ohio. *Campaigns and Elections,* January/February, 40–5.

Williams, J. 2014. Labels & lists offers campaigns Latino-specific targeting. *Campaigns and Elections,* May/June, 59.

Willis, D. 2014. Outside groups set spending record in midterms. *The New York Times,* December 10. Available at http://www.nytimes.com/2014/12/11/upshot/outside-groups-set-spending-record-in-midterms-.html?_r=0&abt=0002&abg=1.

Winston, D. 2010. Creating a winning campaign strategy. In *Campaigns and elections American style,* 3rd ed., ed. J. Thurber and C. Nelson, 35–58. Boulder, CO: Westview Press.

Wisconsin Democracy Campaign. 2014. Money in Wisconsin politics index 2010–2013. Available at http://www.wisdc.org/moneyinpolitics 2010–2013.php. Retrieved January 4, 2015.

Woodruff, B. 2014. Internal emails show DeMaio campaign worried about trackers, spies. *Washington Examiner,* October 17. Available at http://www.washingtonexaminer.com/article/2554895. Retrieved January 4, 2015.

Zagaroli, L. 2008a. Dole's "godless" attack drew boost for Hagan. *Charlotte Observer,* November 12.

Zagaroli, L. 2008b. "Godless" ad sets off war of words between Hagan, Dole. *Charlotte Observer,* October 30. Available at http://www.charlotteobserver.com/politics/story/287745.html.

Zaller, J. 1992. *The nature and origins of mass opinion.* New York: Cambridge University Press.

# Index

Note: Page numbers in *italics* followed by *f* indicate figures; by *t* indicate tables.

analytic groups, 53; 3. membership in a segment suggests shared concerns with others in that segment, 53–54; average party performance (APP), 56–58, 57f; base vote and swing vote, 57–59, 57f, 58f; basic political segments, 55–63; Baum, Ed city council election example, 51–52, 54–55, 63, 219; diagramming the electorate, 55, 56f; ecological inference problem, 55; partisan, soft partisan, toss-up, and split-ticket factor, 59, 59f; performance metrics/formulas, 63–65; predicting individual-level behavior based on aggregate-level research, 53–55; segment ranking, 65, 66t, 67; voter participation/turnout, 60–63; yield analysis, 63–68

September 11, 2001 terrorist attacks, 22, 107, 108

"Serenity Prayer" (Niebuhr), 13

Shaiko, Ronald G., 133

Shaw, Catherine, 108–9

Shaw, Daron R., 4

Shea, Dan, 191

Shea, Rosemary, 191

Shields, Todd G., 105–6

Shrum, Bob, 219

Sides, John, xxiii, 157

Silverberg, Carl, 129

Silver, Nate, 70, 84–85

Simon, Paul, 122–24

Sleeper questions, 83

Smart money, 125

Smith, Nancy, 181

SMS text messaging, xiv, 178, 180, 189, 213

Social media, xvii, 31–34, 36, 137–38, 146; direct voter contact and, 189–91; downsides of using in campaigns, 174; news

media and, 173–74; online tools, 173; social pressure to vote and, 182–83. *See also* Blogging; Digital media; Facebook; Internet; Twitter/tweets; YouTube

Social pressure to vote, 181–83

Social psychology, 93–94

Social voting theory, 179, 180

Sociology, 92–93

"Soft money," 126, 201

Soft-partisan votes, 55, 56f, 59, 59f

"Souls-to-the-Polls" (Ohio, 2014), 194

Sound bites, 160

Specialization, 217–19

Speech modules, xx

*SpeechNow.org v. Federal Election Commission,* 201–2

Split-ticket factor, 59

Squier, Bob, 218

Squier Knapp Ochs media firm, 218

Squire, Bob, 32

Staggers, Harley O., 39

Statistical models, xxi

Stencel, Mark, 33

Stephanopoulos, George, 218

Stereotypes, 16

Stevenson, Adlai, 213

Stock images, 149

Stokes, Donald, 93–94

Stonecash, Jeffrey M., 84, 96

Strauss, Aaron, 179–80

Streyer, Tom, 209

Strickland, Ted, 102

Suffrage, xiii

Sullivan, Margaret, 36

Super PACs. *See* Political action committees (PACs)

Supreme Court campaign finance cases, 126–27, 206–7

"The Supremes' Gift to TV Stations: Big Bucks" (*Media Life Magazine*), 127

## About the Authors

MICHAEL JOHN BURTON, PhD, is associate professor of political science at Ohio University, where he teaches elections and campaigns, political leadership, and political research methods. With Daniel M. Shea, he wrote the previous editions of Praeger's *Campaign Craft* as well as *Campaign Mode: Strategic Vision in Congressional Elections*. Burton spent seven years as a political professional in Washington where he worked in the office of Vice President Al Gore (1993–1998) as special assistant to the chief of staff and assistant political director, the office of Congressman Paul E. Kanjorski (1991–1993), and for the Congressional Research Service (1991). Burton received his bachelor's and master's degrees from Ohio University and his doctorate from the State University of New York at Albany. Current research goes to quantitative analysis and political language.

WILLIAM J. MILLER, PhD, is director of Institutional Research and Effectiveness at Flagler College, Saint Augustine, Florida. He received his bachelor's degree in political science from the Ohio University Honors Tutorial College and his master's degree, also in political science, from Ohio University. He earned a Master of Applied Politics (focusing on political polling and campaign strategy) from the Ray C. Bliss Institute at the University of Akron and a doctorate in public administration and urban studies, also from the University of Akron. Prior to joining Flagler, Miller was assistant professor in the Department of Political Science, Philosophy, and Religion at Southeast Missouri State University and visiting assistant professor at Ohio University and Notre Dame College. He has advised elected officials, agency administrators, and social service agencies, and his special interests include campaigns and elections, polling, board development, grant writing, and the pedagogy of political science and public administration.

DANIEL M. SHEA, PhD, is professor of government and director of the Goldfarb Center for Public Affairs and Civic Engagement at Colby College, Waterville, Maine. An award-winning teacher, Shea has spearheaded numerous initiatives at Colby and other institutions designed to help young Americans better appreciate their potential to affect democratic change. The author or editor for nearly 20 books and dozens of articles and chapters on the American political process, Shea focuses his research on campaigns and elections, political parties, the politics of scandal, and grassroots activism. His coauthored *The Fountain of Youth*, which garnered national attention for its findings on how local party organizations often neglect young citizens. In 2012, his work on civility and compromise was covered by hundreds of media outlets and led to the publication of the coedited volume *Can We Talk? The Rise of Rude, Nasty, Stubborn Politics*. Shea also wrote *Let's Vote: The Essentials of the American Electoral Process* and is the lead author of *Living Democracy*, a text on American government, now in its fifth edition. He earned his doctorate from the University of Albany, State University of New York.